Contents

The Largest U.S. Cities Named after a Food

and Other Mind-Boggling Geography Lists from Around the World

- Countries with the Lowest Number of International Tourists per Year
- States with the Highest Percentage of Individuals Who Call Soft Drinks "Pop"
- Most Populous Cities in the United States without Interstate Highways
- Countries Where the Highest Percentage of Available Food Calories Comes from Sugar
- Hundreds of Additional Lists!

Brandt Maxwell

S A N T A
M O N I C A
P R E S S

Published by:
Santa Monica Press LLC
P.O. Box 1076
Santa Monica, CA 90406-1076
1-800-784-9553
www.santamonicapress.com
books@santamonicapress.com

Printed in the United States

Santa Monica Press books are available at special quantity discounts when purchased in bulk by corporations, organizations, or groups. Please call our Special Sales department at 1-800-784-9553.

Library of Congress Cataloging-in-Publication Data

Maxwell, Brandt, 1968-
    The largest U.S. cities to be named after a food : and other mind-boggling geography lists from around the world / Brandt Maxwell.— 1st ed.
    p. cm.
    Summary: "Hundreds of lists and oddities fill this compendium of geographic trivia. From a list of countries with the lowest number of international tourists per year to information about the largest countries in the world without an FM station, this book of wide-ranging curiosities includes minutia from across the globe"— Provided by publisher.
    Includes bibliographical references.
    ISBN 1-891661-47-7
    1. United States—Geography—Miscellanea. 2. United States—History, Local—Miscellanea. 3. Geography—Miscellanea. 4. Local history—Miscellanea. I. Title.
    E161.3.M34 2004
    917.3'001'4—dc22

                                                                          2004021188

Cover design by Future Studio

Interior design by Lynda "Cool Dog" Jakovich

Chapter Three: Transportation Geography............89

Chapter Four: City Geography.....................................II5

Chapter Six: Demographic Geography........................185

Chapter Eight: Recreation Geography 265

Acknowledgments

I would like to thank Sean Swindler, Miguel Miller and Bobbi Weaver for their ideas and recommendations for interesting lists. Miguel contributed some especially valuable data for "States Where the Highest (and Lowest) Percentage of Cities and Towns Have Spanish Names." I also thank Alan McConchie for allowing me to use his data showing the regional variations between calling soft drinks "soda," "pop," "Coke," and "tonic."

Introduction

When did it snow in the Bahamas? (see page 160)
What is the most populous country in the world to have never won an Olympic medal? (see page 269)
Do palm trees really grow outdoors in London? (see page 347)
What is the largest country in the world to have no FM radio stations? (see page 341)
Which lake borders five countries? (see page 65)
And, of course, what's the largest U.S. city named after a food? (see page 56)

Geography is a subject often overlooked, despite its extreme importance in our increasingly interconnected world. A number of Americans travel frequently, not just to foreign countries where cultures and the physical geography can vary wildly, but also to other parts of their own country, which differ significantly due, in part, to the diversity of the U.S. population. Political and business leaders often deal with other countries, and a better understanding of the world, both in broad and in nuanced terms, will allow them to make better decisions and acquire international respect. But almost more importantly, given people's propensity for exploration, geography is like another set of eyes—we need it to truly see where we are going.

Unfortunately, some people know little about geography. Not only do they know little about the cultures, habits, climates or politics of foreign countries, but some lack knowledge about their own countries, even including where "home" is. According to the National Geographic-Roper 2002 Global Geographic Literacy Survey, 11 percent of

Americans between the ages of 18 and 24 could not identify their own country on an unlabeled world map.

Fortunately, geography does not have to be overlooked. Learning geography can be quite fun for much of the population. (If you don't believe me, just ask any of the six questions at the beginning of this foreword to various people, and you will find many to be instantly fascinated.) Geography encompasses so many topics, from the expected "main courses" (weather, mountains or country locations) to areas people usually do not associate with geography (sports, radio stations, or liquor laws). *If something is associated with a place, then it becomes a part of geography.* These associations can include anything from the tiniest insects (which can cause diseases found in certain *geographic* locations) to the largest cities, continents and oceans, to every single person in the world, whether stationary or nomadic. This book thus contains a wealth of geography-related information.

While the geography basics are important, they are seldom featured in this book, since they are sufficiently covered in almanacs and basic geography texts. Nevertheless, this book is written for a broad audience. Most of the topics are familiar or can be instantly explained to the casual reader, yet will entertain the geography aficionado (partly as a "reward" for the pursuit of this fine hobby). An example would be the 10 largest cities in the United States to share their names (or spellings) with no other cities in the world. The Ballwin, Missouri Web site cites the uniqueness of its name, yet so many larger U.S. cities can claim the same (including Seattle, Fort Worth and Virginia Beach—see page 39 for the remainder) that Ballwin does not even come close to being ranked. While many people have never thought about a topic like this, it becomes instantly recognizable after viewing the list.

The focus here is on the extreme and the surprising (after all, how much excitability comes from "average" things?), so list format is the natural way to present the information (as with polls showing the top 25 NCAA basketball or football teams, or the top 100 pop songs in Billboard magazine). An entire chapter is devoted strictly to things found in an atlas, as many who are fascinated by geography enjoy reading an atlas for purposes other than just to find their destinations. When I was a child, I loved looking at the atlas while on a car ride to see exactly where I was in relation to nearby features. Then, after the excursion, I would draw a map of an imaginary place that I wished existed (or that was similar to a place I wished I could visit). As a meteorologist, I find maps to be of utmost importance and pleasure when determining why a weather feature will move over a specific location (whether that would be "home" or on the other side of the earth).

Some of the lists are here to raise awareness of certain issues or even to shock a bit. Disparity of income is one topic that finds its way onto several lists, including one showing the gaps between rich and poor cities in the United States (for example, Los Angeles neighbor Rolling Hills, one of the richest suburbs in the U.S., if not the world, is within 20 miles of some of the poorest cities and suburbs in the United States). Anyone who visits the L.A. area can see class differences (though they would be even more visible in Guatemala or South Africa) that would be much less extreme in Iowa or North Dakota.

The bulk of this book is about fun, though this is certainly not the first time someone has proclaimed geography to be fun. In 1983, Trivial Pursuit's original classic game, widely played among people of many different backgrounds, had geography as one of its six categories. Nor is this the first time "list books" have been proclaimed to be fun; back in the late 1970s, the authors of the *People's Almanac* created *The Book of Lists* (and eventually several sequels), which sold in the millions. *The Largest U.S. Cities Named after a Food and Other Mind-Boggling Geography Lists from Around the World* is the intersection of these two types of fun, much like the intersection of two winding mountain roads (hopefully with unusual names, like those found on page 35).

Brandt Maxwell
November 2004

For more information (and additional geography lists) please visit www.geographylists.com.

CHAPTER ONE
Name Geography

There are a lot of place names out there, some strange, yet some very ordinary. Some are very common, appearing many thousands of times around the world (especially when street names are considered); some appear only once. Many places are named after people (whether famous, unknown or infamous), plants, geological features, what that place looks like or something as simple as a number. Some names are borrowed from other geographical features (such as a street adopting the name of a city). Sometimes, places will have names of something far away, be it a nation (or its people) halfway around the world or even a distant galaxy. Of course, the thousands of languages around the world contribute to an unbelievable variety of place names.

It is no accident that the first chapter of this book is about place names (though some places are named purely by accident)! Names are very important, especially since many place names reveal something about their locations' histories.

Borrowed Names:
Largest Cities in the United States to Share Their Names with Major World Cities

These are the largest cities (by population) in the United States to have the same name as a well-known city in another country.

U.S. City	World City
1. San Jose, California	San Jose, Costa Rica
2. Toledo, Ohio	Toledo, Spain
3. St. Petersburg, Florida	St. Petersburg, Russia
4. Birmingham, Alabama	Birmingham, U.K.
5. Vancouver, Washington	Vancouver, Canada
6. Alexandria, Virginia	Alexandria, Egypt
7. Manchester, New Hampshire	Manchester, U.K.
8. Athens, Georgia	Athens, Greece
9. Odessa, Texas	Odessa, Ukraine
10. Melbourne, Florida	Melbourne, Australia

All-American Borrowed Names:
Largest Cities in the United States to Share Their Names with a Larger City in Another State

If someone says he or she is from Glendale, without identifying the state, then you probably don't know *which* Glendale, unless you are currently in or near a particular Glendale. These are the largest cities in the United States (by population) to have a larger city of the same name elsewhere in the U.S.

City	Larger City of Same Name
1. Glendale, CA	Glendale, AZ
2. Arlington, VA	Arlington, TX
3. Columbus, GA	Columbus, OH
4. Springfield, MO	Springfield, MA*
5. Kansas City, KS	Kansas City, MO
6. Aurora, IL	Aurora, CO
7. Pasadena, CA	Pasadena, TX
8. Springfield, IL	Springfield, MA*
9. Peoria, AZ	Peoria, IL
10. Richmond, CA	Richmond, VA

* Two Springfields made the list since three cities named Springfield in the United States have at least 100,000 people.

Remote Namesakes: U.S. Towns Named After Distant States, Provinces or Territories

This is only a small snapshot of the many towns in this category.

Alabama, New York
Alaska, New Mexico
Arkansas, West Virginia
California, Maine
Florida, Colorado
Guam, Missouri
Iowa City, California
Kansas, Vermont
Kansas City, Oregon
Minnesota, Georgia
New York, New Mexico
Oklahoma, Pennsylvania
Oregon, Maryland
Puerto Rico, Texas
Quebec, Texas
Texas, New York
Utah, Tennessee
Vermont, Illinois
Wyoming, Rhode Island
Yukon, Florida

Domestic Oddities: Strange U.S. Place Names

The Appalachian states definitely have the highest concentration of strange place names. However, there are plenty of weird place names elsewhere. Many of these places are very small!

Cities and Towns:

Accident, Maryland
Between, Georgia
Bingo, Maine
Bird In Hand, Pennsylvania
Blowout, Texas
Blue Ball, Pennsylvania
Boogertown, North Carolina
Boring, Oregon

Bumpass, Virginia
Buzz, Pennsylvania
Caress, West Virginia
Cocked Hat, Delaware
Crook, Colorado
Cut and Shoot, Texas
Czar, West Virginia
Ding Dong, Texas

Dingy, West Virginia
Disco, Michigan
Dumbell, Wyoming
Eighty Eight, Kentucky
Eighty Four, Pennsylvania
Fickle, Indiana
Firebrick, Kentucky
Fireworks, Massachusetts
Flintstone, Maryland
French Lick, Indiana
Frying Pan, North Carolina
Funk, Ohio
Gasoline, Texas
Glen Campbell, Pennsylvania
Good Intent, Pennsylvania
Greasy Corner, Arkansas
Gun Barrel City, Texas
Hacker Valley, West Virginia
Half Hell, North Carolina
Handshoe, Kentucky
Hell, Michigan
Hundred, West Virginia
Intercourse, Pennsylvania
Jackpot, Nevada
Jot Em Down, Texas
Last Chance, Colorado
Letcher, Kentucky
Lizard Lick, North Carolina
Lower Harmony, New Jersey
Monkey's Eyebrow, Kentucky
Ninety Six, South Carolina
No Name, Ohio

North Pole, Alaska
Odd, West Virginia
Okay, Arkansas
Panic, Pennsylvania
Peach Bottom, Virginia
Penistaja, New Mexico
Polkadot, North Carolina
Poor Town, North Carolina
Poverty, Kentucky
Santa Claus, Indiana
Surprise, Arizona
Telephone, Texas
Ticktown, Virginia
Tightwad, Missouri
Toad Suck, Arkansas
Troublesome, Colorado
Truth or Consequences, New
    Mexico
Umpire, Arkansas
Unalaska, Alaska
Uncertain, Texas
Virgin, Utah
Virginville, West Virginia
Wankers Corner, Oregon
War, West Virginia
What Cheer, Iowa
Why, Arizona
Yeehaw, Florida
Yellville, Arkansas
Zero, Montana
Zilwaukee, Michigan (*not*
    Milwaukee)

Bodies of Water:

Big Bone Lick, Kentucky
    (Spring)
Dork Canal, Oregon
Fryingpan Creek,
    Washington
Ghoul Creek, Washington

Guitar Lake, California
Idiot Creek, Oregon
Kill Creek, Kansas
Liquor Spring, Arizona
Marijuana Tank, New Mexico
    (Reservoir)

Molasses River, Michigan
Pee Pee Creek, Ohio
Poison Creek, Oregon
Poop Creek, Oregon

Shitten Creek, Oregon
Suck Creek, West Virginia
Tickle Creek, North Carolina
Weird Lake, Minnesota

Mountains and Hills:

Bad Marriage Mountain,
Montana
Big Butt, North Carolina
Bitch Mountain, New York
Booger Red Hill, Colorado
Cancer Hill, Maine
Crash-up Mountain, Arizona
Flying W Mountain, New
Mexico
Gag Mesa, New Mexico
Hateful Hill, Vermont
Jim Jones Hill, Texas

Killer Mountain, Oklahoma
Moneyhole Mountain, New
York
Mount Wow, Washington
Peek-A-Boo Hill, Michigan
Pimple Hill, Pennsylvania
Poopout Hill, California
Sex Peak, Montana
Sexy Peak, Idaho
Witch Dance Hill, Mississippi
Xmas Mountain, Utah

Foreign Oddities: Strange Place Names in Other Countries

Of course, in places where languages other than English dominate, some of these names might not be the least bit strange to a local.

Cities and Towns:

Asbestos, Canada (Quebec)
Barton in the Clay, U.K.
(England)
Batman, Turkey
Bled, Slovenia
Blow Clear, Australia (New
South Wales)
Blubberhouses, U.K.
(England)
Catchacoma, Canada (Ontario)
Come-by-Chance, Australia
(New South Wales)
Come by Chance, Canada
(Newfoundland)

Cry, France
Dildo, Canada
(Newfoundland)
Dog Swamp, Australia
(Western Australia)
Giggleswick, U.K. (England)
Howlong, Australia (New
South Wales)
Innaloo, Australia (Western
Australia)
Kill, Ireland
Lower Economy, Canada
(Nova Scotia)

Morón, Cuba (and Mexico, Peru, Venezuela, etc. This is a common town name in Spanish-speaking countries.)
Poor, Nigeria
Primate, Canada (Saskatchewan)

Saint-Louis-du-Ha! Ha!, Canada (Quebec)
Sexmoan, Philippines
The Risk, Australia (New South Wales)
Usa, Japan (and Mozambique, Nigeria and Russia)

Other Places:

Blow Me Down, Canada (a mountain in Newfoundland)
Blow Me Head, Canada (a cape in Newfoundland)
Broke Inlet, Australia (Western Australia)

Cape Foulwind, New Zealand
Nowhere Creek, Australia (Victoria)
Pickle Lake, Canada (Ontario)
Prickly Point, Grenada
Suck River, Ireland

U.S. Towns with the Same Names as Foreign Countries

Numerous towns (some very small, but some quite large) share names with foreign nations. Most of these places have few (if any) people who have emigrated from the namesake nations (except Jamaica, New York).

Angola, Indiana
Belgium, New York
Bolivia, North Carolina
Brazil, Indiana
Britain, Virginia
Canada, Kansas
Chad, Kentucky
China, Maine
Congo, Ohio
Cuba, Missouri
Denmark, Iowa
Egypt, Massachusetts
Egypt Lake, Florida
England, Ohio
Finland, Minnesota
France, Idaho
Germany, Georgia

Greece, New York
Grenada, California
Guinea, Alabama
Holland, Michigan
Honduras, Indiana
Hungary, Connecticut
Iceland, Nevada
India, Texas
Ireland, Washington
Israel, West Virginia
Italy, Texas
Jamaica, New York
Japan, Pennsylvania
Jordan, Minnesota
Korea, Kentucky
Lebanon, Missouri
Malta, Illinois

Mexico, Missouri
Morocco, Indiana
Netherlands, Missouri
Norway, Kansas
Panama City, Florida
Peru, Indiana
Poland, Ohio
Romania, Pennsylvania
Russia, Ohio
Samoa, California

San Marino, California
Spain, South Dakota
Sudan, Texas
Sweden, South Carolina
Switzerland, Florida
Syria, Virginia
Togo, Arkansas
Turkey, Texas
West Jordan, Utah

Most Common Town and City Names in the United States

How one defines what to consider a "town" determines which town names are found most often around the United States. In the first list, only incorporated towns and cities, based on census data, are used.

Town/City Name	Number in U.S.
1. Franklin	29
2. Clinton	23
3. Madison	23
4. Union/Union City	22
4. Washington	22
6. Monroe/Monroe City	21
7. Clayton	19
7. Marion	19
7. Milford	19
7. Oxford	19
7. Salem	19
7. Springfield	19

If any named populated location (based on U.S. Geological Survey data) is considered, the listing changes significantly. This includes many tiny unincorporated towns and villages (though not most subdivisions within larger towns). Often, more than one town with the same name can be found in a given state if everything is included.

Town/City Name	Number in U.S.
1. Midway/Midway City	182
2. Fairview	173
3. Oak Grove	134
4. Five Points	115 (primarily southeastern)
5. Centerville	101
6. Riverside	100
7. Pleasant Hill	99
8. Union/Union City	91
9. Mount Pleasant	88
10. Liberty	87

The word "pleasant" appears twice in this all-inclusive list (plus in No. 13 Pleasant Valley) but not in the list of incorporated towns and cities (though "Mount Pleasant" is an incorporated town in 10 states). While quite a number of people would consider some mid-size and large cities to be pleasant, the largest city in the United States with "pleasant" as part of its name is Pleasanton, California, with about 70,000 people.

Most Common County/Parish Names in the United States

Three of the founding fathers have been honored—their names make up the top three most common counties in the United States.

County Name	Number in U.S.
1. Washington	31
2. Jefferson	26
3. Franklin	25
4. Jackson	24
4. Lincoln	24
6. Madison	20
7. Clay	18
7. Montgomery	18
7. Union	18
10. Marion	17
10. Monroe	17

Despite these county names being common, eight states have none of the above county names: Alaska (no counties), Arizona, California, Connecticut, Delaware, Hawaii, New Hampshire, and North Dakota.

Most Common Counties with the Same Names as States

There are 59 counties in the United States that have the same name as a state. This does not include counties with partial names of states (such as Dakota or Hampshire).

County	Number of Occurrences
1. Washington	31
2. Delaware	6
3. Ohio	3
3. Wyoming	3
5. Iowa	2
5. Mississippi	2
5. Texas	2

Ironically, Wyoming County, which is tied for third place on this list, is only found in the Eastern United States (New York, Pennsylvania and West Virginia).

Counties with the Same Names as the States Where They Are Located

1. Arkansas
2. Hawaii
3. Idaho
4. Iowa
5. New York
6. Oklahoma
7. Utah

Largest U.S. Cities to Share Their Names with No Other World Cities

A number of cities in the United States have completely unique names. Here are the 10 most populous cities in the United States to have no other cities with the same name anywhere in the world.

1. Seattle, Washington
2. Fort Worth, Texas
3. New Orleans, Louisiana*
4. Virginia Beach, Virginia

5. Colorado Springs, Colorado
6. Anaheim, California**
7. Hialeah, Florida
8. Shreveport, Louisiana
9. Lubbock, Texas
10. Newport News, Virginia

This list excludes Oklahoma City, since numerous towns are named Oklahoma, as well as hyphenated names consisting of two redundant names, such as "Nashville-Davidson" or "Winston-Salem" (while those hyphenated names are technically unique, "Nashville," "Davidson," "Winston" and "Salem" are not).

* No other *English-language* New Orleans exists, though there is a Nueva Orleans, Colombia.
** No other city is spelled like Anaheim, though there is an Annaheim in Saskatchewan, Canada.

Cities Whose Names Are in the Titles of Billboard Top 40 Songs

City, State	Song/Artist (Peak Position/Year)
Abilene, Texas	"Abilene"/George Hamilton IV (No. 15/1963)
Allentown, Pennsylvania	"Allentown"/Billy Joel (No. 17/1983)
Atlanta, Georgia	"Atlanta Lady"/Marty Balin (No. 27/1981)
Boston, Massachusetts	"Please Come to Boston" Dave Loggins (No. 5/1974)
Bowling Green, Kentucky	"Bowling Green"/Everly Brothers (No. 40/1967)
Chattanooga, Tennessee	"Chattanooga Choo Choo"/ Tuxedo Junction (No. 32/1978)
Chicago, Illinois	"The Night Chicago Died"/ Paper Lace (No. 1/1974)
Clarksville, Tennessee	"Last Train to Clarksville"/ Monkees (No. 1/1966)

Detroit, Michigan	"Detroit City"/Bobby Bare (No. 16/1963)
Doraville, Georgia	"Doraville"/Atlanta Rhythm Section (No. 35/1974)
El Paso, Texas	"El Paso"/Marty Robbins (No. 1/1960)
Galveston, Texas	"Galveston"/Glen Campbell (No. 4/1969)
Houston, Texas	"Houston"/Dean Martin (No. 21/1965)
Kansas City, Missouri	"Kansas City"/Wilbert Harrison (No. 1/1959)
Key Largo, Florida	"Key Largo"/Bertie Higgins (No. 8/1982)
Kokomo, Indiana	"Kokomo"/Beach Boys (No. 1/1988)
Las Vegas, Nevada	"Viva Las Vegas"/Elvis Presley (No. 29/1964)
Los Angeles, California	"Country Boy (You Got Your Feet in L.A.)"/Glen Campbell (No. 11/1976)
Luckenbach, Texas	"Luckenbach, Texas"/Waylon Jennings (No. 25/1977)
Memphis, Tennessee	"Memphis"/Johnny Rivers (No. 2/1964)
Monterey, California	"Monterey"/Animals (No. 15/1968)
Nashville, Tennessee	"Nashville Cats"/Lovin' Spoonful (No. 8/1967)
New Orleans, Louisiana	"Battle of New Orleans"/Johnny Horton (No. 1/1959)
New York, New York	"New York Groove"/Ace Frehley (No. 13/1979)
Nutbush, Tennessee	"Nutbush City Limits"/Ike & Tina Turner (No. 22/1973)
Philadelphia, Pennsylvania	"Philadelphia Freedom"/Elton John (No. 1/1975)
Phoenix, Arizona	"By the Time I Get to Phoenix"/Glen Campbell (No. 26/1967)

San Francisco, California	"San Francisco"/Scott McKenzie (No. 4/1967)
San Jose, California	"Do You Know the Way to San Jose"/Dionne Warwick (No. 10/1968)
Tallahassee, Florida	"Tallahassee Lassie"/Freddie Cannon (No. 6/1959)
Tulsa, Oklahoma	"Tulsa Time"/Eric Clapton (No. 30/1980)
Wichita, Kansas	"Wichita Lineman"/Glen Campbell (No. 3/1969)
Woodstock, New York	"Woodstock"/Crosby, Stills, Nash & Young (No. 11/1970)

Some Cities outside the United States

City, State	Song/Artist (Peak Position/Year)
Bangkok, Thailand	"One Night in Bangkok"/ Murray Head (No. 3/1985)
Calcutta (Kolkata), India	"Calcutta"/Lawrence Welk (No. 1/1961)
Ipanema, Brazil	"Girl from Ipanema"/Stan Getz & Astrud Gilberto (No. 5/1964)
London, United Kingdom	"London Town"/Paul McCartney & Wings (No. 39/1978)
Marrakesh, Morocco	"Marrakesh Express"/Crosby, Stills & Nash (No. 28/1969)
Nassau, Bahamas	"Funky Nassau"/Beginning Of The End (No. 15/1971)
Paris, France	"Free Man in Paris"/Joni Mitchell (No. 22/1974)
Rio de Janeiro, Brazil	"Rio"/Duran Duran (No. 14/1983)
Saigon (Ho Chi Minh City), Vietnam	"Still in Saigon"/Charlie Daniels Band (No. 22/1982)
Scarborough, United Kingdom	"Scarborough Fair"/Simon & Garfunkel (No. 11/1968)

Tijuana, Mexico | "Tijuana Jail"/Kingston Trio (No. 12/1959)

Vienna, Austria | "It's All Down to Goodnight Vienna"/Ringo Starr (No. 31/1975)

Winchester, United Kingdom | "Winchester Cathedral"/New Vaudeville Band (No. 1/1966)

Only one song per city is listed. Chart positions are based on *Billboard Magazine*'s Hot 100.

North, East, South or West: States Where the Highest Percentage of Town Names Have Directions as Their First Words

In New England, names like "North Franklin" or "West Hartford" are quite common (and often accompanied by "South Franklin" and "East Hartford"). The Western and Southern United States have most of the lowest ranking states, though Utah and Washington rank fairly high (tied at No. 11).

State	Percentage of North, East, South or West Towns
1. Vermont	22.4
2. Maine	17.2
3. New Hampshire	15.5
4. Massachusetts	15.1
5. Connecticut	11.2
6. New York	9.6
7. Rhode Island	7.1
8. New Jersey	3.9
9. Ohio	3.8
10. Pennsylvania	3.5

This list does not account for names like "Westminster" or "Easton," where the direction is a part of a word.

States Where the Lowest Percentage of Town Names Have Directions as Their First Words

State	Percentage of North, East, South or West Towns
1. Hawaii	none
2. Idaho	0.7
3. Alaska	0.9
3. Kansas	0.9
5. Mississippi	1.0
5. Nevada	1.0
6. Kentucky	1.1
6. Oklahoma	1.1
6. Tennessee	1.1
10. Louisiana	1.2
10. North Dakota	1.2

States Where the Highest Percentage of Towns Contain an Early U.S. President's Name

In the United States, about 0.8 percent of towns contain a U.S. president's name (among the first 16 presidents from Washington through Lincoln), and more than half the states deviate little from normal, having between 0.5 and 1 percent. The Northeast and the Midwest have the highest percentages of towns containing a U.S. president's name, while the western states had the lowest (with Hawaii having none).

This list includes towns and cities sharing the last name (or "Quincy") of presidents from Washington through Lincoln (1789–1865) and variations, such as "Washingtonville" or "Jefferson Hills" (but not "Taylorsville"; note the extra "s"). A few places, especially those named Jackson or Taylor, may have been named for someone other than the president, yet they still share the same name.

One might ask if the western states would increase in this list if later presidents were included. That would generally not be the case as fewer towns were named after the later presidents (and many were still in the Midwest and Northeast). Some later presidents had common last names (Johnson, Wilson, Clinton, etc.) where the namesake towns almost certainly would have been named after someone else, which would have made the data somewhat less meaningful.

State	Percentage of Presidential Towns
1. New Hampshire	2.0
2. Ohio	1.8
3. Maine	1.5
4. Indiana	1.4
5. New Jersey	1.3
5. Rhode Island	1.3
7. North Dakota	1.2
7. Vermont	1.2
9. Delaware	1.1
9. Pennsylvania	1.1

States Where the Lowest Percentage of Towns Contain an Early U.S. President's Name

State	Percentage of Presidential Towns
1. Hawaii	none
2. Nevada	0.3
2. New Mexico	0.3
4. Arizona	0.4
4. Arkansas	0.4
4. Minnesota	0.4
7. Alaska	0.5
7. California	0.5
7. Montana	0.5
7. Texas	0.5
7. Washington	0.5
7. Wyoming	0.5

States Where the Highest Percentage of Town Names End in "Ville"

The French word for "city" appears in over 5 percent of the town and city names in the United States, especially in the Northeast and Midwest. Ironically, "ville" is rarely used in town or city names in France, though it is common in Quebec.

Despite containing Jacksonville, the largest city in the United States with its name ending with "ville," Florida ranks only No. 35 out of the 50 states. The western states generally rank lowest.

State	Percentage of "Ville" Towns
1. Rhode Island	12.6
2. Vermont	10.8
3. New York	10.2
4. Connecticut	9.9
4. Pennsylvania	9.9
6. Ohio	9.3
7. Indiana	8.5
8. Massachusetts	8.4
9. Georgia	7.3
10. New Jersey	7.2

States Where the Lowest Percentage of Town Names End in "Ville"

State	Percentage of "Ville" Towns
1. Hawaii	0.7
2. New Mexico	1.0
3. Alaska	1.2
4. Arizona	1.5
4. Wyoming	1.5
6. Washington	1.6
7. Montana	1.9
7. Nevada	1.9
9. North Dakota	2.0
10. Colorado	2.2
10. Idaho	2.2

States Where the Highest Percentage of Town Names End in "Town" or "Ton"

Just like "ville," cities with names ending in "town" or "ton" are primarily in the Northeast and the Midwest. Western states, especially those with large numbers of names representing languages other than English, such as Spanish, Hawaiian or the Native-American languages, rank lowest.

State	Percentage of "Town"/"Ton" Towns
1. New Jersey	11.4
2. Rhode Island	10.7
3. New Hampshire	10.3
4. Pennsylvania	9.7
5. Vermont	8.8
6. Massachusetts	8.4
7. Connecticut	8.3
8. Ohio	8.1
9. Maryland	8.0
10. Indiana	7.2

States Where the Lowest Percentage of Town Names End in "Town" or "Ton"

State	Percentage of "Town"/"Ton" Towns
1. Hawaii	0.5
2. Alaska	1.1
3. New Mexico	1.8
4. Arizona	2.1
5. California	3.2
6. Nevada	3.4
7. Oregon	3.5
8. Florida	3.6
9. Washington	3.7
10. Colorado	3.8
10. Idaho	3.8
10. Montana	3.8

States Where the Highest Percentage of Cities and Towns Have Spanish Names

Nationwide, 4.8 percent of all cities and towns have Spanish names, including some of the largest cities in the United States, such as Los Angeles, San Diego and San Antonio. The southwestern United States, which used to be part of Mexico, has the highest percentage of cities with Spanish-language names (despite the fact that many of the cities and their names were created after much of the Southwest was ceded from Mexico to the United States in 1848).

State	Percentage of Cities and Towns with Spanish Names
1. New Mexico	44.2
2. California	28.4
3. Texas	18.9
4. Arizona	17.9
5. Colorado	12.6
6. Florida	6.2
7. Nevada	5.6
8. Utah	3.1*
9. Illinois	2.8*
10. Missouri	2.7*
10. Washington	2.7*

* Even though these states rank in the top 10, they are actually below the national average of 4.8 percent, since Spanish city names are so heavily concentrated in a few states.

States Where the Lowest Percentage of Cities and Towns Have Spanish Names

The East Coast (north of Florida) contains most of the states with the fewest Spanish names.

State	Percentage of Cities and Towns with Spanish Names
1. Connecticut	none
1. Delaware	none
1. Hawaii	none
1. New Hampshire	none
1. Rhode Island	none
1. Vermont	none
7. Massachusetts	0.4
8. North Carolina	0.6
8. Pennsylvania	0.6
10. Alaska	0.9

Arboreal Monikers: States with the Highest Percentage of Towns Named After Trees

Towns in the southeastern United States, the Mid-Atlantic, and California are most likely to be named after trees, while towns in parts of the West, Plains and (somewhat surprisingly) New England are least likely. This includes both Spanish and English tree names and towns with trees making up part of the name (such as "Oakdale" or "Poplar Bluff").

State	Percentage of Tree-Named Towns
1. Tennessee	6.6
2. Florida	6.2
3. Delaware	5.5
4. New Jersey	5.0
4. North Carolina	5.0
6. California	4.9
6. Maryland	4.9
8. Virginia	4.4
9. Arkansas	4.3
9. Louisiana	4.3

States with the Lowest Percentage of Towns Named After Trees

State	Percentage of Tree-Named Towns
1. Hawaii	0.2
2. North Dakota	1.0
3. Montana	1.1
4. Alaska	1.2
5. Wyoming	1.3
6. Nevada	1.7
6. South Dakota	1.7
6. New Hampshire	1.7
9. Kansas	1.9
9. Nebraska	1.9
9. Vermont	1.9

Atypical Avenues: Weird Street Names

Nobody will ever get these street names confused with Main Street or Second Street!

5000th Street—Bronson, KS 66716
Aaahi Street—Mililani, HI 96789
Alphabet Street—Islip, NY 11741
Assembly of God Lane—Buras, LA 70041
Beep Dump Road—Nyssa, OR 97913
Big Mac Road—Lakeview, AR 72642
Bingo Road—Sutherlin, OR 97479
Breath Lane—Bay St. Louis, MS 39520
Burrito Drive—Hillsborough County, FL 33569
Candy Cane Lane—Redding, CA 96003
Cannibal Road—Loleta, CA 95551
Cokain Road—Harrisville, PA 16038
Conservative Street—New Albany, IN 47150
Daddy Drive—Leesville, LA 71446
Daddy Rabbit Road—Royston, GA 30662
Double Trouble Road—Toms River, NJ 08757
Drunk Horse Lane—Westcliffe, CO 81252
Drunkard Road—Jetersville, VA 23083
Ego Avenue—Eastpointe, MI 48021
Gang Road—Holden, ME 04429
Gasoline Alley—Victorville, CA 92394
Geeker Street—Pensacola, FL 32514
Getta Way—Mocksville, NC 27028
Her Street—North Pole, AK 99705
His Way—Bakersfield, CA 93308
Hitler Street—Kimmell, IN 46760
Jokers Wild Lane—Grass Valley, CA 95945
Keepa Way—Mocksville, NC 27028
Leaky Pond Road—Sewanee, TN 37375
Liquid Laughter Lane—Columbia, MD 21044
Livewire Lane—Amado, AZ 85645
Lizard Head Lane—Sedona, AZ 86336
Monopoly Street—Silverdale, WA 98383
Monster Lane—Canton, IL 61520
My Way—San Diego, CA 92154
Old Paint Drive—Victorville, CA 92392
Outatha Way—Mocksville, NC 27028

Peoples Court—Burlington, KY 41005
Poison Ivy Drive—Bruceville, TX 76630
Poison Oak Lane—Redding, CA 96003
Pothole Road—Goldendale, WA 98620
Queen of Hearts Court—Jacksonville, FL 32210
Radical Road—Sumter, SC 29153
Seinfeld Court—Houston, TX 77069
Sesame Street—Plattsburgh, NY 12901
Shades Of Death Road—Andover, NJ 07821
Star Trek Drive—Pelham, AL 35124
Staya Way—Mocksville, NC 27028
Stock Market Road—Pine Bush, NY 12566
Taco Street—Ulmito, TX 78575
That A Way—Newport, TN 37821
This A Way—Newport, TN 37821
Ticket Street—San Diego, CA 92126
Tiger Whip Road—Stockton, IL 61085
Tornado Alley—Parrish, AL 35580
Ugly Creek Road—Duck River, TN 38454
Wanta Drive—Plover, WI 54467
Weatherman Avenue—Port Charlotte, FL 33954
Weird Road—Shepherdsville, KY 40165
Wolftongue Road—Nederland, CO 80466
Wow Road—Corpus Christi, TX 78413
Wreck Avenue—Salem, NH 03079
Your Way—Grants Pass, OR 97527
Zzyzx Road—Baker, CA 92309

Street-Naming Conventions

Streets sometimes are seemingly named at random, but other times, there is a clear pattern to the names. Here are a few examples.

1. 1st Street, 2nd Street, 30th Street, etc.

Using numbers for street names is a phenomenon primarily found only in the United States and Canada (especially when the numbers are in order), though Bogota, Colombia has many ordered numbered streets (e.g., Calle 1). In the United States, numbered streets are especially common in the Midwest, but less so in the Appalachians and New England. Using single letters (e.g., E Street) is also primarily a U.S. phenomenon.

Washington, D.C., was the trendsetter for orderly numbered and lettered streets in 1800, when it was first the capital of the United States. This even included diagonal directions (NE, NW, SE, SW) from the capitol in the addresses. New York, NY followed 12 years later with the numbering of many of Manhattan's streets.

Some cities, such as Miami, Florida, take the numbering of streets to an extreme. Streets oriented east-west are called NW 1st Street, NE 20th Street, etc., while streets oriented north-south are called avenues, like SW 12th Avenue or NW 44th Avenue (all of these geographically placed in numerical order). In addition, some east-west streets are called terraces, such as NW 12th Terrace, due to an extra street needed between NW 12th Street and NW 13th Street (and likewise, courts are used as "fillers" between north-south avenues).

2. Streets named after presidents.

Most sizable cities in the United States have at least a few streets named after presidents of the United States. A few place the streets in the order that they served. In the northeastern part of Minneapolis, Minnesota, a series of north-south streets are named after presidents sequentially from Washington Street through Hoover Street (with a few streets using names other than the last name, such as Quincy Street or Benjamin Street, since there are two presidents named Adams and two Harrisons).

3. Streets named in alphabetical order.

A number of larger cities in the United States name some of their streets in alphabetical order (first street name in a series starting with the letter A, second street name starting with the letter B, etc.). This makes streets easier to find.

In Washington, D.C., this method is taken a step further. Traveling south to north from the Capitol, one would cross east-west-oriented streets sequentially from A Street through W Street (with a few other streets mixed in and with J Street missing). Next, one would cross Adams Street, then Bryant Street, and the pattern of alphabetical two-syllable words would continue through Webster Street (again with a few other streets mixed in and a missing street starting with the letter J). Then, after Webster Street, one would cross the first three-syllable street, Allison Street, then Buchanan Street, Crittenden Street, up through Whittier Street (this time with Jefferson Street used for a name starting with J). What's next, a four-syllable street name? No. Instead, plant names are used after Whittier Street, but still in alphabetical order, up to the very northernmost point of the District of Columbia.

4. Address-like street names in Utah.

In most cities in Utah, including Salt Lake City, Provo and St. George, numerous street names are based on the address (where each block equals 100) and direction from the city center. A street name of W 500 S indicates that the street is west of the location five blocks directly south of the city center. An address of 600 S 700 E would indicate that the location is six blocks south and seven blocks east of the city center.

5. State street names of Lawrence, Kansas.

Many of the streets that run north-south in older parts of Lawrence, Kansas are named after states. While numerous cities (including Washington, D.C.) have a lot of state street names, Lawrence's follows a particular order.

The "main street" is Massachusetts Street, named after the state from which most of Lawrence's founders originated. State streets to the east of Massachusetts Street were named after the original 13 colonies but without the Confederate states (Lawrence was founded in 1854 as an anti-slavery town shortly before the Civil War). The first street east of Massachusetts Street, New Hampshire Street, was the named after the most northern of the colonies, while the furthest east state street in Lawrence (originally) was Maryland Street, the most southern of the colonies that remained in the union (Oregon Street was later added).

State streets to the west of Massachusetts Street were named based on states achieving statehood after the original 13 colonies (from east to west, in order of statehood, from Vermont through Florida). West of Florida Street are a few other state streets, though out of order.

6. Cigarette streets in Dallas, Texas

Though the streets do not follow any particular pattern, a small section of Dallas, Texas has five streets in a row named after cigarette brands (past or present). They are (from north to south) Fatima Avenue, Kool Avenue, Camel Court, Lucky Lane and Pall Mall Avenue.

What "States" Are Called in Other Countries

Most countries refer to their divisions as "states," "provinces," "parishes" or sometimes just "divisions" (or at least, that is the English-language equivalent). Here are some less common English-equivalent names of "states" (all names are listed in the plural form):

Cantons—Switzerland
Communes—Liechtenstein (believe me, these aren't very big "states"!)
Governorates—Egypt, Jordan, Kuwait, Lebanon, Tunisia, Yemen
Juletule—Moldova *
Oblasti—Ukraine *
Oblasts—Russia, Tajikistan
Oblystar—Kazakhstan, Kyrgyzstan *
Prefectures—Central African Republic, Chad, Greece, Guinea, Japan, Rwanda
Rayons—Azerbaijan, Georgia
Voblastsi—Belarus *
Welayatlar—Turkmenistan *
Wiloyatlar—Uzbekistan *

* Singular forms are juletul, oblast, oblysy, voblasts, welayat and wiloyat, respectively.

Home Away from Home: Names of States and Larger U.S. Cities Found in Other Countries

Some names used for large cities and states in the United States, including California, Colorado, Florida, San Antonio, San Francisco and San Jose are found in numerous Spanish-speaking countries. However, many other names are rarely found outside the United States. In some cases, the foreign place was named first (and sometimes resulted in the name of the United States place). All the cities on this list are much smaller than their U.S. counterparts (except "Philadelphia," an alternate name for Amman, Jordan).

Alabama Camp, Liberia
Albuquerque, Spain
Alaska, Zimbabwe
Arizona—numerous instances, including Argentina and Brazil
Atlanta, Nicaragua
Austin, Canada (Manitoba)
Baltimore, South Africa
Boston, United Kingdom (England)
Buffalo—numerous instances, including rivers in Australia and South Africa
Cabo San Diego, Argentina

California—numerous instances, including Baja California
Charlotte Lake, Canada (British Columbia)
Chicago, Philippines
Cleveland River, Canada (Southampton Island)
Colorado—numerous instances, including Costa Rica and Cuba
Dallas, Canada (Manitoba)
Denver, United Kingdom (England)
Florida—numerous instances, including a city and department of
   Uruguay
Georgia—the name of a nation
Houston, Canada (British Columbia)
Indiana, Brazil
Jacksonville, Cuba
Long Beach, Canada (Newfoundland)
Los Angeles—numerous instances, including Chile and Mexico
Maryland, Nigeria
Memphis, Egypt
Miami, Colombia
Montana—numerous instances, including Bulgaria and Switzerland
Nevada—numerous instances, including Bosnia & Herzegovina and
   Mexico
Norfolk—numerous instances, including a South Pacific Island
Orlando, South Africa
Philadelphia, Jordan (alternate name for Amman)
Phoenix, South Africa
Pittsburgh, Canada (Ontario)
Portland, Australia (New South Wales)
Rochester, United Kingdom (England)
Sacramento, Mexico (Coahuila)
St. Louis, Senegal
San Antonio—numerous instances, including Philippines and Spain
San Francisco—numerous instances, including Argentina and Mexico
San Jose—numerous instances, including Costa Rica and Philippines
Springfield, Canada (Nova Scotia)
Tampa, Indonesia
Texas, Australia (Queensland)
Utah, Papua New Guinea
Virginia, South Africa
Washington Land, Greenland
Wyoming, Canada (Ontario)

Largest U.S. Cities Named after a Food

Despite America's love affair with eating, not that many cities are named after food. Fruits are the most commonly used foods in city names, while meats are rarely used. Somehow, "Porktown" just doesn't seem like an appealing place to live.

City	Population
1. Orange, CA	128,821
2. Citrus Heights, CA	85,071
3. Appleton, WI	70,087
4. Walnut Creek, CA	64,296
5. Sugar Land, TX	63,328
6. Apple Valley, CA	54,239
7. Port Orange, FL	45,823
8. Apple Valley, MN	45,527
9. Coconut Creek, FL	43,566
10. Pearland, TX	37,640

Note: East Orange (69,824) and West Orange (44,943), New Jersey were named after Holland's Duke of Orange.

This list does not include cities that have contributed to food names, like "K.C. Strip" or "Philly Cheesesteak."

Source of Population: U.S. Census, 2000.

Largest U.S. Cities with One-Syllable Names

Despite the abundance of one-syllable words in the English language, just 1.6 percent of U.S. cities (50,000 people or more) have only one syllable in their names. Even cities named after people are rarely monosyllabic as Washington, Clinton, and Franklin are common city and town names, while names like Smith, Polk, and Pierce are almost exclusively reserved for counties.

City	Population
1. Flint, MI	124,943
2. Lynn, MA	89,050
3. Troy, MI	80,959
4. Kent, WA	79,524
5. Sparks, NV	66,346

6. Burke, VA	57,737
7. Wayne, NJ	54,069
8. Bend, OR	52,029
9. Ames, IA	50,731
10. Troy, NY	49,170

Largest World Cities with One-Syllable Names

Most other parts of the world also have few cities with one-syllable names as only 1.7 percent of large cities in the world (500,000 people or more) have monosyllabic names. Central and Eastern Europe and the Middle East are areas most likely to have one-syllable names, while Latin America has almost no places (including very small villages) that are monosyllabic.

City	Population
1. Seoul, South Korea*	10,280,523
2. Minsk, Belarus	1,677,137
3. Wien, Austria**	1,550,123
4. Omsk, Russia	1,133,900
5. Perm, Russia	1,000,100
6. Köln, Germany**	967,940
7. Qom, Iran	777,677
8. Fès, Morocco	769,014
9. Hims, Syria	540,133
10. Jos, Nigeria	510,300

If Rome, Italy, and Prague, Czech Republic were their true names, they would rank No. 2 and No. 6, respectively. Their names (using the Italian or Czech languages) are actually Roma and Praha.

* Seoul can be pronounced with either one or two syllables.

** Wien and Köln are one-syllable names in their home countries, even though English speakers usually call those cities Vienna and Cologne, respectively.

Liquid Language: What Are Streams Called? Creeks? Brooks? Branches? Runs?

In some parts of the country, streams are referred to as creeks; in others, they are referred to as brooks, runs or branches. The next few lists are percentages of the streams (moving bodies of water smaller than a river, including some that occasionally become dry) called a certain name (based on U.S. Geological Survey data). These are based on the official names (as "Oak Creek" would be considered a "creek" or "Adams Brook" would be considered to be called a "brook").

These lists do not include names such as "canyon," "gulch" or "hollow," which refer to the ravines where the streams flow and not the streams themselves (even though they will sometimes be used more often than the stream name).

States Where the Highest Percentage of Streams Are Called "Creeks"

States in the northwestern U.S. are most likely to call their streams "creeks."

State	Percentage of Streams Which Are Called "Creeks"
1. Montana	98.1
2. Idaho	98.0
3. Washington	97.2
4. Oregon	96.7
5. Wyoming	96.6
6. South Dakota	96.5
7. Alaska	95.2
8. Colorado	93.8
9. Kansas	93.1
10. North Dakota	92.0
10. California	92.0

States Where the Highest Percentage of Streams Are Called "Brooks"

New England contains most of the "brooks" in the United States.

State	Percentage of Streams Which Are Called "Brooks"
1. Connecticut	95.8
2. New Hampshire	95.1
3. Rhode Island	91.3
4. Massachusetts	90.6
5. Vermont	90.2
6. Maine	81.7
7. New York	42.1
8. New Jersey	30.5
9. Minnesota	7.6
10. Indiana	3.4

States Where the Highest Percentage of Streams Are Called "Branches"

The Southeast contains most of the "branches" in the United States. However, in only two states are a majority of streams called "branches."

State	Percentage of Streams Which Are Called "Branches"
1. Tennessee	58.3
2. Kentucky	54.0
3. Delaware	48.3
4. Alabama	43.2
5. North Carolina	42.3
6. South Carolina	41.6
7. Missouri	35.7
8. Georgia	35.0
9. Florida	32.7
10. Virginia	32.6

This list does not include combination names, such as "East Branch Oak Creek."

States Where the Highest Percentage of Streams Are Called "Runs"

It is rare for anyplace outside of the Middle Atlantic States or the Lower Midwest to have a "run" (unless it's a 10-K!).

State	Percentage of Streams Which Are Called "Runs"
1. Pennsylvania	65.7
2. Ohio	50.2
3. West Virginia	45.5
4. Maryland	25.2
5. Indiana	20.4
6. Virginia	15.6
7. New Jersey	12.4
8. Delaware	7.9
9. Illinois	3.6
10. Kentucky	3.2

States with the Highest Density of "Gulches"

A "gulch" is a Western United States term for a ravine. States with a lot of mountains rank high here, but only those in the Western U.S.

While Colorado leads the nation in number of gulches (2,565), Hawaii has a greater density. Figures given below are in gulches (based on U.S. Geological Survey names) per 10,000 square miles, which is the same as a 100-mile by 100-mile area.

State	Gulches per 10,000 Sq. Mi.
1. Hawaii	883 *
2. Colorado	247
3. Idaho	159
4. California	129
5. Oregon	122
6. Montana	117
7. Wyoming	43
8. Washington	31
9. South Dakota	27
10. Utah	26

* State has fewer than 10,000 square miles.

States with the Highest Density of "Hollows"

"Hollow" is the equivalent to "gulch" in the Eastern United States. However, the term is occasionally used in the West (unlike "gulch" which is rarely used in the East), especially in Utah.

Tennessee has the largest number of "hollows" (4,516) and the greatest density of "hollows" of any state in the United States. Most states on this list contain either parts of the Appalachians or the Ozarks. Figures given below are in hollows (based on U.S. Geological Survey names) per 10,000 square miles, again the same as a 100-mile by 100-mile area.

State	Hollows per 10,000 Sq. Mi.
1. Tennessee	1,096
2. Missouri	438
3. Kentucky	408
4. West Virginia	396
5. Pennsylvania	328
6. Arkansas	276
7. Virginia	262
8. Ohio	157
9. Utah	153
10. Alabama	127

States with the Highest Density of "Canyons"

"Canyon" is based on the Spanish word "cañon," so it is not surprising (partly due to the rugged terrain) that this term is most commonly used in the Southwest, which was formerly owned by Mexico (and, previously, Spain). However, "canyon" is used for some gorges in the Pacific Northwest and northern Rockies.

While New Mexico has the largest number of canyons (4,256), Utah has the highest density of canyons. While Arizona has the largest and most famous canyon in the United States, it ranks only No. 4. Figures given below are in canyons (based on U.S. Geological Survey names) per 10,000 square miles and include cases where they are spelled "canon" or "cañon."

State	Canyons per 10,000 Sq. Mi.
1. Utah	427
2. New Mexico	351
3. California	265
4. Arizona	232
5. Nevada	188
6. Colorado	144
7. Oregon	139
8. Idaho	135
9. Washington	96
10. Wyoming	61

Unusually Pronounced Places in the United States

Many places in the United States have "local" pronunciations that would be quite unexpected a few states away. Accented syllables below are printed in capital letters.

1. Albany, Georgia—In New York, it's pronounced "ALL-bin-knee." In Georgia, it's pronounced "All-BANE-knee."

2. Arkansas River, Kansas—In Kansas, this river is pronounced "Ar-KAN-sas" (rhyming with Kansas), not "AR-kan-saw" like the state. However, where the Arkansas River flows through Colorado, Oklahoma and (of course) Arkansas, the favored pronunciation is "AR-kan-saw."

3. Berlin, New Hampshire and Berlin, Wisconsin—During World War I, both towns changed their pronunciations from "Ber-LIN" to "BURR-lin."

4. Buena Vista, Colorado—Like California, Colorado has "anglicized" many of Spanish city names. Buena Vista is "BYOO-nuh VIS-tuh" in central Colorado.

5. Cairo, Illinois—Unlike the large city in Egypt, this town (made famous by "Huckleberry Finn") is pronounced "CAY-row."

6. Du Bois, Pennsylvania—Excellent French pronunciation will get you far in Paris or Montreal (maybe) but not Du Bois (pronounced "DEW-boyz"), Pennsylvania.

7. Nevada, Missouri—This small town in extreme Western Missouri (closer to the state of Nevada than almost any other town in Missouri) is pronounced "Nuh-VAY-duh."

8. New Madrid, Missouri—Another Missouri town (the one near the epicenter of the severe 1811–1812 earthquakes) uses a unique pronunciation of a Spanish town name. Instead of "Muh-DRID," it's pronounced "MAD-rid."

9. Peru, Indiana—Locals in this Northern Indiana town call their home "PEE-rue" instead of "Pay-RUE."

10. Quincy, Massachusetts—When is the letter C pronounced like a Z? When it's in the name of the Massachusetts city "QUIN-zee."

CHAPTER TWO
Atlas Geography

This chapter (and entire book, for that matter) is for anyone who becomes fascinated just by opening an atlas. We will explore borders, distances, mountains and other things found on maps (though most of the "road atlas geography" will be saved for Chapter 3). Much of the material for this chapter "bleeds" into the other chapters, since everything explored in geography's realm can somehow be depicted on a map.

States and Similarly Sized Nations

These paired states and nations are similar in size. However, on a map, they might not always appear to be the same size, due to shape (and scale) differences. Often, a foreign nation, viewed on a global or continental scale, looks smaller than a similarly sized U.S. state, viewed on a national scale. Ecuador, a small nation in South America, is nearly the same size as Nevada, a large state.

Alabama—Greece
Alaska—Mongolia
Arizona—Italy
Arkansas—Bangladesh
California—Paraguay
Colorado—New Zealand
Connecticut—Bahamas
Delaware—Trinidad & Tobago
Florida—Nepal

Georgia—Suriname
Hawaii—Kuwait
Idaho—Guyana
Illinois—Tajikistan
Indiana—Portugal
Iowa—Tajikistan (again)
Kansas—Oman
Kentucky—Iceland
Louisiana—North Korea

Maine—Austria
Maryland—Burundi
Massachusetts—El Salvador
Michigan—Tunisia
Minnesota—Uganda
Mississippi—Honduras
Missouri—Cambodia
Montana—Japan
Nebraska—Kyrgyzstan
Nevada—Ecuador
New Hampshire—Djibouti
New Jersey—Slovenia
New Mexico—Poland
New York—Nicaragua
North Carolina—Eritrea
North Dakota—Syria
Ohio—Bulgaria

Oklahoma—Uruguay
Oregon—Romania
Pennsylvania—Benin
Rhode Island—Samoa
South Carolina—U.A.E.
South Dakota—Senegal
Tennessee—Cuba
Texas—Burma
Utah—Laos
Vermont—Macedonia
Virginia—Serbia and
   Montenegro
Washington—Cambodia
   (again)
West Virginia—Sri Lanka
Wisconsin—Nepal (again)
Wyoming—Ghana

Hope They're a Good Neighbor: Enclaves

An enclave is a nation completely surrounded by one other nation. In this list, the nation in parentheses surrounds the enclave.

1. Lesotho (South Africa)
2. San Marino (Italy)
3. Vatican City (Italy)

The Split: Exclaves

When a portion of a country is separated from another portion, it is called an exclave. That portion of a country must be separated by another nation, not just by water. Only exclaves of independent nations are listed here. One former exclave is West Berlin (when West Germany and East Germany were separate).

1. Alaska (United States)

This is the largest exclave in the world. Alaska is separated from the 48 contiguous states by Canada.

2. Cabinda (Angola)

Along the west coast of Africa, a small piece of the Democratic Republic of Congo (the only section connecting the rest of that nation with the ocean) separates Cabinda from the rest of Angola.

There is a large movement for independence of Cabinda (including an expatriate Cabindese government), but Angola keeps a tight grip on Cabinda due to resources (mostly oil and forest), which supply the Angolan economy with about $4 billion per year.*

3. Kaliningrad (Russia)

Formerly known as Königsberg, and once part of Prussia and Germany, Kaliningrad became, at the end of World War II, part of the Russian Soviet Federal Socialist Republic, which, in turn, was a part of the U.S.S.R. After the Soviet Union split, the newly independent nations of Lithuania, Latvia and Belarus all stood between the Russian exclave of Kaliningrad and the main part of Russia.

4. Musandam Peninsula (Oman)

The Musandam Peninsula is separated from the rest of Oman by the United Arab Emirates.

5. Naxcivan (Azerbaijan)

Naxcivan is separated from the rest of Azerbaijan by Armenia. In addition, a very small exclave of Armenia exists within Azerbaijan.

6. Eastern Uzbekistan

Four mountainous exclaves of Uzbekistan are completely surrounded by Kyrgyzstan.

Source: Forces of Liberation of the State of Cabinda (F.L.E.C.), 2000.

Five Lakes in the World That Border Three or More Nations

Lake		Nations Touching the Lake
1. Caspian Sea*	5	Azerbaijan, Iran, Kazakhstan, Russia, Turkmenistan
2. Lake Chad	4	Cameroon, Chad, Niger, Nigeria

2. Lake Tanganyika	4	Burundi, Congo (Dem. Rep.), Tanzania, Zambia
4. Lake Malawi	3	Malawi, Mozambique, Tanzania
4. Lake Victoria	3	Kenya, Tanzania, Uganda

* The Caspian Sea is actually a salt lake, not a sea.

Longest Borders Between Countries

The United States shares two of the longest borders in the world with Canada and Mexico. While the U.S.-Canada border is the longest in the world, the Kazakhstan-Russia border is the longest *continuous* border in the world. One border on this list, India-Bangladesh, looks short; however, it is quite jagged (which adds length) and encircles most of Bangladesh.

Border	Border Length (Mi.)
1. U.S.-Canada	5,526 *
2. Kazakhstan-Russia	4,254
3. Argentina-Chile	3,200
4. China-Mongolia	2,904
5. India-Bangladesh	2,518
6. China-Russia	2,265 **
7. Russia-Mongolia	2,138
8. Bolivia-Brazil	2,113
9. China-India	2,100
10. U.S.-Mexico	2,067

* Includes 3,987 miles of border between Canada and the 48 contiguous states and 1,539 miles of border between Canada and Alaska.

** Twenty-eight miles of the border are west of Mongolia; the remainder is east of Mongolia.

Source: CIA World Factbook, 2003.

Shortest Borders Between Countries

Border	Border Length (Mi.)
1. Spain-Gibraltar	0.7
2. Italy-Vatican City	2.0
3. France-Monaco	2.7
4. Turkey-Azerbaijan	6
5. Guadeloupe-Netherland Antilles (Saint Martin-St. Maarten)	6.3
6. Egypt-Gaza Strip	7
7. Morocco-Spain (Ceuta and Melilla)	9.9
8. Russia-North Korea	12
9. Austria-Liechtenstein	22
9. Iran-Armenia	22

In addition, the internal border between China and Macau is 0.2 miles, and the internal border between China and Hong Kong is 19 miles.

Includes territories with international land borders. Malaysia-Singapore is not considered a border, since Singapore is an island.

Source: CIA World Factbook, 2003.

Nations That Border the Most Other Nations

Large nations surrounded by a lot of small nations are the winners on this list (unlike the U.S. or Canada, which are surrounded by oceans and one or two large countries). Only independent nations are counted here (so Macau and Hong Kong would not count as bordering nations with China).

Country	Bordering Nations
1. China	14
1. Russia	14
3. Brazil	9
3. Congo (Dem. Rep.)	9
3. Germany	9
3. Sudan	9
7. France	8
7. Turkey	8
9. Hungary	7

9. Iran	7
9. Mali	7
9. Niger	7
9. Poland	7
9. Saudi Arabia	7
9. Serbia and Montenegro	7
9. Tanzania	7
9. Ukraine	7
9. Zambia	7

Counties in the U.S. That Border the Largest Number of Other Counties (and/or Parishes)

San Juan County, in southeastern Utah, borders 11 other counties (including some in Colorado and Arizona). If one includes the three counties touching diagonally at an infinitesimally small point, the grand total is 14.

County	Bordering Counties
1. San Juan, Utah	11
2. Worcester, Massachusetts	10
3. Baker, Florida	9
3. Caddo, Louisiana	9
3. Cherry, Nebraska	9
3. Custer, Nebraska	9
3. Elko, Nevada	9
3. Grafton, New Hampshire	9
3. Idaho, Idaho	9
3. Lea, New Mexico	9
3. Lycoming, Pennsylvania	9
3. Mono, California	9
3. Nye, Nevada	9
3. Park, Wyoming	9
3. Saguache, Colorado	9
3. Washington, Pennsylvania	9

And, by the way, Cimarron County, Oklahoma borders four other states: Colorado, Kansas, New Mexico and Texas. However, it only borders seven counties.

Good Day Trips: Towns within 100 Miles of Five or More Foreign Countries

Kurd, Hungary is the only place in the world within 100 miles (in fact, 95 miles) of seven different foreign nations. The places listed are within 100 miles (by air) of at least five foreign (independent) countries.

Town, Country		Countries within 100 Miles
1. Kurd, Hungary	7	Austria, Bosnia & Herzegovina, Croatia, Romania, Slovakia, Slovenia, Yugoslavia

Kurd is approximately 80 miles SSW of Budapest.

2. Durrës, Albania	6	Bosnia & Herzegovina, Croatia, Greece, Italy, Macedonia, Yugoslavia

3. Az-Zalaf, Syria	5	Iraq, Israel, Jordan, Lebanon, Saudi Arabia

Az-Zalaf is approximately 80 miles SE of Damascus.

3. Krusevac, Yugoslavia	5	Albania, Bosnia & Herzegovina, Bulgaria, Macedonia, Romania

Krusevac is approximately 100 miles SSE of Belgrade.

3. Zurich, Switzerland	5	Austria, France, Germany, Italy, Liechtenstein

Zurich is among many other cities in Switzerland, including Bern and Lucerne, within 100 miles of five foreign countries.

In addition, if places like Anguilla, Guadeloupe, Martinique or Montserrat became independent nations, several Caribbean towns would also be on this list.

Land of State Lines: Towns within 100 Miles of Six or More Other States

Numerous locations in Western Connecticut and a few places in southeastern New York and southwestern Massachusetts are within 100 miles (as the crow flies—or maybe other common New England birds, like the cardinal or blue jay) of seven other states. A very tiny section of Tennessee is also within 100 miles of seven other states.

Town, State		States within 100 Miles
1. Waterbury, Connecticut	7	Massachusetts,New Hampshire, New Jersey, New York, Pennsylvania, Rhode Island, Vermont

Bristol, Hamden, Meriden, Southington, Torrington and Wallingford are other large towns in Connecticut within 100 miles of seven other states.

1. Great Barrington, Massachusetts	7	Connecticut, New Hampshire, New Jersey, New York, Pennsylvania, Rhode Island, Vermont

Great Barrington is approximately 40 miles west of Springfield, Massachusetts.

1. Amenia, New York	7	Connecticut, Massachusetts, New Hampshire, New Jersey, Pennsylvania, Rhode Island, Vermont

Amenia is approximately 80 miles north of NYC.

1. Nobles, Tennessee	7	Alabama, Arkansas, Illinois, Indiana, Kentucky, Mississippi, Missouri

This small hamlet just west of Kentucky Lake (or six miles NE of Paris, Tennessee) is just barely within 100 miles of seven other states. A large number of towns in Western Tennessee are within 100 miles of six other states, including Humboldt, McKenzie, Milan and Paris.

5. Spruce Pine, North Carolina	6	Georgia, Kentucky, South Carolina,Tennessee, Virginia, West Virginia

A few locations in Western North Carolina are within 100 miles of these six states listed, including Spruce Pine, about 40 miles NE of Asheville.

5. Sweetwater, Tennessee	6	Alabama, Georgia, Kentucky, North Carolina, South Carolina, Virginia

In addition to Western Tennessee, a small part of southeastern Tennessee is within 100 miles of six other states. Sweetwater is approximately 40 miles SW of Knoxville. Erwin, in northeastern Tennessee just south of Johnson City, is within 100 miles of Georgia, Kentucky, North Carolina, South Carolina, Virginia and West Virginia.

5. Washington, D.C.	6	Delaware, Maryland, New Jersey, Pennsylvania, Virginia, West Virginia

Capitol Hill is conveniently located for at least 12 senators (of course, it is very distant for some senators, such as those from Alaska or Hawaii).

5. Concord, New Hampshire	6	Connecticut, Maine, Massachusetts, New York, Rhode Island, Vermont

5. West Glocester, Rhode Island	6	Connecticut, Maine, Massachusetts, New Hampshire, New York, Vermont
5. Brattleboro, Vermont	6	Connecticut, Maine, Massachusetts, New Hampshire, New York, Rhode Island

Many places of New England are within 100 miles of 6 states, including those in parts of southern New Hampshire, southeastern Vermont and a small section of northwestern Rhode Island (plus parts of Connecticut and Massachusetts, which go the extra step by having sections within 100 miles of 7 states).

Some Places are Closer to Each Other Than...

In the United States:

El Paso, Texas is closer to San Diego, California than it is to Brownsville, Houston or Tyler, Texas.

Ewing, a small town in the far southwest corner of Virginia, is closer to St. Louis, Missouri than it is to Virginia Beach, Virginia.

Pensacola, Florida is closer to Evansville, Indiana than it is to Miami, Florida.

Bristol, Tennessee is closer to parts of the South Jersey Shore than it is to Memphis, Tennessee.

Cairo, Illinois is closer to Jackson, Mississippi than it is to Chicago, Illinois.

Crescent City, California is closer to Vancouver, British Columbia than it is to Santa Barbara, California.

Ironwood, Michigan is closer to Jamestown, North Dakota than it is to Detroit, Michigan.

Kansas City, Kansas is closer to Florence, Alabama than it is to Scottsbluff, Nebraska.

Harpers Ferry, West Virginia is closer to Stamford, Connecticut than it is to Huntington, West Virginia.

Brownsville, Texas is closer to Mexico City, Mexico than it is to Dallas, Texas.

Honolulu, Hawaii is closer to Portland, Oregon than it is to San Diego, California.

Attu Island, Alaska, at the west end of the Aleutians, is closer to Harbin, China than it is to Ketchikan, Alaska.

In Other Parts of the World:

Mumbai (Bombay), India is closer to Muscat, Oman, on the Arabian Peninsula than it is to Kolkata (Calcutta), India.

Merauke, Indonesia (on the island of New Guinea) is closer to all places in New Zealand than it is to Banda Aceh, Indonesia (on the island of Sumatra).

Copenhagen, Denmark is closer to Kaliningrad, Russia than it is to Amsterdam, Netherlands.

Milan, Italy is closer to Prague, Czech Republic than it is to Naples, Italy. Milan is also closer to Heidelberg, Munich and Stuttgart, Germany than it is to Rome, Italy.

Recife, Brazil is closer to Freetown, Sierra Leone than it is to several locations in extreme southern Brazil, including Uruguaiana and Rio Grande.

Recife, Brazil is also closer to Bamako, Mali, the capital of an African nation that is not even on the Atlantic Coast, than it is to several locations in extreme western Brazil, including Cruzeiro do Sul and Benjamin Constant.

St. Johns, Newfoundland, in Canada, is closer to Prague, Czech Republic than it is to Vancouver, British Columbia, in Canada.

The east tip of Africa (in Somalia) is closer both to Hong Kong and even parts of Taiwan than it is to Dakar, Senegal, in extreme western Africa.

The northernmost point in Chile is closer to the southernmost point in Cuba than it is to Cape Horn, at the very southernmost point in Chile.

Some Places Are Further East, West, North or South Than...

It's fairly common knowledge that Reno, Nevada is further west than Los Angeles, California. However, these other city geographical orientations are less known. If some of these seem too good to be true, open up the atlas (or find the latitudes and longitudes).

In the United States:

Libby, Montana is further *west* than both Las Vegas, Nevada and Needles, California.

Crescent City, California is further *north* than New Bedford, Massachusetts.

San Diego, California is at the same latitude as Charleston, South Carolina.

Jacksonville, Florida is further *west* than Youngstown, Ohio.

Old Faithful, in Yellowstone National Park, Wyoming, is further *west* than Cabo San Lucas, Mexico, at the tip of Baja California.

Wichita, Kansas is further *east* than Tampico, Mexico, on the Gulf Coast.

In Other Parts of the World:

Brindisi, Italy is further *east* than Bratislava, the capital of Slovakia.

Venice, Italy is at the same latitude as Ottawa, Canada.

Parts of Kazakhstan are further *west* than the extreme east tip of Ethiopia.

Lima, Peru is further *east* than Nassau, Bahamas.

San Jose, Costa Rica, in Central America is further *south* than Cartagena, Colombia and Caracas, Venezuela, both in South America.

In fact, the north tip of South America is further *north* than parts of Nicaragua (including its capital, Managua) and all of Costa Rica and Panama.

Parts of Hokkaido, Japan are further *east* than Guam.

Possibly the Most Amazing of All:

Algiers, Algeria (in Africa), is further *north* than the Midwest town of Branson, Missouri.

An Easy Attack? Capital Cities That Border Other Nations

The capital cities of most countries are either in the interior or along the coast (away from any international border). Here are countries where the capital city is along (or very near) an international border. This list does not include capital cities of small countries (less than 1,000 square miles).

Capital City, Country	Neighboring Country
Gaborone, Botswana	South Africa
Bangui, Central African Republic	Congo (Rep.)
N'Djamena, Chad	Cameroon
Kinshasa, Congo (Dem. Rep.)	Congo (Rep.)
Brazzaville, Congo (Rep.)	Congo (Dem. Rep.)
Nicosia, Cyprus	Turkish Cyprus*
Vientiane, Laos	Thailand
Maseru, Lesotho	South Africa
Asuncion, Paraguay	Argentina
Bratislava, Slovakia	Austria
Lome, Togo	Ghana

* Turkish Cyprus is not officially recognized as an independent nation, though it is usually considered separate from the rest of Cyprus.

Backroads and Hiking: 10 Locations in the U.S. Furthest from Any State or National Numbered Highway

1. Kabuch Point, Alaska, near Cold Bay: 549 miles

This is the furthest one can go in the United States (as an airplane would fly) from a highway (excluding islands—the Aleutians extend so far west that the furthest west islands are closer to some Japanese highways than Alaskan highways). The nearest highway is Alaska Highway 1 at Anchor Point, near Homer.

Because Alaska has such an extreme amount of land without highways (a plus for the environment), only one location from that state is listed here.

2. Central Idaho: 52 miles

One point, near the middle of the Frank Church-River of No Return Wilderness Area, is 52 miles from Idaho Highways 14 and 21 and U.S. Highway 93. This is the furthest one can get from a highway in the "lower 48."

3. Western Utah: 51 miles

At a point in western Juab county, one is 51 miles from Utah Highways 196 and 199 (to the northeast), U.S. combination Highway 6 and 50 (to the south) and Alternate U.S. Highway 93 (to the northwest, in Nevada). Parts of this highway-sparse area are restricted territory (including the Deseret Test Center), and most of it is desert.

4. Northwestern Arizona: 50 miles

One must go far to get from one rim of the Grand Canyon to the other. To the west of the Grand Canyon (much more than to the east), there are few roads (and no highways until around the Nevada border). One location in the eastern part of Grand Canyon-Parashant National Monument is exactly 50 miles from both Arizona Highways 66 and 389 and Interstate Highway 15 (I-15).

5. Extreme southwestern Idaho: 44 miles

In this "no man's land" covering the area near where Idaho, Nevada and Oregon meet, one spot is no closer than 44 miles from Idaho Highway 51 and two separate sections of U.S. Highway 95 (not exactly a straight road).

6. Northwestern Nevada: 43 miles

If it weren't for Nevada Highway 447, sticking into the middle of the vast northwestern Nevada expanse, this area would rank No. 2, only behind Alaska. Regardless, a spot west of the Black Rock Range is 43 miles from the end of Nevada Highway 447 and sections of Nevada Highway 140.

7. Northern Maine: 41 miles

Surprise! A state "back east" made it to this list. Of course, this is the remote section of Northern Maine, near the Canadian border, where all roads are privately run toll roads. A scenic spot in Piscataquis County is 41 miles from combined Maine Route 6 and 15 at Rockwood, the end of Maine Route 159 at Shin Pond and, across the border, Quebec's Route Provinciale 204.

8. Northeastern Minnesota: 38 miles

Parts of extreme northeastern Minnesota are closer to Trans-Canada Highway 11 than to any U.S. highway. A location in the Boundary Waters Canoe Area, almost due north of Schroeder, is 38 miles from Canada's Highway 11 and Minnesota Highways 1 and 61. Some numbered county highways are closer, however.

8. Eastern Utah: 38 miles

A spot in southern Uintah County is 38 miles from the end of Utah Highway 123 at Sunnyside, the end of Utah Highway 88 at Ouray and Interstate Highway 70 (I-70).

10. Southern Nevada: 37 miles

A spot at the far northern end of the Nevada Test Site is 37 miles from Nevada Highway 375 and two points along U.S. Highway 95.

This includes all numbered U.S., plus adjacent Canadian and Mexican highways. "Secondary state highways" (as in Montana) were included, but numbered county roads (as in Minnesota) were not. Islands and water locations (such as over lakes considered part of a state) were not included.

States with the Largest and Smallest Counties

The large states of the Western United States have the largest counties (by area), many of which are sparsely populated. Maine is the only state east of the Mississippi to have mostly large counties.

The smallest counties are in the Ohio Valley and Mid-Atlantic States. These are older states that tend to have a large number of small and mid-sized towns (which can act as county seats).

Largest-County States:

State	Average County Size (Sq. Mi.)
1. Alaska	21,183 *
2. Arizona	7,576
3. Nevada	6,855 **
4. Wyoming	4,084
5. New Mexico	3,677
6. Utah	2,833
7. California	2,689
8. Oregon	2,667
9. Montana	2,599
10. Maine	1,929

Smallest-County States:

State	Average County Size (Sq. Mi.)
1. Rhode Island	209
2. Kentucky	331
3. New Jersey	353
4. Georgia	364
5. Indiana	390
6. Virginia	399 **
7. Maryland	421 **
8. Tennessee	434
9. West Virginia	438
10. Ohio	465

* Alaskan boroughs/census areas.
** Does not include cities independent from any county.

Very Steep Mountains: Shortest (Horizontal) Distances in the U.S. Where the Elevation Changes by 10,000 Feet

Here are the mountains in the United States with elevation gains of 10,000 feet in less than 10 miles (less than five miles in Alaska). Not only does Alaska have the highest mountains in the United States, but it also has the steepest. The south and west slopes of Mt. St. Elias, in southeastern Alaska are the steepest in the country (based on the criteria used here), slightly edging out the north slope of Mt. McKinley. Those slopes average approximately 45 degrees for over two miles—in both the horizontal and the vertical!

These horizontal distances are, of course, as the crow flies and not as the hiker climbs.

Mountain Slope	Horizontal Distance
1. South/west slopes of Mt. St. Elias, Alaska	slightly under 2 miles
2. Wickersham Wall, north slope of Mt. McKinley, Alaska	2 miles
3. East slope of Mt. Foraker, Alaska	2 ½ miles
3. Southwest slope of Mt. Sanford, Alaska	2 ½ miles
3. Southwest slope of Mt. Fairweather, Alaska	2 ½ miles
6. Southwest slope of Mt. Blackburn, Alaska	3 miles
7. Southeast slope of Mt. Augusta, Alaska	3 ½ miles
8. South slope of Mt. Rainier, Washington	4 miles
8. Southwest slope of Mt. Bona, Alaska	4 miles
10. Southwest slope of Mt. Shasta, California	6 miles
11. From Palm Springs to Mt. San Jacinto, California	7 miles
11. From the south coast of Maui to Red Hill, Hawaii	7 miles
13. Southeast slope of Mt. Baker, Washington	8 miles

Honorable Mention:
East slope of Mt. Whitney, California   11 miles

Surprisingly Long Distance:
Southeast slope of Pikes Peak, Colorado   93 miles

Pikes Peak has the shortest horizontal distance for any elevation gain of 10,000 feet in Colorado.

Highest "Highest Points" of Nations

Here are the nations that can claim the true mountains of the world. With Mount Everest standing tall along an international border, two nations can claim the ultimate trophy.

Country	Highest Point (Ft.)
1. China	29,035
1. Nepal	29,035
3. Pakistan	28,250
4. India	28,208
5. Bhutan	24,784
6. Tajikistan	24,590
7. Afghanistan	24,557
8. Kyrgyzstan	24,406
9. Kazakhstan	22,949
10. Argentina	22,834

Lowest "Highest Points" of Nations

This list is for those who don't like to climb mountains (though there are plenty of stairs in the Vatican). The key to making this list is being a small island nation (and certainly not one of volcanic origin) or a small nation on a coastal plain. The highest point does not include places to which one can ascend in buildings (which in several cases, such as in Maldives or Vatican City, *would* be the true highest point).

Country	Highest Point (Ft.)
1. Maldives	8
2. Tuvalu	16
3. Marshall Islands	33

4. The Gambia	174
5. Nauru	200
6. Bahamas	207
7. Vatican City*	246
8. Kiribati	266
9. Qatar	338
10. Bahrain	400

* Vatican City is the only landlocked nation on this list.

Highest "Lowest Points" of Nations

The key to making this list is being a small, mountainous and (of course) landlocked nation.

Country	Lowest Point (Ft.)
1. Lesotho	4,592
2. Rwanda	3,116
3. Andorra	2,755
4. Burundi	2,532
5. Uganda	2,037
6. Mongolia	1,699
7. Botswana	1,683
8. Liechtenstein	1,410
9. Armenia	1,312
10. Central African Republic	1,099

Lowest "Lowest Points" of Nations

One must "climb" to the ocean from the lowest points of these countries. Note that these elevations will vary when a fluctuating salt lake is at the lowest point (in the case of Turkmenistan, the lowest point has dropped to as low as 361 feet below sea level).

Country	Lowest Point (Ft.)
1. Israel	-1,339
1. Jordan	-1,339
3. Syria	-656
4. Djibouti	-509
5. China	-505
6. Egypt	-436

7. Kazahkstan	-433
8. Ethiopia	-410
9. United States	-282
10. Turkmenistan	-266

Highest Locations in the U.S. Where the Terrain Is Flat or Gently Sloping

These are the places that have the highest elevations in which flat or gently sloping terrain extends for at least a few miles in all directions. In most of these cases, there are mountains not too far away.

1. South Park, Colorado—9,500 feet

This broken valley in central Colorado has several areas that have gently rolling terrain extending for at least a few miles, including areas near Jefferson and south of Fairplay. There are many open cattle grazing areas here. Large mountains are just miles away. And no—Kenny wasn't just killed here!

2. North Park, Colorado—8,400 feet

This 20-mile-wide, mostly flat valley, centered around Walden, near the Wyoming border, reaches as high as about 8,400 feet at its south end.

3. San Luis Valley, Colorado—7,800 feet

Near the source of the Rio Grande River, this highland valley of Southern Colorado is completely surrounded by mountains, but it is 40 miles wide in a few spots. Crops can be grown here, despite the high elevation and a very short growing season, including potatoes and barley. This gently sloping valley reaches 7,800 feet in the western parts before losing its flatness.

4. Green River Valley, Wyoming—7,400 feet

While parts of the Green River further downstream have deep gorges, after leaving its source, one section, the Wind River Range in Western Wyoming, broadens and forms a swampy plain (with a little help from some creeks). This area is north of Daniel along U.S. Highways 189/191. There are other scattered areas of flatness further south, but large mountains can be found in the other directions.

5. Western New Mexico—slightly over 7,200 feet

There are several flat areas in Western New Mexico, the largest being the Plains of San Agustin, which contains the Very Large Array telescopes of the National Radio Astronomy Observatory. The nearby North Plains reach elevations of over 7,200 feet.

6. Laramie, Wyoming—7,200 feet

A number of small lakes and the Laramie River valley combine to make areas (up to about 10 miles wide) both north and southwest of Laramie rather flat.

7. Palmer Divide, Colorado—7,000 feet (highest part of the Great Plains)

Some areas up to about 7,000 feet above sea level are moderately flat in this "highest of the High Plains" area near Peyton, Colorado, northeast of Colorado Springs. This is the highest part of the United States that can be approached without going through any mountains (and from three directions—north, east and south).

8. Northeastern New Mexico—7,000 feet

There is much less of an abrupt transition from the High Plains to the mountains in northeastern New Mexico than in other areas along the eastern extremes of the Rocky Mountains. Instead, most of this area is quite hilly with many mesas, buttes, canyons and small mountains. However, some areas around 6,500 feet above sea level, and a few localities to around 7,000 feet along Highways 64/87 west of Capulin, could be considered "flat," though there are a few mountains scattered in the distance in most directions.

9. Great Divide Basin, Wyoming—6,900 feet

Parts of the Continental Divide, surrounding the Great Divide Basin, appear to be little more than small hills. Much of the Great Divide Basin, up to 70 miles wide, consists of flat basins separated by desolate-looking hills with gentle slopes.

10. Central New Mexico—6,500 feet

East of the Sandia Mountains, which are east of Albuquerque, lies a north-south basin extending from Stanley through Moriarty (where I-40 crosses) to Willard. Some higher parts of this basin are 6,500 feet above sea level.

Honorable Mention:

Grand Mesa, Colorado—10,000 feet

Grand Mesa, southeast of Grand Junction, is a high mountain with a fairly flat top. However, the flat top of the mountain is small enough so that one can never be more than about 1 ½ miles (as a crow—or ingenious human—would fly) from the edge. So South Park (being somewhat more expansive) makes it to the list, and Grand Mesa does not. The mesa extends further east-southeast from its flat area; however, it becomes hillier in that direction.

Is the Highest Point of a State Necessarily the Steepest?

In most cases, the answer is a resounding "no." In a few cases, the highest point hardly even qualifies as a hill, with other parts of the state having more impressive terrain. Here are examples:

1. Indiana: Northwest of Bethel—1,257 feet

There is no name for the highest point in Indiana, because it is not even really a hill. It wouldn't even be called a "mesa" out west—it is simply a flat area which is a little bit higher than the surrounding flat areas. This is the second lowest "highest point" of a state which does not border the ocean. Illinois is No. 1 in that category; however, its highest point is a legitimate hill. Indiana does have some large hills near the Ohio River in the southern part of the state.

2. Iowa: Northwest of Allendorf—1,670 feet

This high point (without a name) is even flatter than the highest point in Indiana. There are some sections of Iowa, especially near the Mississippi River, that are quite hilly, but not in this part of northwestern Iowa.

3. Kansas: Mt. Sunflower—4,039 feet

Mt. Sunflower, near the Kansas-Colorado border, is barely a hill. Much steeper hills (and larger, if you go by vertical climb between the valley and the peak) can be found at much lower elevations further east in Kansas, such as in the Flint Hills or along the Missouri River bluffs. In fact, "mole hills" just on the Colorado side of the Kansas-Colorado border are larger than Mt. Sunflower, and one only needs to travel about 1,000 feet into Colorado to reach an elevation higher than the highest point in Kansas. However, despite this knoll's lackluster performance, its elevation above sea level is still higher than the highest points of 21 other states.

4. Nebraska: Near the southwest corner—5,426 feet

This unimpressive, unnamed hill is near where Colorado, Nebraska and Wyoming meet. One only needs to travel about half a mile into nearby Wyoming to reach an elevation higher than the highest point in Nebraska. Nebraska is not known for its hills, but there are some steep ones, including Chimney Rock, more than 1,000 feet lower in elevation than Nebraska's highest summit. Even though Nebraska's highest point is in the Great Plains, it is higher than the highest points of 30 states.

5. Florida: Near Paxton—345 feet

At 345 feet, the highest point in Florida is the lowest of its kind. While parts of Northern Florida have some rolling hills, including near Tallahassee, not many areas are hillier than around Florida's massif.

Large Mountains Very Near Coastlines

Here are some notable large mountains (greater than 12,000 feet) around the world which are within 20 miles of the coast (including fjords, bays and other sea-level inlets).

Mountain	Elevation (Ft.)	Distance from Coast (Mi.)
Mt. St. Elias, U.S.A. (Alaska)/Canada	18,008	16
Mt. Vancouver, U.S.A. (Alaska)/Canada	15,700	20
Mt. Fairweather, U.S.A. (Alaska)/Canada	15,300	15
Mauna Kea, U.S.A. (Hawaii)	13,796	18
Mt. Cook, U.S.A. (Alaska)/Canada	13,760	17
Mt. Minto, Antarctica	13,664	12
Mt. Cameroon (Fako), Cameroon	13,435	13
Mt. San Valentin, Chile	13,313	16
Mt. Crillon, U.S.A. (Alaska)	12,726	10
Mt. Erebus, Antarctica	12,444	6
Mt. Fuji, Japan	12,388	16
Mt. Cook, New Zealand	12,349	20
Gunung Rindjani, Indonesia (Lombok)	12,224	12
Mt. Huxley, U.S.A. (Alaska)	12,216	15

Gavaher Deh, Iran *	12,201	13
Pico del Teide, Canary Islands	12,198	7
Mt. Suckling, Papua New Guinea	12,060	19

* Gavaher Deh, in Iran, is not technically 13 miles from a coastline. Instead, it is 13 miles from the Caspian Sea, a large inland salt lake, which has a shoreline similar to a true "coastline." Since the Caspian Sea is below sea level, this mountain is included in this list.

Digging to China: Antipodes

If one were to dig straight through the center of the earth to a point directly on the opposite side of the earth, one would arrive at the antipode. If that person started in the United States, then in almost all cases, the end result of the long dig would be water, because the antipodes for most locations in the United States lie in various parts of the Indian Ocean. In order to dig straight to China, one would have to start either in parts of Argentina or Chile (or nearby oceans).

Only about 10 percent of the world's land area has an antipode that is not in an ocean. Many of these places are remote; for example, much of Greenland and the northern Arctic islands of Canada lie opposite parts of Antarctica.

With latitudes and longitudes, one can easily determine an antipode for any location in the world. Simply flip hemispheres for the latitude (from northern to southern, or vice versa), and flip the hemispheres for the longitude (from western to eastern, or vice versa) and subtract from 180. So, an antipode for 40 degrees North, 110 degrees West would be 40 degrees South, 70 (or 180 minus 110) degrees East.

Here are some antipodes where both points are on land:

Auckland, New Zealand—Gibraltar
Beijing, China—Bahia Blanca, Argentina
Djakarta, Indonesia—northern Colombia, about 100 miles northeast of Bogota
Fiji—central Mali
Hong Kong—The Andes of extreme northwestern Argentina
Honolulu, Hawaii—western Botswana
Manila, Philippines—Rural southwestern Brazil
Perth, Australia—Bermuda
Santiago, Chile—Xian, China
Singapore—eastern Ecuador

Tahiti—northern Sudan, about 200 miles northwest of Khartoum
Taipei, Taiwan—The Formosa province of northeastern Argentina
(Ironically, Taiwan has been called "Formosa" in the past.)

The most famous antipodes are almost certainly the North Pole and the South Pole! And, of course, the Antipodes Islands are opposite Guernsey, one of the Channel Islands, which are not too far from Britain.
Hmm...just who might have named the Antipodes Islands?

Nations Where the Capital Cities Are on Islands, Yet Other Parts of the Nations Are on the Mainland

1. Denmark
2. Equatorial Guinea
3. United Arab Emirates

Does not include islands in rivers or deltas.

Landlubbers: Six Landlocked Countries in Which All Land Area (Including Rivers and Lakes) Drains Internally (No Outlet to the Ocean)

Most rivers have an ultimate destination to the ocean, either directly or by flowing into another river that flows into the ocean (or again, yet another river that flows into the ocean). Some rivers, especially in dry parts of the world, do not have an ultimate destination to the ocean; instead they usually end abruptly in the desert or drain into a salt lake (or salt flat, if the lake is dry). Here are six countries in which *all* rivers and lakes have no outlet to the ocean. In some of these cases, the rivers drain into the Caspian Sea, which is below sea level, salty, and has no outlet.

Note that all of these countries are landlocked, as even desert nations (such as Saudi Arabia) that border an ocean (or a sea or gulf connected to an ocean), will have at least a razor-thin area along the coast that drains into the ocean.

1. Armenia
2. Azerbaijan
3. Kyrgyzstan
4. Tajikistan

5. Turkmenistan
6. Uzbekistan

Chad, in Africa, almost places in this category, except that a very small section (less than 1 percent of the total land area of Chad) in the southwest drains toward the Atlantic Ocean.

CHAPTER THREE
Transportation Geography

A nyone who has wanted to explore geography (beyond books, or pictures, or walking/running distance) must use some sort of transportation. This chapter has some fun statistics about roads, railways and aviation (and how cities and countries relate to them) and a few not-so-fun statistics (such as various states' mortality rates for those in accidents).

Most Populous Cities in the United States without Interstate Highways

Most larger U.S. cities are served by the Interstate Highway system. The cities listed below have no Interstate Highways within the city limits (or within 10 miles), though all have at least one other highway that is built as a freeway.

1. Fresno, CA
2. Anchorage, AK *
3. Bakersfield, CA
4. Modesto, CA
5. Oxnard, CA
6. Salinas, CA *
7. Santa Rosa, CA

8. Brownsville, TX *
9. Lancaster, CA
10. Thousand Oaks, CA

* These are cities that one must reach by using a road that is (for at least part of the distance) not a freeway.

Five Most Populous U.S. Cities Where All Interstate Highways Connecting the Cities with the Rest of the Interstate Highway System Are Toll Roads (or Have Toll Bridges)

To travel outside of these cities using only Interstate Highways, one must pay a toll at least once, regardless of the route.

1. New York, NY *
2. Tulsa, OK **
3. Aurora, IL **
4. Naperville, IL **
5. Coral Springs, FL **

* New York City is kind of weird—there's actually a way to exit the city (to the north) via an expressway without paying a toll, but not by exclusively using the Interstate Highway system.

** These are cities where not only are the exiting Interstate Highways toll roads, but all other limited-access highways connecting the city with other freeways or Interstate Highways are also toll roads (meaning you either support your local toll-collector or take a regular highway to get out of the area).

Now or Never: Longest Distances Between Exits on Limited Access Roads (Freeways, Turnpikes, Etc.) in the United States

If driving along these roads, better not miss the exit—it will be a long drive until the next one. Of the roads listed here, all are toll roads except No. 3 and No. 10.

1. Florida's Turnpike: 51 miles

This is the distance between adjacent exits along the southbound section of Florida's Turnpike from St. Cloud and Yeehaw Junction, to the southeast of the Orlando area. The northbound section has 49 miles between exits.

2. Florida's Turnpike: 40 miles

Florida's Turnpike appears twice on this list. The next section to the south, between Yeehaw Junction and Fort Pierce, lasts for 40 miles without an exit.

3. Interstate 80 (I-80) in Western Utah: 37 miles

Between Exit 4 near Wendover and Exit 41 near Knolls, in the Great Salt Lake Desert, lies 37 miles of freeway without an exit.

4. Pennsylvania Turnpike: 36 miles

This section of the oldest turnpike in the United States, between Somerset and Bedford in southwestern Pennsylvania, has no exits for 36 miles. I-70 and I-76 both share this stretch of road.

5. Kansas Turnpike: 34 miles

Between Emporia and Cassoday, the Kansas Turnpike (I-35, along this portion) goes for 34 miles without an exit.

6. Turner Turnpike in Oklahoma: 31 miles

The westbound lanes of Turner Turnpike (I-44) between Chandler and Oklahoma City have no exit for 31 miles. However, the eastbound lanes have an exit during this 31-mile stretch, at Wellston.

7. Alligator Alley in Southern Florida: 30 miles

Between exits 14 and 14a (both with relatively few towns nearby), Alligator Alley (I-75) goes for 30 miles without an exit.

7. Kansas Turnpike: 30 miles

The Kansas Turnpike appears once again (this time along its I-335 section) with 30 miles separating the south Topeka and Admire exits.

7. Massachusetts Turnpike: 30 miles

The Mass Turnpike (I-90), between Lee and Westfield in the Berkshires, has 30 miles without an exit.

10. I-40 in southeastern California: 28 miles

Along I-40 between the town of Ludlow and Kelbaker Road, there's nowhere to go except further down the freeway for 28 miles.

Does not include service areas, where one cannot exit away from the turnpike.

Is It a "Route" or a "Highway"?

Most federal and state roads that are assigned a number (except sometimes those that are part of the Interstate Highway system) are either called routes or highways. For example, U.S. 40 is usually referred to as either "Highway 40" or "Route 40" (though sometimes the number is used alone, without "highway" or "route"). However, there is a strong preference for "route" (or sometimes "state route") to be used in the Northeast and a strong preference for "highway" to be used in the South, the Plains and the West. Here are state-by-state preferences (with emphasis on media reference; note that road signs do not always follow the public or media preference).

Alabama—highway
Alaska—highway (but uses names, such as "The Alaska Highway" more than numbers)
Arizona—highway (mostly)
Arkansas—highway
California—highway (mostly)
Colorado—highway
Connecticut—route
Delaware—route (mostly)
Florida—highway
Georgia—highway
Hawaii—highway (but uses names, such as "The Pali Highway" more than numbers)
Idaho—highway
Illinois—route (mostly)
Indiana—"state road" is most popular
Iowa—highway
Kansas—highway (though state highways are sometimes named with a K, such as "K-10")
Kentucky—highway (except some preference for route in the east)
Louisiana—highway
Maine—route

Maryland—route
Massachusetts—route
Michigan—M is used for Michigan highways (such as M 66), and
U.S. is used for U.S. highways (such as U.S. 41)
Minnesota—highway (mostly)
Mississippi—highway
Missouri—highway
Montana—highway
Nebraska—highway
Nevada—highway
New Hampshire—route
New Jersey—route
New Mexico—highway
New York—route
North Carolina—highway (mostly)
North Dakota—highway
Ohio—route
Oklahoma—highway
Oregon—highway
Pennsylvania—route
Rhode Island—route
South Carolina—highway
South Dakota—highway
Tennessee—highway
Texas—highway
Utah—highway
Vermont—route
Virginia and West Virginia—route
Washington, Wisconsin and Wyoming—highway

Where Do You Want Your Steering Wheel? Left or Right?

It is certainly basic knowledge that people in the United States drive on the right-hand side of the road, and people in Britain drive on the left-hand side of the road. What is less known is that about a third of the world's population drives on the left. In general, the areas of the world where left-hand-side driving is common include the British Isles, southern and eastern Africa, Japan, a wide swath from India and Pakistan to Australia and New Zealand and parts of the Caribbean. Many, but not all of the countries originally colonized by Britain drive on the left.

Most nations where driving is on the right side of the road have drivers sitting in the left side of the car, and most nations where driving is on the left have drivers sitting in the right side of the car. However, this is not always the case. In the Bahamas, U.S. Virgin Islands and Cyprus, among a few other places where people drive on the left side of the road, the drivers also sit in the left side of the car because most of the cars are imported from nations where driving is on the right side of the road. Conversely, in Burma, where people drive on the right side of the road, most cars are imported from Japan with steering wheels on the right side of the car.

Most Populous Countries Where Driving Is on the Left Side of the Road

1. India
2. Indonesia
3. Pakistan
4. Bangladesh
5. Japan
6. Thailand
7. United Kingdom
8. South Africa
9. Tanzania
10. Kenya

Two South American Countries Where Driving Is on the Left Side of the Road

1. Guyana
2. Suriname

Two Mediterranean Countries Where Driving Is on the Left Side of the Road

1. Cyprus
2. Malta

Nine British Commonwealth Countries Where Driving Is on the Right Side of the Road

1. Belize
2. Cameroon
3. Canada
4. The Gambia
5. Ghana
6. Nigeria
7. Samoa
8. Sierra Leone
9. Vanuatu

In addition, the British Indian Ocean Territory and Gibraltar, both British territories, drive on the right. The remaining 45 British Commonwealth countries drive on the left.

Twelve Countries and Locations Not in the British Commonwealth Where Driving Is on the Left Side of the Road

1. Bhutan *
2. East Timor
3. Hong Kong *
4. Indonesia
5. Ireland
6. Japan
7. Macau
8. Nepal
9. Somaliland (a part of Somalia claiming independence) *
10. Suriname
11. Thailand
12. U.S. Virgin Islands

* A British protectorate/territory at some point in the past 100 years.

Five Places That Switched from Left-Side to Right-Side Driving

1. Burma (1970)
2. Sweden (1967)

3. Newfoundland (1947)
4. British Columbia and Atlantic Provinces of Canada (1920s)
5. Falkland Islands (early 1980s, during Argentine rule—but have since switched back to driving on the left)

Nations with the Highest Density of Highways

Here are the nations with the most highway mileage in a given area (miles of highway per 1,000 square miles of land). A highway is loosely defined and usually includes rural roads and major city streets. Small, densely populated countries rank highest.

Country	Miles of Highway per 1,000 Sq. Mi. Land
1. Monaco	42,300
2. Malta	8,870
3. Belgium	7,759
4. Bahrain	7,655
5. Singapore	7,424
6. Barbados	6,160
7. San Marino	5,784
8. Netherlands	5,532
9. Japan	4,947
10. Grenada	4,864

Source: CIA World Factbook, 2003 (using mostly data from 1999–2001).

Dependencies that would rank here include Bermuda (13,600), Gibraltar (11,400) and Aruba (6,670).

Nations with the Lowest Density of Highways

Conversely, these nations have the lowest total highway mileage (miles) per unit area (1,000 square miles). Mostly sparse desert nations are on this list.

Country	Miles of Highway per 1,000 Sq. Mi. Land
1. Vatican City	0 *
2. Mongolia	4

3. Sudan	8
4. Mauritania	12
5. Niger	13
6. Mali	20
7. Libya	22
8. Ethiopia	35
9. Chad	43
10. Suriname	45

* The Vatican has no highways, just minor city streets.

Source: CIA World Factbook, 2003 (using mostly data from 1999–2001).

Dependencies that would rank here include Western Sahara, a territory under control by Morocco (38).

Countries with No Paved Highways

1. Equatorial Guinea
2. Tuvalu
3. Vatican City (no highways, paved or unpaved)

Source: CIA World Factbook, 2003 (using mostly data from 1999–2001).

Speed Limits in Various Countries Around the World

These are the maximum speed limits (usually on a rural limited-access expressway) in various countries around the world.

Country	Highest Speed Limit
Argentina	130 km/hr (81 mph)
Australia	110 km/hr (68 mph) [1]
Austria	130 km/hr (81 mph)
Barbados	80 km/hr (50 mph)
Belarus	100 km/hr (62 mph)
Belize	55 mph [2, 3]
Belgium	120 km/hr (75 mph)
Bermuda	35 km/hr (21 mph)
Botswana	120 km/hr (75 mph)
Brazil	110 km/hr (68 mph)

Bulgaria	120 km/hr (75 mph)
Canada	100 km/hr (62 mph) [4]
Chile	100 km/hr (62 mph)
China	120 km/hr (75 mph)
Costa Rica	100 km/hr (62 mph)
Croatia	120 km/hr (75 mph)
Cyprus	100 km/hr (62 mph)
Czech Republic	130 km/hr (81 mph)
Denmark	110 km/hr (68 mph)
Egypt	100 km/hr (62 mph)
Estonia	110 km/hr (68 mph)
Fiji	80 km/hr (50 mph)
Finland	120 km/hr (75 mph)
France	130 km/hr (81 mph)
Georgia	100 km/hr (62 mph)
Germany	no maximum in some areas
Greece	120 km/hr (75 mph)
Hungary	120 km/hr (75 mph)
Iceland	90 km/hr (56 mph)
India	no maximum in some areas
Iran	110 km/hr (68 mph)
Ireland	70 mph [3]
Israel	100 km/hr (62 mph) [5]
Italy	150 km/hr (93 mph)
Japan	100 km/hr (62 mph)
Latvia	90 km/hr (56 mph)
Lithuania	130 km/hr (81 mph)
Luxembourg	120 km/hr (75 mph)
Malaysia	110 km/hr (68 mph)
Mexico	110 km/hr (68 mph)
Namibia	120 km/hr (75 mph)
Netherlands	120 km/hr (75 mph)
New Zealand	100 km/hr (62 mph)
Nigeria	100 km/hr (62 mph)
Norway	90 km/hr (56 mph) [6]
Oman	120 km/hr (75 mph)
Pakistan	120 km/hr (75 mph)
Palau	25 mph [3]
Poland	130 km/hr (81 mph)
Portugal	120 km/hr (75 mph)
Romania	120 km/hr (75 mph)
Russia	110 km/hr (68 mph)

Singapore	80 km/hr (50 mph)
Slovakia	130 km/hr (81 mph)
Slovenia	120 km/hr (75 mph)
South Africa	120 km/hr (75 mph)
South Korea	100 km/hr (62 mph)
Spain	120 km/hr (75 mph)
Sudan	120 km/hr (75 mph)
Sweden	110 km/hr (68 mph)
Switzerland	120 km/hr (75 mph)
Thailand	100 km/hr (62 mph)
Turkey	130 km/hr (81 mph)
Ukraine	120 km/hr (75 mph)
United Kingdom	70 mph [3]
United States	up to 75 mph [3]
Yugoslavia	120 km/hr (75 mph)
Zimbabwe	120 km/hr (75 mph)

[1] On some highways in the Northern Territory of Australia, there is no speed limit.

[2] Until recently, some roads in Belize had no speed limit.

[3] Note that speeds are in miles per hour.

[4] Except in Alberta, which has a top speed limit of 110 km/hr (68 mph).

[5] An Israeli highway with planned completion in 2004 will have a speed limit of 110 km/hr (68 mph).

[6] A few motorways have a test speed limit of 100 km/hr (62 mph) in Norway.

Ten Countries with the Most Expressway Mileage

Due largely to the Interstate Highways, the United States has almost as high of expressway mileage as the other nine nations ranked in the top 10. China, with a similar land area to the U.S. but with a much greater population density, has recently leaped to No. 2 as the populace has a newfound love for the automobile.

Country	Expressway Mileage
1. United States	46,048
2. China	12,000 *
3. Canada	10,299
4. Germany	7,085

5. France	6,153
6. Spain	5,633
7. Italy	4,015
8. Mexico	3,937
9. Japan	3,800
10. United Kingdom	2,053

* China's value is approximate as of 2003 with the mileage increasing at a rate greater than 1,000 miles per year.

Source of Most Data: CIA World Factbook, 2003 (using data mostly from 1999–2001).

States in the U.S. Where All Roadside Billboards Are Banned

No billboards will hide the scenery along the highways in these states (all of which are especially known for their spectacular scenery). In addition, Rhode Island has banned all *new* billboards.

1. Alaska
2. Hawaii
3. Maine
4. Vermont

States with the Highest Average Number of Lanes on State Highways

This is the total number of "lane miles" (both directions) divided by the total number of "highway miles." States ranked the highest are primarily urban states where highways with more lanes are needed.

State	Average Number of Lanes on State Highways
1. New Jersey	3.52
2. Florida	3.31
3. California	3.25
4. Massachusetts	3.05
5. Maryland	2.83
6. Michigan	2.81
7. Arizona	2.63

7. Connecticut   2.63
9. Washington   2.62
10. Utah   2.58

Source: U.S. Department of Transportation Statistics, 2002.

States with the Lowest Average Number of Lanes on State Highways

States ranked the lowest are either rural states or have a dense network of small state highways (such as Missouri or Virginia). Note that the minimum number of lanes possible on standard highways is two.

State	Average Number of Lanes on State Highways
1. Alaska	2.06
1. West Virginia	2.06
3. Maine	2.11
4. North Carolina	2.12
5. Missouri	2.15
5. South Carolina	2.15
7. Arkansas	2.19
7. Delaware	2.19
7. Virginia	2.19
10. New Hampshire	2.21
10. Pennsylvania	2.21

Source: U.S. Department of Transportation Statistics, 2002.

Countries with No Unpaved Highways

Instead of countries with no paved highways, we will look at the opposite—countries where *all* highways are paved. The U.S. is not among them; numerous state (and county) highways are unpaved in rural areas.

1. Austria
2. Brunei
3. Czech Republic
4. Denmark
5. France

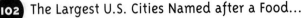

6. Germany
7. Israel
8. Italy
9. Jordan
10. Liechtenstein
11. Luxembourg
12. Monaco
13. San Marino
14. Singapore
15. Switzerland
16. United Arab Emirates
17. United Kingdom
18. Vatican City

Source: CIA World Factbook, 2003 (using mostly data from 1999–2001).

Ten Largest Countries (by Area) without Railroads

These are all countries with large areas of low population density. Except for Libya, Oman and Iceland, these are among the poorest countries in the world.

1. Libya *
2. Niger
3. Chad
4. Somalia
5. Central African Republic
6. Yemen
7. Papua New Guinea
8. Laos
9. Oman
10. Iceland

* Libya has had plans for two rail lines, but nothing has been built yet. Libya had railroads before 1965, but all have been removed.

If dependencies were included, Western Sahara (a territory under control by Morocco) would be No. 8.

End of the Line: Largest U.S. Metropolitan Areas Along or at the End of a "Dead-End" Railroad Route

Here are the largest metropolitan areas (by population) where only one railroad link to the outside rail network exists. In some cases, the railroad link continues in the other direction but eventually ends without intersecting any other railroads that connect with the "outside world."

1. Miami-Ft. Lauderdale, FL *
2. San Diego, CA **
3. Sarasota-Bradenton, FL
4. McAllen-Edinburg-Mission, TX
5. Fort Myers-Cape Coral, FL
6. Anchorage, AK ***
7. Myrtle Beach, SC
8. Barnstable-Yarmouth, MA
9. Panama City, FL
10. State College, PA

* There is a slight caveat here, as there are two rail lines linking Miami with the rest of Florida to the north. However, they are only about a mile apart, so this could almost be considered the rail equivalent of a "dead-end superhighway."

** The rail line between San Diego and El Centro, California, which was out of service for many years, is being restored as of 2004.

*** Railroads in Alaska only connect internally (such as the link between Anchorage and Fairbanks).

Beyond the End of the Line: U.S. Metropolitan Areas without Any Connecting Railroads

Only two metropolitan areas have no railroads that exit the area. Naples once had a railroad connecting to the north, but it has since been removed.

1. Honolulu, HI
2. Naples, FL

Other Sizable Towns (Not in Any Metropolitan Areas) without Railroads

Many of these towns are either on islands or near mountainous terrain, both of which make railroads inefficient.

Carson City, NV
Farmington, NM
Hilo, HI
Juneau, AK
Key West, FL
Lake Havasu City, AZ
St. George, UT
South Lake Tahoe, CA

Nations with the Highest Density of Railroads

Europe has the highest density of railroads in the world, which makes travel by rail quite efficient for most visitors. However, not all of the countries listed here are in Europe; some are small island nations where railroads are used to transport minerals or sugar cane (but not people). The figures below represent the number of miles of railroads per thousand square miles of land.

Country	Miles of Railroads per 1,000 Sq. Mi. Land
1. Vatican City	3,145
2. Monaco	1,403
3. Nauru	383
4. St. Kitts & Nevis	308
5. Antigua & Barbuda	280
6. Germany	210
7. Czech Republic	197
8. Liechtenstein	186
9. Switzerland	183
10. Luxembourg	170

Source: CIA World Factbook, 2003 (using mostly data from 2002).

Largest Countries (by Area) without Any Waterways Used for Transportation

These are countries with no navigable inland rivers or lakes (not including any ocean waters). Most consist of primarily desert or mountains.

1. Algeria
2. Saudi Arabia
3. Libya
4. Ethiopia
5. Namibia

6. Pakistan
7. Somalia
8. Botswana
9. Yemen
10. Morocco

Source: CIA World Factbook, 2003.

If Greenland were counted as a country, it would rank No. 2.

States with the Highest Number of Traffic Deaths (per Million People)

Rural states, especially in the South, generally have more traffic deaths per million people than urban states. While urban driving may appear more dangerous, rural driving is often done at higher speeds (and longer distances). Public transportation also is usually less readily available in areas with low population density. In addition, many of the states with the highest traffic deaths per million are low-income, while many states with the fewest traffic deaths per million are high-income. The figures below are from 1995-1998.

State	Annual Traffic Deaths (per Million)
1. Mississippi	325
2. Alabama	266
3. Arkansas	259
4. Wyoming	254
5. New Mexico	243
6. South Carolina	238
7. Oklahoma	235
8. Montana	229
9. Tennessee	228
10. Delaware	227

Source: National Center for Health Statistics, Center for Disease Control, 2002.

States with the Lowest Number of Traffic Deaths (per Million People)

State	Annual Traffic Deaths (per Million)
1. Massachusetts	78
2. Rhode Island	86
3. New York	95
4. New Jersey	101
5. Connecticut	104
6. New Hampshire	110
7. Hawaii	111
8. California	122
9. Ohio	124
10. Alaska	126

If the District of Columbia were a state, it would rank No. 2 with 79.

Source: National Center for Health Statistics, Center for Disease Control, 2002.

States with the Highest Number of Deaths from Train Collisions (per Million People)

On average, about 400 people are killed each year in the U.S. by collisions between vehicles and trains. Most occur in the Midwest and in the South. The states below have the highest number of deaths per year per million people (1995–1998).

State	Train-Vehicle Collision Deaths (per Million)
1. North Dakota	7.4
2. Mississippi	7.3
3. Arkansas	6.4
4. Louisiana	5.5
5. Oklahoma	5.1
6. Kansas	4.3
7. Nebraska	3.8
8. Indiana	3.2
8. Iowa	3.2

| 10. Montana | 3.1 |
| 10. New Mexico | 3.1 |

Source: National Center for Health Statistics, Center for Disease Control, 2002.

States with the Highest Number of Deaths from Air and Space Transport Accidents (per Million People)

Most "air and space transport" accidents are from small planes. States in the rural Northwest, especially Alaska, use small aircraft frequently for transportation, including in areas of rough terrain. The figures below are for deaths per year per million people from 1995–1998 and do not include accidents for planes departing from the United States but occurring outside the U.S.

State	Air and Space Transport Deaths (per Million)
1. Alaska	54.5
2. Idaho	11.2
3. Montana	8.5
4. Nevada	7.6
5. Colorado	7.5
6. Oregon	6.1
7. Utah	5.7
7. Wyoming	5.7
9. North Dakota	5.5
10. Washington	5.1

Source: National Center for Health Statistics, Center for Disease Control, 2002.

Highest Airports in the United States

Airplanes have more trouble lifting off from the runway at a higher elevation. Therefore, they must fly with lighter loads (especially on a warm day when the temperature combines with the altitude to produce a low density, or high "density altitude").

Of the 10 highest airports in the United States, only one has commercial flights—Telluride. The rest are primarily for private airplanes.

Airport City	Elevation (Ft.)
1. Leadville, Colorado	9,927
2. Telluride, Colorado	9,078
3. Creede, Colorado	8,680
4. Angel Fire, New Mexico	8,380
5. Westcliffe, Colorado	8,290
6. Granby, Colorado	8,203
7. Walden, Colorado	8,149
8. Del Norte, Colorado	7,949
9. Buena Vista, Colorado	7,946
10. Saguache, Colorado	7,826

Highest Airports in the United States with Commercial Flights

Airport City	Elevation (Ft.)
1. Telluride, Colorado	9,078
2. Aspen, Colorado	7,820
3. Gunnison, Colorado	7,678
4. Bryce Canyon, Utah	7,586
5. Alamosa, Colorado	7,539
6. Laramie, Wyoming	7,278
7. Los Alamos, New Mexico	7,171
8. Taos, New Mexico	7,091
9. Flagstaff, Arizona	7,011
10. Rock Springs, Wyoming	6,760

Highest Commercial Airports in the World

Seven of the 10 highest commercial airports are in the Andes, a mountain range with numerous high-elevation cities. Two are in relatively sparse Tibet.

Airport City	Elevation (Ft.)
1. Bangda, Tibet	14,219
2. La Paz, Bolivia	13,314
3. Juliaca, Peru	12,546
4. Gonggar, Tibet (near Lhasa)	11,621
5. Cuzco, Peru	10,630

6. Sucre, Bolivia	9,528
7. Quito, Ecuador	9,222
8. Telluride, Colorado, U.S.A.	9,078
9. Arequipa, Peru	8,406
10. Bogota, Colombia	8,361

U.S. Capital Cities without Commercial Airports

These capital cities are more than 30 miles from the nearest airport with regularly scheduled commercial flights.

1. Dover, Delaware
2. Montpelier, Vermont
3. Olympia, Washington
4. Salem, Oregon

Airports to Which Walking Is Almost an Option: Cities Where Downtown (City Hall) Is Closest to the Airport

Smaller cities (especially those that are part of a large metropolitan area but have their own commercial airports) and cities with older airports tend to be on this list.

City	Distance
1. San Diego, California	2 ½ miles
1. San Jose, California	2 ½ miles
3. Newark, New Jersey	3 miles
4. Boston, Massachusetts	3 ½ miles
5. Washington, D.C.	4 miles *
6. Omaha, Nebraska	4 ½ miles
7. Albuquerque, New Mexico	5 miles
7. Honolulu, Hawaii	5 miles
7. Phoenix, Arizona	5 miles
10. Anchorage, Alaska	5 ½ miles
10. Fresno, California	5 ½ miles

* Distance given is to Ronald Reagan Airport.

Cities listed have at least 250,000 people. Distances are standard driving distances between city hall and the largest airport.

Long Shuttle Ride: U.S. Cities Where Downtown (City Hall) Is Furthest from the Airport

Generally, cities that are a part of larger metropolitan areas are further from their airports than their smaller counterparts (Toledo definitely excepted).

City	Distance
1. Washington, D.C.	26 miles [1]
2. Fort Worth, Texas	24 miles [2]
3. Denver, Colorado	23 miles
4. Dallas, Texas	22 miles [3]
4. Houston, Texas	22 miles [4]
6. Kansas City, Missouri	21 miles
6. Toledo, Ohio	21 miles
8. Aurora, Colorado	19 miles [5]
8. Los Angeles, California	19 miles [6]
10. New York, New York	18 miles [7]
10. Virginia Beach, Virginia	18 miles [8]

[1] Distance given is to Dulles International. Ronald Reagan Airport is only four miles from city hall.

[2] Distance given is to DFW.

[3] Distance given is to DFW. Love Field is only 8 miles from city hall.

[4] Distance given is to Houston Intercontinental. Houston Hobby is only 12 miles from city hall.

[5] Distance given is to Denver International Airport.

[6] Distance given is to LAX. Burbank Airport is only 16 miles from the Los Angeles city hall.

[7] Distance given is to JFK. La Guardia is only 11 miles from city hall.

[8] Distance given is to Norfolk International Airport.

Cities listed have at least 250,000 people. Distances are standard driving distances between city hall and the largest airport. In some cases, alternate commercial airports will be closer.

Hard to Reach Countries: Most Populous Countries without Non-Stop Commercial Flights to or from the United States

While some passenger planes have the ability to fly to all these destinations non-stop from at least some point in the United States, it is considered economically unfeasible (by the airlines) to do that. Therefore, people flying from the United States to these countries must either change planes or (in some cases, like India, Ethiopia or Thailand) have at least a stop on a direct flight.

1. India
2. Indonesia *
3. Pakistan
4. Bangladesh
5. Vietnam
6. Iran
7. Ethiopia
8. Thailand
9. Congo (Dem. Rep.)
10. Ukraine

* Non-stop flights occur between Guam and Jakarta, Indonesia.

Harder to Reach Countries: Most Populous Countries without Non-Stop Commercial Flights to or from the U.S. or the U.K.

London's Heathrow airport offers many flights to places which the airports in the United States do not. However, there are still some large nations beyond a non-stop flight from the U.S. or U.K.

1. Indonesia
2. Vietnam
3. Ethiopia
4. Congo (Dem. Rep.)
5. Burma
6. Sudan
7. Afghanistan
8. Nepal
9. Iraq
10. North Korea

Hardest to Reach Countries: Most Populous Countries without Non-Stop Commercial Flights to or from the U.S., the U.K., Canada, France, Germany, Hong Kong, Italy, Japan, The Netherlands, Singapore, South Korea, Spain or Thailand

These are places with no non-stop flights to countries that are represented by many of the busiest airports in the world. Thus, to reach the countries listed below, one must connect through a somewhat smaller airport (or, in the case of a few countries, such as Iraq, simply use other transportation).

1. Sudan
2. Afghanistan
3. Iraq
4. North Korea
5. Mozambique
6. Malawi
7. Somalia
8. Tajikistan
9. Burundi
10. Paraguay

Most Remote by Flight: Countries to Which One Must Take a Minimum of Three Commercial Flights* from the United States

These countries can be reached, but more time (and money) are needed than for most international destinations. Multiple airlines must be used to reach these places, except that Air France can be taken the entire way from the U.S. to the Central African Republic.

1. Bhutan
2. Burundi
3. Central African Republic
4. East Timor
5. Liberia

* Direct flights with a stop between the initial and final points count as two flights.

This list does not include countries unreachable by commercial flights, either because of international sanctions (Iraq), turmoil (Somalia) or lack of airport (Andorra).

Countries with No Airports

All are very small European countries.

1. Andorra
2. Liechtenstein
3. Monaco *
4. San Marino
5. Vatican City

* Monaco has a public heliport.

Source: CIA World Factbook, 2003.

Largest U.S. Metropolitan Areas to Have No Regularly Scheduled Non-Stop International Flights from Their Airports

Most sizable metropolitan areas have non-stop international flights, even if they are only to Canada or Mexico. However, many smaller metropolitan areas do not.

1. Norfolk—Virginia Beach, Virginia
2. Greensboro—Winston-Salem, North Carolina
3. Buffalo, New York
4. Jacksonville, Florida
5. Oklahoma City, Oklahoma *
6. Louisville, Kentucky
7. Greenville—Spartanburg, South Carolina
8. Fresno, California
9. Birmingham, Alabama
10. Tulsa, Oklahoma

* Limited non-stop flights between Oklahoma City and Cancun, Mexico occur during summer.

This list does not include cities with direct flights to international destinations that first stop in another city.

CHAPTER FOUR
City Geography

The majority of people in the United States (58 percent, as of the 2000 Census) live in metropolitan areas of at least one million people. In some countries, this total is much higher (in the city-state of Singapore, it's 100 percent), and our world is becoming increasingly urbanized.

Most of the cities ranked in this chapter are in the United States, and they vary enormously. Some are suburban; some are stand-alone; some are rich, while others are poor; some reached their heyday in the 1700s or 1800s, and others have yet to even appear on most maps.

For comparison purposes, many of the U.S. cities were split into two categories: those with 250,000 or more people (all of which are fairly well-known) and those with 20,000 or more people (most of which are unknown by most people, but are still large enough to provide a good statistical sample for some interesting lists). U.S. Census data from 2000 was used for a majority of the lists. Cities of less than 20,000 people are occasionally explored in this chapter, but usually only if they show a definite regional trend (such as the sparseness of household telephones on Indian Reservations in the Southwest or extreme poverty in essentially "highly populated camps" along the Mexican border).

Note that this certainly is not the only chapter of this book in which cities are compared, though *only* cities are compared in this chapter.

Most Densely Populated Cities and Towns in the United States

Coastal areas, especially the East Coast, overwhelmingly have the most densely populated cities. Most of these cities are suburbs of New York. The figures below are people per square mile.

Most maps do not show Friendship Village, Maryland, a very compact suburb near Bethesda with only 0.06 square miles.

City, State	People per Sq. Mi.
1. Friendship Village, Maryland	81,992 *
2. Guttenberg, New Jersey	56,012 *
3. Union City, New Jersey	52,978
4. West New York, New Jersey	44,995
5. Hoboken, New Jersey	30,239
6. New York, New York	26,403
7. Buena Vista, California	24,099 *
8. Maywood, California	23,887
9. Cliffside Park, New Jersey	23,848 *
10. East Newark, New Jersey	23,330 *

* The town has less than one square mile, so the total population is less than the population per square mile.

Source: 2000 U.S. Census.

Most Densely Populated Heartland Cities and Towns

There are some densely populated cities and towns away from the coasts, too. This list will be restricted to states neither on the East nor the West Coast. More than half of these places are in the Chicago metropolitan area. The others are suburbs of Cincinnati, Dallas, Detroit, or Louisville.

City, State	People per Sq. Mi.
1. Poplar Hills, Kentucky	17,036 *
2. Stone Park, Illinois	15,378 *
3. Cicero, Illinois	14,645
4. Berwyn, Illinois	13,876
5. Elmwood Park, Illinois	13,328
6. Chicago, Illinois	12,750
7. Mobile City, Texas	11,911 *

8. Oak Park, Illinois	11,173
9. Hamtramck, Michigan	10,901
10. Lakewood, Ohio	10,209

* The town has less than one square mile, so the total population is less than the population per square mile.

Source: 2000 U.S. Census.

Most Densely Populated Larger Cities in the United States

Since the previous lists contain some small, compact suburbs, one might want to see a list containing only more well-known cities. This list will be restricted to cities with more than 100,000 people.

City, State	People per Sq. Mi.
1. New York, New York	26,403
2. Paterson, New Jersey	17,675
3. East Los Angeles, California	16,697
4. San Francisco, California	16,634
5. Jersey City, New Jersey	16,094
6. Cambridge, Massachusetts	15,766
7. Daly City, California	13,704
8. Chicago, Illinois	12,750
9. Santa Ana, California	12,452
10. Inglewood, California	12,324

Source: 2000 U.S. Census.

Most Densely Populated Larger Heartland Cities in the United States

As with the list on page 116, we will remove all cities in East Coast and West Coast states (in addition to all cities with populations below 100,000).

City, State	People per Sq. Mi.
1. Chicago, Illinois	12,750
2. Minneapolis, Minnesota	6,970
3. Detroit, Michigan	6,855

4. Metairie, Louisiana	6,297
5. Milwaukee, Wisconsin	6,214
6. Cleveland, Ohio	6,167
7. St. Louis, Missouri	5,623
8. St. Paul, Minnesota	5,442
9. Grand Rapids, Michigan	4,431
10. Cincinnati, Ohio	4,249

Source: 2000 U.S. Census.

Least Densely Populated Cities and Towns in the United States (with Populations of at Least 10,000)

These are cities and towns whose official boundaries have expanded far beyond their urban areas. One of these cities, Butte, has consolidated with an entire county, Silver Bow.

City, State	People per Sq. Mi.
1. Juneau, Alaska	11
2. Butte-Silver Bow, Montana	48
3. Boulder City, Nevada	74
4. Pahrump, Nevada	83
5. Hibbing, Minnesota	94
6. Black Forest, Colorado	104
7. Canyon Lake, Texas	117
8. Sierra Vista, Arizona	128
9. Eloy, Arizona	145
10. St. Marys, Pennsylvania	146

Source: 2000 U.S. Census. Does not include townships or military forts.

Least Densely Populated Cities in the United States (with Populations of at Least 100,000)

City, State	People per Sq. Mi.
1. Anchorage, Alaska	153
2. Chesapeake, Virginia	585
3. Augusta-Richmond County, Georgia	617
4. Peoria, Arizona	784

5. Oklahoma City, Oklahoma	834
6. Athens-Clarke County, Georgia	840
7. Columbus, Georgia	861
8. Huntsville, Alabama	909
9. Lexington-Fayette, Kentucky	916
10. Columbia, South Carolina	929

Source: 2000 U.S. Census. Does not include townships.

Fallen Giants: Cities That Have Fallen Far in the Rankings of Largest U.S. Cities

Here are some cities that used to rank somewhere in the top 100 most populous U.S. cities (of course, this was back when the United States had a relatively small population and relatively few large cities). Somehow, these cities failed to keep up with the Joneses (or Burgs or Villes or especially Sans and Santas), as all but two listed here are now well below the No. 100 mark.

The population of many of these cities is actually higher now than when they ranked high among other U.S. cities (for example, Albany had 33,721 people in 1840 when it ranked No. 9, but in 2000 it had about 95,658 people despite ranking only No. 258).

Albany, NY
1840 ranking: No. 9
2000 ranking: No. 258

Camden, NJ
1880 ranking: No. 44
2000 ranking: No. 341

Charleston, SC
1790 ranking: No. 4
2000 ranking: No. 253
(This is actually an increase
from No. 277 since 1990.)

Cincinnati, OH
1850 ranking: No. 6
2000 ranking: No. 55

Gloucester, MA
1790 ranking: No. 12
2000 ranking: No. 1,209

Hudson, NY
1790 ranking: No. 24
2000 ranking: No. 4,467

Johnstown, PA
1910 ranking: No. 98
2000 ranking: No. 1,566

Lancaster, PA
1800 ranking: No. 25
2000 ranking: No. 558

Newburyport, MA
1800 ranking: No. 12
2000 ranking: No. 2,199

Newport, RI
1790 ranking: No. 8
2000 ranking: No. 1,410

Petersburg, VA
1790 ranking: No. 21
2000 ranking: No. 1,071

Portsmouth, NH
1790 ranking: No. 14
2000 ranking: No. 1,841

St. Louis, MO
1910 ranking: No. 4
2000 ranking: No. 49

Scranton, PA
1870 ranking: No. 35
2000 ranking: No. 366

Troy, NY
1830 ranking: No. 19
2000 ranking: No. 686

Wilmington, DE
1880 ranking: No. 42
2000 ranking: No. 388

York, PA
1800 ranking: No. 33
2000 ranking: No. 845

Youngstown, OH
1930 ranking: No. 45
2000 ranking: No. 329

Note that many cities have been annexed by another (such as New York's annexation of Brooklyn, which from the 1860 until the 1880 census ranked No. 3 behind New York and Philadelphia), so they would instantly lose their rankings.

Source: U.S. Census, various years.

Capital Cities That Contain the Highest Percentage of Their Countries' Total Populations

Three of these countries are city-states, so that the whole nation is comprised of just the capital city. The remaining countries are mostly very small.

City, Country	Percentage of Total National Population
1. Monaco, Monaco	100
1. Singapore, Singapore	100
1. Vatican City, Vatican City	100
4. Nassau, Bahamas	67.5
5. Djibouti, Djibouti	66.7

6. Koror, Palau	58.3
7. Doha, Qatar	50.6
8. Paramaribo, Suriname	47.7
9. Funafuti, Tuvalu	45.5
10. Montevideo, Uruguay	42.5

Data based on the most recent population statistics available. Only capital cities of independent nations are listed.

Capital Cities That Contain the Lowest Percentage of Their Countries' Total Populations

There are two ways to make this possible; either have a very large nation (India, China) or a small capital city (Kuwait).

City, Country	Percentage of Total National Population
1. New Delhi, India *	0.03
2. Abuja, Nigeria	0.1
3. Washington, United States	0.2
4. Islamabad, Pakistan	0.4
5. Beijing, China	0.5
6. Ottawa, Canada	1.1
7. Brasilia, Brazil	1.2
8. Bern, Switzerland	1.6
8. Canberra, Australia	1.6
8. Kuwait, Kuwait	1.6

* Part of a large metropolitan area (Delhi).

Data based on the most recent population statistics available.

Big Fish: The Largest Small Cities in the United States

These are the most populous cities in the United States that have less than 50 square miles (approximately a seven-mile by seven-mile area). Note that if Manhattan and the Bronx were individual cities, instead of boroughs, they would rank No. 1 and No. 2, respectively.

1. San Francisco, California
2. Boston, Massachusetts

3. Miami, Florida
4. Santa Ana, California
5. Anaheim, California
6. Buffalo, New York
7. Newark, New Jersey
8. Jersey City, New Jersey
9. Hialeah, Florida
10. Rochester, New York

Source: 2000 U.S. Census.

Smaller Ponds: The Biggest Really Small Cities in the United States

Here are the most populous cities in the United States with less than 10 square miles (approximately a three-mile by three-mile area). All are suburbs. All cities in this and the previous list are either in the Northeast, California or the Miami area.

1. Paterson, New Jersey
2. East Los Angeles, California
3. El Monte, California
4. Inglewood, California
5. Daly City, California
6. Norwalk, California
7. Cambridge, Massachusetts
8. South Gate, California
9. Miami Beach, Florida
10. Alhambra, California

Honorable Mention:

12. Trenton, New Jersey (largest that is not a suburb)

Source: 2000 U.S. Census.

Stand-Alone Cities: 10 Largest U.S. Cities That Have No Large Suburbs or Adjacent Cities

1. San Antonio, Texas
2. Jacksonville, Florida
3. Austin, Texas
4. Charlotte, North Carolina
5. Wichita, Kansas
6. Toledo, Ohio
7. Corpus Christi, Texas
8. Lexington, Kentucky
9. Anchorage, Alaska
10. Baton Rouge, Louisiana

A large suburb or adjacent city is defined as a city (whether incorporated or not) within 10 miles with more than 25,000 people.

Completely Stand-Alone Cities: Largest U.S. Cities to be Disconnected from All Other Cities or Towns

Most larger cities in the United States are connected with suburbs or other cities as a continuous urban area. However, those listed below are completely stand-alone cities that have at least a few miles of rural area (or water) between them and the nearest incorporated (or large unincorporated) towns or cities.

1. Corpus Christi, Texas
2. Lexington-Fayette, Kentucky
3. Anchorage, Alaska
4. Stockton, California
5. Lincoln, Nebraska
6. Montgomery, Alabama
7. Lubbock, Texas
8. Amarillo, Texas
9. Salinas, California
10. Tallahassee, Florida

Small Central City, Larger Metropolitan Area

Some Metropolitan Statistical Areas (MSA) and Combined Metropolitan Statistical Areas (CMSA), as defined by the U.S. Census Bureau, have small central cities relative to the metropolitan areas. This is especially true where there are several central cities.

Below are the 10 metropolitan areas with the smallest central cities as a percentage of the total metro population. The central cities are in parentheses.

Metropolitan Statistical Area	Percentage of Metro Population in Central City
1. Greenville-Spartanburg-Anderson, SC (Greenville)	5.8
2. Benton Harbor, MI (Benton Harbor)	6.9
3. West Palm Beach-Boca Raton, FL (West Palm Beach)	7.3
4. Harrisburg-Lebanon-Carlisle, PA (Harrisburg)	7.8
5. Naples, FL (Naples)	8.3
6. Washington-Baltimore, D.C.-MD-VA-WV (Baltimore)	8.6
7. Sarasota-Bradenton, FL (Sarasota)	8.9
8. Miami-Ft. Lauderdale, FL (Miami)	9.4
9. Atlanta, GA (Atlanta)	10.1
9. Punta Gorda, FL (Punta Gorda)	10.1
9. Boston-Worcester-Lawrence, MA-NH-ME-CT (Boston)	10.1

Source: 2000 US Census.

U.S. Cities with the Highest Percentage of Households Lacking Telephone Service

Telephone service is nearly universal in the United States—only 2.4 percent of occupied households were without telephone service in 2000. Here are cities well above that average.

City, State	Percentage of Households with No Telephone Service
1. Camden, New Jersey	14.0
2. East St. Louis, Illinois	10.0
3. Opelousas, Louisiana	9.3
4. Greenwood, South Carolina	9.2
5. Newark, New Jersey	8.9

Cities listed have at least 20,000 people.

Source: 2000 U.S. Census.

Larger U.S. Cities with the Highest Percentage of Households Lacking Telephone Service

City, State	Percentage of Households with No Telephone Service
1. Newark, New Jersey	8.9
2. Detroit, Michigan	7.1
3. Chicago, Illinois	5.4
4. Baltimore, Maryland	5.3
5. Miami, Florida	5.2

Cities listed have at least 250,000 people.

Source: 2000 U.S. Census.

Towns with the Highest Percentage of Households Lacking Telephone Service

This includes all places (towns and villages) with 1,000 people or more. All of these places are either in the Navajo Nation or on Indian Reservations in the southwestern United States, and all have low average incomes.

City, State	Percentage of Households with No Telephone Service
1. Houck, Arizona	79.1
2. Cibecue, Arizona	63.6

3. Lukachukai, Arizona	59.3
4. Alamo, New Mexico	57.0
5. Kaibito, Arizona	51.4

Source: 2000 U.S. Census.

Richest Cities in the United States

These are the highest per capita incomes (total income earned by all people living in the city divided by the population) of cities of 20,000 people or more in the United States. All of these are suburbs of large cities.

City, State	Per Capita Income
1. Lake Forest, Illinois	$77,092
2. Westport, Connecticut	$73,664
3. Los Altos, California	$66,776
4. Beverly Hills, California	$65,507
5. Saratoga, California	$65,400
6. Potomac, Maryland	$64,875
7. University Park, Texas	$63,414
8. McLean, Virginia	$63,209
9. Newport Beach, California	$63,015
10. Bloomfield, Michigan	$62,716

Source: 2000 U.S. Census, based on 1999 income.

Richest Towns in the United States

These are the richest places with 1,000 people or more. All have populations of around 10,000 or less and are suburban. Most are in states with large populations.

City, State	Per Capita Income
1. Belvedere, California	$113,595
2. Rancho Santa Fe, California	$113,132
3. Atherton, California	$112,408
4. Rolling Hills, California	$111,031
5. Barton Creek, Texas	$110,504
6. Palm Beach, Florida	$109,219
7. Bloomfield Hills, Michigan	$104,920

8. Belle Meade, Tennessee	$104,908
9. Woodside, California	$104,667
10. Oyster Bay Cove, New York	$103,203

Source: 2000 U.S. Census, based on 1999 income.

Richest Towns in States with Lower Populations

Most of the richest towns in the United States are in states with higher populations. However, there are also towns with high per capita incomes in smaller states. These are the richest places with 1,000 people or more that are in states ranked between No. 26 and No. 50 in population.

Again, all of these places are suburban. All except Nichols Hills, Oklahoma (a suburb of Oklahoma City) share a metropolitan area with a larger state.

City, State	Per Capita Income
1. Mission Hills, Kansas	$95,405
2. Greenville, Delaware	$83,223
3. Darien, Connecticut	$77,519
4. Westport, Connecticut	$73,664
5. Nichols Hills, Oklahoma	$73,661

Source: 2000 U.S. Census, based on 1999 income.

Poorest Cities in the United States

These are the lowest per capita incomes of cities of 20,000 people or more in the United States. These cities are heavily populated by immigrants from Mexico. All cities ranked between No. 4 and No. 10 are within 10 miles to the southeast of the Los Angeles Civic Center (except Lennox, which is about 10 miles southwest), despite the appearances of cities from the same metropolitan area on the "richest cities in the United States" list (page 126).

City, State	Per Capita Income
1. Socorro, Texas	$7,287
2. Coachella, California	$7,416
3. San Juan, Texas	$7,945
4. Florence-Graham, California	$8,092
5. Bell Gardens, California	$8,415

6. Lennox, California	$8,499
7. Cudahy, California	$8,688
8. Maywood, California	$8,926
9. Huntington Park, California	$9,340
10. Lynwood, California	$9,542

Source: 2000 U.S. Census, based on 1999 income.

Poorest Towns in the United States

These are the poorest places in the United States with 1,000 people or more. Most of these places are unincorporated. All are either along the Texas-Mexico border or are on Indian reservations.

The Mexican border towns listed here are so poor that they have lower per capita incomes than the average for the country many of their inhabitants just left, Mexico.

City, State	Per Capita Income
1. South Alamo, Texas	$3,162
2. Muniz, Texas	$3,230
3. Lukachukai, Arizona	$3,380
4. Indian Hills, Texas	$3,583
5. El Cenizo, Texas	$3,610
6. Oglala, South Dakota	$3,824
7. Las Lomas, Texas	$3,877
8. Fort Thompson, South Dakota	$4,030
9. Alamo, New Mexico	$4,039
10. Cameron Park, Texas	$4,103

Source: 2000 U.S. Census, based on 1999 income.

Poorest Towns in the United States Where the Population Is More Than 90 Percent White (Non-Latino)

All of the poorest towns in the United States are either predominantly Latino (mostly very recent Mexican immigrants) or Native American (on Indian reservations). One common link among predominantly white (and non-Latino) towns with low per capita incomes is a very large average family size (the average among these five is 6.5

people per family, and children in a household usually earn little or no income). Towns listed here have populations of at least 1,000.

City, State	Per Capita Income
1. Kiryas Joel, New York	$4,355
2. Hildale, Utah	$4,782
3. Kaser, New York	$5,147
4. New Square, New York	$5,237
5. Colorado City, Arizona	$5,293

Source: U.S. Census, 2000, based on 1999 income.

Cities in the U.S. with the Highest Percentage of People Possessing Graduate or Professional Degrees

University towns and upscale suburbs of Boston and Washington, D.C. lead the list of cities with high percentages of people with graduate or professional degrees (such as an M.A., M.S., Ph.D., M.D. or J.D., among others). Bethesda, with the National Naval Medical Center and the National Institutes of Health, has many medical doctors, while Brookline doubles as a university town (Hebrew University and Hellenic College, near Harvard and Boston University) and upscale suburb. The Washington, D.C. area, with its demand for highly educated people in its government and high-tech jobs, has three of the top four cities.

City, State	Percentage of People Over 25 with Graduate or Professional Degrees
1. Bethesda, Maryland	48.8
2. Brookline, Massachusetts	45.3
3. Potomac, Maryland	44.2
4. McLean, Virginia	43.9
5. Palo Alto, California	43.0
6. Lexington, Massachusetts	42.2
7. Wellesley, Massachusetts	41.2
8. Chapel Hill, North Carolina	40.5
9. State College, Pennsylvania	40.4
10. West Lafayette, Indiana	40.2

Cities listed have at least 20,000 people. People counted were over 25.

Source: 2000 U.S. Census.

Larger Cities in the U.S. with the Highest Percentage of People Possessing Graduate or Professional Degrees

City, State	Percentage of People over 25 with Graduate or Professional Degrees
1. Washington, D.C.	21.0
2. Seattle, Washington	17.3
3. San Francisco, California	16.4
4. Boston, Massachusetts	15.3
5. Austin, Texas	14.7

Cities listed have at least 20,000 people. People counted were over 25.

Source: 2000 U.S. Census.

Crowded Houses: Cities and Towns in the U.S. with the Highest Average Number of People per Household

Most of these places are military, where large numbers of people are housed in barracks. Other places have different types of communal living, such as prisons (Avenal, Florence, Gatesville), a university (Storrs) or a Jewish village (Kiryas Joel).

City, State	Average Number or People per Household
1. Avenal, California	7.1
2. Fort Bragg, North Carolina	6.6
3. Storrs, Connecticut	6.5
4. Kiryas Joel, New York	5.9
5. Fort Stewart, Georgia	5.8
5. Fort Benning South, Georgia	5.8
7. Fort Carson, Colorado	5.7
7. Fort Hood, Texas	5.7
9. Fort Lewis, Washington	5.4
10. Florence, Arizona	5.3

Cities listed have populations of at least 10,000.

Source: 2000 U.S. Census.

Empty Nests: Cities and Towns in the U.S. with the Lowest Average Number of People per Household

This list consists entirely of resort communities, where many homes are "second homes."

City, State	Average Number or People per Household
1. North Myrtle Beach, South Carolina	0.61
2. Ocean City, New Jersey	0.76
3. East Hampton, New York	1.00
3. Marco Island, Florida	1.00
5. Destin, Florida	1.05
5. Palm Beach, Florida	1.05
7. Rancho Mirage, California	1.12
8. Dennis, Massachusetts	1.13
9. Kings Point, Florida	1.16
10. Sunny Isles Beach, Florida	1.18

Cities listed have populations of at least 10,000.

Source: 2000 U.S. Census.

U.S. Cities with the Highest Percentage of One-Room Housing Units*

Usually these one-room units are apartments.

City, State	Percentage of Housing Units with Only One Room
1. Miami Beach, Florida	28.0
2. Huntington Park, California	20.1
3. Lennox, California	16.2
4. Hawthorne, California	15.8
4. Miami, Florida	15.8
6. Maywood, California	15.0
7. East Palo Alto, California	14.6
8. San Francisco, California	13.6
9. Honolulu, Hawaii	13.3
10. Bell, California	13.1
10. Los Angeles, California	13.1

* Not including strip or Pullman kitchens, bathrooms, open porches, balconies, halls or foyers, half-rooms, utility rooms, unfinished attics or basements, or other unfinished space used for storage.

Cities listed have at least 20,000 people.

Source: 2000 U.S. Census.

Larger U.S. Cities with the Highest Percentage of One-Room Housing Units *

City, State	Percentage of Housing Units with Only One Room
1. Miami, Florida	15.8
2. San Francisco, California	13.6
3. Honolulu, Hawaii	13.3
4. Los Angeles, California	13.1
5. Washington, D.C.	10.2
6. Long Beach, California	9.6
7. Santa Ana, California	9.3
8. Oakland, California	8.9
9. Seattle, Washington	8.3
10. New York, New York	8.1

* Not including strip or Pullman kitchens, bathrooms, open porches, balconies, halls or foyers, half-rooms, utility rooms, unfinished attics or basements, or other unfinished space used for storage.

Larger U.S. Cities with the Lowest Percentage of One-Room Housing Units *

City, State	Percentage of Housing Units with Only One Room
1. Virginia Beach, Virginia	0.7
2. Toledo, Ohio	1.0
3. Cleveland, Ohio	1.5
3. Memphis, Tennessee	1.5
5. Indianapolis, Indiana	1.6
5. Nashville-Davidson, Tennessee	1.6

* Not including strip or Pullman kitchens, bathrooms, open porches, balconies, halls or foyers, half-rooms, utility rooms, unfinished attics or basements, or other unfinished space used for storage.

Cities listed have at least 250,000 people.

Source: 2000 U.S. Census.

U.S. Cities with the Most Rooms per Housing Unit

Cities with the most rooms per house are mostly upscale family suburbs. In the statistics below, "median" (where half the houses have more, half have less) is used instead of "average" or "mean."

City, State	Median Number of Rooms per Housing Unit
1. Brentwood, Tennessee	8.5
1. McLean, Virginia	8.5
1. Potomac, Maryland	8.5
1. Southlake, Texas	8.5
5. Hudson, Ohio	8.3
5. North Potomac, Maryland	8.3
5. South Jordan, Utah	8.3
8. Dix Hills, New York	8.2
8. Germantown, Tennessee	8.2
8. Leawood, Kansas	8.2
8. Mountain Brook, Alabama	8.2
8. Olney, Maryland	8.2

* Not including strip or Pullman kitchens, bathrooms, open porches, balconies, halls or foyers, half-rooms, utility rooms, unfinished attics or basements, or other unfinished space used for storage.

Cities listed have at least 20,000 people.

Source: 2000 U.S. Census.

Larger U.S. Cities with the Most Rooms per Housing Unit

City, State	Median Number of Rooms per Housing Unit
1. Virginia Beach, Virginia	6.0
2. Colorado Springs, Colorado	5.7
3. Philadelphia, Pennsylvania	5.6
4. Baltimore, Maryland	5.5
4. Buffalo, New York	5.5
4. Detroit, Michigan	5.5
4. Toledo, Ohio	5.5

* Not including strip or Pullman kitchens, bathrooms, open porches, balconies, halls or foyers, half-rooms, utility rooms, unfinished attics or basements, or other unfinished space used for storage.

Cities listed have at least 250,000 people.

Source: 2000 U.S. Census.

U.S. Cities with the Highest Percentage of Households Heated by Natural Gas

Cities with the most households heated by (utility) natural gas are generally Midwestern suburbs.

City, State	Percentage of Households Heated by Utility Natural Gas
1. Romeoville, Illinois	97.8
2. Algonquin, Illinois	97.0
3. Dearborn Heights, Michigan	96.4
3. Redford, Michigan	96.4
5. West Seneca, New York	96.3
6. Allen Park, Michigan	96.1
6. South Holland, Illinois	96.1
8. Streamwood, Illinois	95.9
9. Burbank, Illinois	95.8
10. Bolingbrook, Illinois	95.6
10. Hamtramck, Michigan	95.6

Cities listed have at least 20,000 people.

Source: 2000 U.S. Census.

Larger U.S. Cities with the Highest Percentage of Households Heated by Natural Gas

City, State	Percentage of Households Heated by Utility Natural Gas
1. Detroit, Michigan	90.2
2. Buffalo, New York	90.1
3. Cleveland, Ohio	88.2
4. Pittsburgh, Pennsylvania	87.2
5. Albuquerque, New Mexico	85.3

Cities listed have at least 250,000 people.

Source: 2000 U.S. Census.

U.S. Cities with the Lowest Percentage of Households Heated by Natural Gas (in Climates with Cold Winters)

In Florida (except the far north) and Hawaii, few places have natural gas heating (and some places have no heating source at all). For this list, the average January temperature must be below 40 degrees Fahrenheit (average of the high and low temperatures).

City, State	Percentage of Households Heated by Utility Natural Gas
1. Bainbridge Island, Washington	0.4
2. Bangor, Maine	0.9
3. Juneau, Alaska	1.4
4. Shirley, New York	2.1
5. Biddeford, Maine	2.3

Cities listed have at least 20,000 people.

Source: 2000 U.S. Census.

U.S. Cities with the Highest Percentage of Households Heated by Fuel Oil*

The Northeast, especially near the coast and in smaller cities and towns, has the highest percentages of houses heated by oil.

City, State	Percentage of Households Heated by Heating Oil
1. Shirley, New York	91.1
2. Bangor, Maine	86.8
2. Biddeford, Maine	86.8
4. Levittown, New York	85.9
5. Levittown, Pennsylvania	83.4
6. Ronkonkoma, New York	81.6
7. Medford, New York	81.0
8. Lewiston, Maine	80.3
9. Auburn, Maine	77.5
10. Westport, Connecticut	75.8

Two Other Notable Locations:

Juneau, Alaska	70.4
Fairbanks, Alaska	69.8

*Includes kerosene.

Cities listed have at least 20,000 people.

Source: 2000 U.S. Census.

Larger U.S. Cities with the Highest Percentage of Households Heated by Fuel Oil*

City, State	Percentage of Households Heated by Heating Oil
1. New York, New York	33.0
2. Boston, Massachusetts	26.3
3. Newark, New Jersey	19.6
4. Portland, Oregon	17.1
5. Baltimore, Maryland	15.2

* Includes kerosene.

Cities listed have at least 250,000 people.

Source: 2000 U.S. Census.

U.S. Cities with the Highest Percentage of Households Using Coal or Coke as the Primary Source of Heating

Very few households in the U.S. are heated by coal or coke. Many are places with cold winters. All cities below, except Grand Forks, North Dakota, are near areas with coal mines.

City, State	Percentage of Households Heated by Coal or Coke
1. Hazleton, Pennsylvania	5.5
2. Back Mountain, Pennsylvania	4.1
3. Fairbanks, Alaska	2.5
4. Grand Forks, North Dakota	1.4
5. Cumberland, Maryland	0.8
5. Scranton, Pennsylvania	0.8
5. Wilkes-Barre, Pennsylvania	0.8

Cities listed have at least 20,000 people.

Source: 2000 U.S. Census.

U.S. Cities with the Highest Percentage of Households Heated by Electricity

Florida has the top 53 cities in the United States in this category. The only other areas even remotely competing in the number of households heated by electricity are in coastal areas of the Carolinas and in the Pacific Northwest, where electricity is relatively cheap due to hydroelectric power.

City, State	Percentage of Households Heated by Electricity
1. Golden Gate, Florida	98.5

1. Wekiwa Springs, Florida	98.5
3. Palm Coast, Florida	98.4
4. Citrus Park, Florida	98.0
5. Yeehaw Junction, Florida	97.9

Cities listed have at least 20,000 people.

Source: 2000 U.S. Census.

U.S. Cities with the Highest Percentage of Households Heated by Electricity (outside of Florida)

City, State	Percentage of Households Heated by Electricity
1. Hilton Head Island, South Carolina	94.0
2. Mount Pleasant, South Carolina	91.7
3. Myrtle Beach, South Carolina	91.3
4. Longview, Washington	90.7
5. Jacksonville, North Carolina	89.8

Cities listed have at least 20,000 people.

Source: 2000 U.S. Census.

U.S. Cities with the Highest Percentage of Households Using Wood as a Primary Heat Source

Wood is rarely used as a primary source of heating, though fireplaces are often second sources. The Pacific Northwest, Northern California, and some Intermountain West resorts are areas with higher percentages of wood-heated houses than the U.S. as a whole.

City, State	Percentage of Households Heated by Wood
1. Paradise, California	10.9
2. Bend, Oregon	9.3
3. North Marysville, Washington	7.1
4. Bainbridge Island, Washington	7.0
5. Eureka, California	5.8

Cities listed have at least 20,000 people.

Source: 2000 U.S. Census.

U.S. Cities with the Highest Percentage of Households Using No Fuel or Electricity for Heating

Even in the few tropical parts of the United States, many households have available heating (usually electricity).

City, State	Percentage of Households Using No Fuel or Electricity for Heat
1. Kailua, Hawaii	59.4
2. Hilo, Hawaii	48.7
3. Waimalu, Hawaii	45.7
4. Kahului, Hawaii	44.7
5. Kaneohe, Hawaii	44.4
6. Honolulu, Hawaii	42.2
7. Mililani Town, Hawaii	41.4
8. Pearl City, Hawaii	39.4
9. Key West, Florida	31.1
10. Waipahu, Hawaii	28.4

Cities listed have at least 20,000 people.

Source: 2000 U.S. Census.

Larger U.S. Cities with the Highest Percentage of Households Using No Fuel or Electricity for Heating

City, State	Percentage of Households Using No Fuel or Electricity for Heat
1. Honolulu, Hawaii	42.2
2. Miami, Florida	6.9
3. Santa Ana, California	6.6
4. Los Angeles, California	3.9
5. Long Beach, California	2.9

Cities listed have at least 250,000 people.

Source: 2000 U.S. Census.

Extended Families: Cities in the U.S. with the Highest Percentage of Their Populations Consisting of Grandparents Living with Their Grandchildren

This phenomenon tends to be more prevalent in lower income areas and in immigrant communities. These figures are so high that in some other communities, the *total* number of grandparents is less than the percentages below (whether they live with grandchildren or not).

City, State	Percentage of People Who are Grandparents Living with Their Grandchild(ren)
1. Waipahu, Hawaii	8.1
2. Valinda, California	7.8
3. West Puente Valley, California	7.6
4. Calexico, California	7.0
5. West Little River, Florida	6.8
6. Maywood, Illinois	6.6
7. Socorro, Texas	6.3
8. Carol City, Florida	6.2
8. Carson, California	6.2
10. Pico Rivera, California	6.0

Cities listed have at least 20,000 people.

Source: 2000 U.S. Census.

Larger Cities in the U.S. with the Highest Percentage of Their Populations Consisting of Grandparents Living with Their Grandchildren

City, State	Percentage of People Who are Grandparents Living with Their Grandchild(ren)
1. El Paso, Texas	4.3
2. Detroit, Michigan	4.1
2. Santa Ana, California	4.1
4. Baltimore, Maryland	4.0
4. Newark, New Jersey	4.0

Cities listed have at least 250,000 people.

Source: 2000 U.S. Census.

U.S. Cities with the Highest Percentage of Mobile Home Households

With the exception of the locations along the Mexican border, these are places with large retirement communities.

City, State	Percentage of Households in Mobile Homes
1. Fortuna Foothills, Arizona	57.1
2. North Fort Myers, Florida	51.0
3. Apache Junction, Arizona	50.0
4. Pahrump, Nevada	48.8
5. Bullhead City, Arizona	44.7
6. Socorro, Texas	33.3
7. Largo, Florida	31.1
8. Pharr, Texas	29.4
9. South Bradenton, Florida	29.0
10. Hemet, California	28.1

Cities listed have at least 20,000 people.

Source: 2000 U.S. Census.

Larger U.S. Cities with the Highest Percentage of Mobile Home Households

City, State	Percentage of Households in Mobile Homes
1. Mesa, Arizona	17.6
2. Tucson, Arizona	7.8
3. Jacksonville, Florida	7.1
4. Anchorage, Alaska	5.8
5. Santa Ana, California	5.2

Cities listed have at least 250,000 people.

Source: 2000 U.S. Census.

Largest U.S. Cities with No Residential Mobile Homes

City, State	Population
1. Alhambra, California	85,804
2. Passaic, New Jersey	67,861
3. Irvington, New Jersey	60,695
4. Hempstead, New York	56,554
5. Ellicott City, Maryland	56,397
6. Medford, Massachusetts	55,765
7. Towson, Maryland	51,793
8. Orland Park, Illinois	51,077
9. Aspen Hill, Maryland	50,228
10. Hoffman Estates, Illinois	49,495

Source: 2000 U.S. Census.

Larger U.S. Cities with the Lowest Percentage of Mobile Home Households

City, State	Percentage of Households in Mobile Homes
1. Baltimore, Maryland	0.05
2. New York, New York	0.07
2. Washington, D.C.	0.07
4. Cincinnati, Ohio	0.09
5. Buffalo, New York	0.11
5. Honolulu, Hawaii	0.11
5. San Francisco, California	0.11

Cities listed have at least 250,000 people.

Source: 2000 U.S. Census.

U.S. Cities with the Highest Percentage of No-Vehicle Households

In the United States, not having a vehicle in the household is very much a northeastern phenomenon, with the New York metropolitan

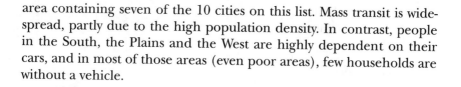

area containing seven of the 10 cities on this list. Mass transit is wide-spread, partly due to the high population density. In contrast, people in the South, the Plains and the West are highly dependent on their cars, and in most of those areas (even poor areas), few households are without a vehicle.

City, State	Percentage of Households with No Vehicles
1. New York, New York	55.7
2. Atlantic City, New Jersey	50.3
3. Union City, New Jersey	46.3
4. Newark, New Jersey	44.2
5. West New York, New Jersey	43.1
6. Jersey City, New Jersey	40.7
7. Camden, New Jersey	40.6
8. Hoboken, New Jersey	38.3
9. East Orange, New Jersey	37.1
10. Washington, D.C.	36.9

Cities listed have at least 20,000 people.

Source: 2000 U.S. Census.

Larger U.S. Cities with the Highest Percentage of No-Vehicle Households

Again, most cities where many people do not drive are in the Northeast. Even dense, compact San Francisco ranked only No. 10 (with all other California cities with 250,000 people or more ranking much lower).

City, State	Percentage of Households with No Vehicles
1. New York, New York	55.7
2. Newark, New Jersey	44.2
3. Washington, D.C.	36.9
4. Baltimore, Maryland	35.9
5. Philadelphia, Pennsylvania	35.7
6. Boston, Massachusetts	34.9
7. Buffalo, New York	31.4
8. Pittsburgh, Pennsylvania	29.4

9. Chicago, Illinois	28.8
10. San Francisco, California	28.6

Cities listed have at least 250,000 people.

Source: 2000 U.S. Census.

U.S. Cities with the Lowest Percentage of No-Vehicle Households

Suburbs (especially outer suburbs) are places where nearly all households have at least one vehicle.

City, State	Percentage of Households with No Vehicles
1. Leawood, Kansas	0.4
2. Riverton, Utah	0.5
3. Brentwood, Tennessee	0.7
4. North Potomac, Maryland	0.8
5. Flower Mound, Texas	0.9
5. Missouri City, Texas	0.9
5. Sammamish, Washington	0.9
8. Highland Ranch, Colorado	1.0
8. Chanhassen, Minnesota	1.0
10. Fishers, Indiana	1.1
10. Maple Grove, Minnesota	1.1

Cities listed have at least 20,000 people.

Source: 2000 U.S. Census.

Larger U.S. Cities with the Lowest Percentage of No-Vehicle Households

City, State	Percentage of Households with No Vehicles
1. Arlington, Texas	4.3
2. Virginia Beach, Virginia	4.7
3. San Jose, California	6.1

4. Colorado Springs, Colorado	6.3
5. Anchorage, Alaska	6.4
6. Mesa, Arizona	6.5
7. Aurora, Colorado	7.0
8. Raleigh, North Carolina	7.1
9. Albuquerque, New Mexico	7.2
10. Wichita, Kansas	7.4

Cities listed have at least 250,000 people.

Source: 2000 U.S. Census.

U.S. Cities with the Highest Percentage of Householders Who Moved into Their Current (2000) Residences Before 1970

These cities have a lot of people who "stay put."

City, State	Percentage of 2000 Householders Who Moved into Their Residences Before 1970
1. Pearl City, Hawaii	31.6
2. West Mifflin, Pennsylvania	30.8
3. Rotterdam, New York	29.1
4. Paramus, New Jersey	29.0
5. Allen Park, Michigan	28.9
6. Plainview, New York	28.6
7. Dundalk, Maryland	27.9
8. Brook Park, Ohio	27.6
8. Hicksville, New York	27.6
10. Levittown, Pennsylvania	27.0

Cities listed have at least 20,000 people.

Source: U.S. Census, 2000.

Larger U.S. Cities with the Highest Percentage of Householders Who Moved into Their Current (2000) Residences Before 1970

City, State	Percentage of 2000 Householders Who Moved into Their Residences before 1970
1. Philadelphia, Pennsylvania	17.8
2. Pittsburgh, Pennsylvania	17.5
3. Baltimore, Maryland	14.6
4. Cleveland, Ohio	14.4
5. Honolulu, Hawaii	14.2

Cities listed have at least 250,000 people.

Source: 2000 U.S. Census.

Very Flat Cities in the United States

The following cities are quite flat, though a few small hills, especially near rivers (or bayous) can be found. No parts of these cities are even remotely considered "hilly." Most of the flattest cities in the United States are found along the Gulf or Atlantic Coasts of the Southeast, though some are located in the Central and Salinas Valleys of California (even though mountains are nearby). Bicycling should generally be easy, unless other factors interfere, such as wind, traffic or heat. See the next list for the most extreme examples.

Charleston, South Carolina
Chicago, Illinois
Corpus Christi, Texas
Detroit, Michigan
Fargo, North Dakota
Houston, Texas
Jacksonville, Florida
Modesto, California
Norfolk, Virginia
Sacramento, California (some suburbs are hillier, though)
Salinas, California
Tampa, Florida
Virginia Beach, Virginia

The Very Flattest Cities in the United States

The following cities are nearly completely flat, with little variation in elevation between highest and lowest points. Any (rare) hills in these places are very small and barely noticeable. Even most creeks and river banks are shallow here.

Brownsville, Texas
Fort Lauderdale, Florida
Fresno, California
Miami, Florida
New Orleans, Louisiana
Stockton, California

CHAPTER FIVE
Climate Geography

This chapter focuses on the climate extremes—the hottest, coldest and wettest (or maybe even loudest, because of thunderstorms) cities, the lowest or highest temperatures of the year, or places that have weather uncharacteristic of their parts of the world. The emphasis here is on the unusual; people can go to the Internet or a weather almanac to view something ordinary (albeit important), such as the average high temperature in April in Los Angeles or London.

Climate, of course, is subject to change (weather is not constant, so why should climate be?), and as a result, the latest statistics possible are included (fortunately, an easier task with the Internet).

Hottest Capital and Major Cities in the World

These are the hottest cities, based on average annual temperature (using daytime highs and lows). Most of these cities are either in the Middle East or North Africa, arid (or semi-arid) areas that get very hot in the abundant sunshine.

City, Country	Average Annual Temp. (°F)
1. Mecca, Saudi Arabia	88
2. Djibouti, Djibouti	86
2. Khartoum, Sudan	86
4. Aden, Yemen	85
4. Niamey, Niger	85
6. Bangkok, Thailand	84

6. Muscat, Oman   84
6. Ouagadougou, Burkina Faso   84
6. Port-au-Prince, Haiti   84
6. Timbuktu (Tombouctou), Mali 84 *

* Yes—this is neither a capital nor a major city, but it is well-known, nevertheless!

Capital and Major Cities in the World with the Highest "Winter" Temperatures

Note that "winter" is in quotation marks! These are the cities with the warmest "coolest month of the year" (in the Northern Hemisphere, that is typically around January; in the Southern Hemisphere, that is typically around July), using average daily high and low temperatures. Not surprisingly, these cities are near the equator, far beyond the reach of winter, and most of these places are on islands, especially in the western part of the Pacific. All are humid year-round.

City, Country	Average Coolest Monthly Temp. (°F)
1. Funafuti, Tuvalu	83
1. Tarawa, Kiribati	83
3. Yaren, Nauru	82
4. Colombo, Sri Lanka	81
4. Koror, Palau	81
4. Kuala Lumpur, Malaysia	81
4. Majuro, Marshall Islands	81
4. Palikir, Micronesia	81
4. Panama City, Panama	81
4. Port-au-Prince, Haiti	81

Coldest Capital and Major Cities in the World

These are cities at northern latitudes where summers are short and winters are long. The temperatures listed are average annual temperatures (based on daily highs and lows).

City, Country	Average Annual Temp. (°F)
1. Fairbanks, Alaska, U.S.A.	27

2. Ulaanbaatar, Mongolia	31
3. Novosibirsk, Russia	35
3. Regina, Saskatchewan, Canada	35
5. Anchorage, Alaska, U.S.A.	36
6. Edmonton, Alberta, Canada	37
6. Winnipeg, Manitoba, Canada	37
8. Moscow, Russia	40
8. Reykjavik, Iceland	40
10. Helsinki, Finland	41
10. Juneau, Alaska, U.S.A.	41

Capital and Major Cities in the World with the Lowest Summer Temperatures

This list has a combination of northern oceanic cities, where the chilly water keeps the air cool during the short summers, and tropical highland places that stay cool throughout the year, despite the heat at lower elevations. The temperatures listed are average (based on daily highs and lows) temperatures in the warmest month of the year.

City, Country	Average Warmest Monthly Temp. (°F)
1. Reykjavik, Iceland	52
2. La Paz, Bolivia	54
3. Juneau, Alaska, U.S.A.	56
3. Cusco, Peru	56
5. Bogota, Colombia	57
6. Anchorage, Alaska, U.S.A.	59
6. Edinburgh, Scotland, U.K.	59
6. Glasgow, Scotland, U.K.	59
6. Quito, Ecuador	59
10. Belfast, Northern Island, U.K.	60
10. Dublin, Ireland	60

And among cities in the United States...

City, Country	Average Warmest Monthly Temp. (°F)
1. Juneau, Alaska	56

2. Eureka, California	58
3. Anchorage, Alaska	59
4. Bellingham, Washington	62
4. Fairbanks, Alaska	62
6. Olympia, Washington	63
6. Monterey, California	63
6. San Francisco, California	63
9. Laramie, Wyoming	64
9. Santa Maria, California	64

Capital and Major Cities in the World with the Lowest Winter Temperatures

Not surprisingly, the cities with the coldest winters are at northerly latitudes far from the moderating effects of the ocean. Below are the average temperatures in the average coldest month of the year.

City, Country	Average Coldest Monthly Temp. (°F)
1. Fairbanks, Alaska, U.S.A.	-8
2. Ulaanbaatar, Mongolia	-4
3. Harbin, China	0
3. Regina, Saskatchewan, Canada	0
5. Winnipeg, Manitoba, Canada	2
6. Novosibirsk, Russia	4
7. Quebec, Quebec, Canada	10
8. Edmonton, Alberta, Canada	11
9. Minneapolis, Minnesota, U.S.A.	13
10. Montreal, Quebec, Canada	14
10. Ottawa, Ontario, Canada	14

Wettest Capital and Major Cities in the World

The wettest major cities in the world lie near the equator, either in the West Pacific or in Africa.

City, Country	Annual Rainfall (In.)
1. Palikir, Micronesia	189
2. Monrovia, Liberia	183
3. Douala, Cameroon	150

4. Conakry, Guinea	149
5. Koror, Palau	148
6. Funafuti, Tuvalu	137
7. Majuro, Marshall Islands	134
8. Freetown, Sierra Leone	118
9. Bandar Seri Begawan, Brunei	114
10. Apia, Samoa	112

Wettest Capital and Major Cities (North of 50-Degree N. Latitude)

Most places far from the equator receive relatively little rainfall, since cold air usually contains less moisture than warm air. The wettest cities in the high latitudes, not surprisingly, are located near warm ocean currents, such as the Gulf Stream (North Atlantic Drift) or the Alaska Current.

City, Country	Annual Rainfall (In.)
1. Juneau, Alaska, U.S.A.	55
2. Cardiff, U.K.	36
2. Manchester, U.K.	36
4. Amsterdam, Netherlands	32
4. Brussels, Belgium	32
4. Reykjavik, Iceland	32

Driest Capital and Major Cities in the World

While the Middle East has most of the following cities, it doesn't top the list. The driest part of the world is along the Pacific Coast of northern Chile and Peru due to the cold ocean current and the Andes (see below for more details).

City, Country	Annual Rainfall (In.)
1. Lima, Peru	0.3
2. Cairo, Egypt	1.0
3. Aden, Yemen	1.7
4. Abu Dhabi, United Arab Emirates	2.2
4. Jeddah, Saudi Arabia	2.2
6. Manama, Bahrain	3.0
7. Doha, Qatar	3.2

8. Dubai, United Arab Emirates   3.7
9. Muscat, Oman   3.8
10. Kuwait City, Kuwait   4.2

Why Are the Coasts of Northern Chile and Peru So Dry?

The north part of Chile's Pacific Coast (the Atacama Desert) is the driest part of the world, and the Peruvian coast is almost as dry. There are three main factors contributing to this extreme desert.

1. Cold Ocean Current.

The Peru Current, which is a cold ocean current off the coast of South America (due to a process called "upwelling" where cold water from the depths of the ocean is forced up to the surface), limits evaporation of ocean water into the atmosphere. In addition, the cold ocean water lowers the air temperature near the surface, which makes the atmosphere more stable. This keeps whatever precious little ocean water that does evaporate in the lowest layer of the atmosphere (the "marine layer"). Even during El Niño, the ocean water over northern Chile and southern Peru usually fails to warm enough to bring any significant precipitation.

2. Andes.

The Andes Mountains are a formidable block to any moisture attempting to enter from the east. Some of the mountains are more than 20,000 feet above sea level, and even if moisture from above 20,000 feet were successful at reaching the Pacific Coast from the east, it would not be enough for sprinkles.

3. Subtropical Latitude.

Many of the world's deserts lie in the subtropics (around 20 or 30 degrees latitude, either north or south of the equator). The Atacama has a perfect fit into this definition. The jet stream (which helps to steer weather systems) is almost always further from the equator, and the tropical moisture is almost always closer to the equator in these subtropical deserts. Of course, we mustn't forget (and therefore offend) the "subtropical high." After all, these persistent subtropical high-pressure systems have the power to bring extreme drought since the air aloft slowly subsides from higher altitudes to lower altitudes, which normally keeps the atmosphere rather dry.

Warmest and Coldest Climates Relative to Latitude

Highest Average Annual Temperatures at Weather Stations:

The hottest places in the world lie at tropical latitudes. As one moves north (or south) from those latitudes, the climate becomes progressively colder. Below are the outliers, which are much warmer than their comparative latitudinal counterparts.

North of 30° N latitude in the U.S.:
Death Valley, California (76° F)

North of 30° N latitude anywhere in the world:
Abadan, Iran (78° F)

North of 35° N latitude in the U.S.:
Death Valley, California (76° F)

North of 35° N latitude anywhere in the world:
also Death Valley, California (76° F)

North of 40° N latitude in the U.S.:
Redding, California (64° F)

North of 40° N latitude anywhere in the world:
also Redding, California (64° F)

North of 45° N latitude in the U.S.:
John Day Dam, Washington, along the Columbia River east of the Cascades (55° F)

North of 45° N latitude anywhere in the world:
Trieste, Italy (58° F)

North of 50° N latitude:
Pendennis Point, (southwestern) England (53° F)

North of 55° N latitude:
Greenock, Scotland (50° F)

North of 60° N latitude:
Flora, Norway (46° F)

North of the Arctic Circle:
Sorvagen, Norway (42° F)

South of 30° S latitude:
Cape Hermes (near Port St. Johns), South Africa (68° F)

South of 40° S latitude:
San Antonio Oeste, Argentina (60° F)

South of 50° S latitude:
Santa Cruz, Argentina (50° F)

South of the Antarctic Circle:
Stonington, Antarctica (19° F)

Lowest Average Annual Temperatures at Weather Stations near Sea Level (Below 300 Feet in Elevation):

One can usually navigate to a colder climate by either moving closer to the North (or South) Pole or by increasing in elevation. Here are locations that are unusually cold for the latitude (yet are near sea level). All locations are near cold ocean currents (and the Chinese and Russian locations receive massive amounts of Siberian air during winter).

Between 10° S and 10° N latitude:
Trujillo, Peru (68° F)

Between 20° S and 20° N latitude:
Paramunga, Peru (65° F)

Between 30° S and 30° N latitude:
La Serena, Chile (59° F)

Between 40° S and 40° N latitude:
Zhuanghe (at the north end of Korea Bay), China (49° F)

Between 50° S and 50° N latitude:
Tumnin (in the very far eastern part of Siberia along the Tumnin River), Russia (32° F)

Here is one way to think of how extremely cold Tumnin, Russia is compared to the warmest parts of southwestern England, both of which are at about the same latitude and elevation. The difference in average temperatures between those two places is as great as the difference in the average temperatures between New York City and Death Valley.

Places That Have Never Recorded 100-Degree Temperatures

Quite a few places in the world (especially in polar and mountain areas, but also some oceanic areas) have never reached 100 degrees. Here are some of those places.

United States:

Aspen, Colorado
Buffalo, New York
Fairbanks, Alaska
Flagstaff, Arizona
Honolulu, Hawaii
Jackson, Wyoming
Juneau, Alaska
Miami, Florida
North Bend, Oregon
Santa Fe, New Mexico
Tahoe City, California

Other Countries (Plus Puerto Rico):

Amsterdam, Netherlands
Auckland, New Zealand
Copenhagen, Denmark
Guatemala City, Guatemala
Hong Kong
Johannesburg, South Africa
Kingston, Jamaica
Lima, Peru
Luxembourg City, Luxembourg
Mexico City, Mexico
Moscow, Russia
Munich, Germany
Nairobi, Kenya

Oslo, Norway
Port Moresby, Papua New Guinea
San Juan, Puerto Rico
Stockholm, Sweden
Vancouver, Canada

Places That Have Never Recorded 90-Degree Temperatures

Now we will become even more extreme and list some places that have never seen a 90-degree day.

United States:

Anchorage, Alaska
Barrow, Alaska
Eureka, California
Leadville, Colorado
Mauna Loa Slope Observatory, Hawaii (all-time warmest: 71 degrees)

Other Countries:

Bergen, Norway
Bogota, Colombia
Cuzco, Peru
Dublin, Ireland
La Paz, Bolivia
Ponta Delgada, Azores
Quito, Ecuador
Reykjavik, Iceland
Wellington, New Zealand

And, lastly, Vostok, Antarctica (not only at a polar latitude, but also at a high elevation), which hasn't even recorded a temperature above zero.

* Mauna Loa Slope Observatory, at around 11,000 feet, has never reached higher than 71 degrees, at least when a thermometer was present.

Big Chill: Largest U.S. Cities with Cold Winter Climates

These are the largest cities where the average January daily high temperature is 32 degrees F or below. About 18 percent of Americans live in these cold climates, and a little over 10 percent of the largest cities are listed here.

The ranking among all U.S. cities (regardless of January temperatures) is in parentheses.

1. Chicago, IL (3)
2. Detroit, MI (10)
3. Milwaukee, WI (19)
4. Omaha, NE (44)
5. Minneapolis, MN (45)
6. Toledo, OH (57)
7. Buffalo, NY (59)
8. St. Paul, MN (60)
9. Anchorage, AK (66)
10. Rochester, NY (80)

Largest U.S. Cities with Mild Winter Climates

These are the largest cities where the average January daily high temperature is 60 degrees F or above. The largest cities in the U.S. are much more likely to be mild in winter than cold, even though about 19 percent of Americans live in these mild climates (almost the same as the 18 percent of Americans in cold climates).

The ranking among all U.S. cities (regardless of January temperatures) is in parentheses.

1. Los Angeles, CA (2)
2. Houston, TX (4)
3. Phoenix, AZ (6)
4. San Diego, CA (7)
5. San Antonio, TX (9)
6. Jacksonville, FL (14)
7. Austin, TX (16)
8. Tucson, AZ (30)
9. New Orleans, LA (31)
10. Long Beach, CA (34)

One city that did not make the list: Las Vegas, Nevada. Despite the palm trees planted there, its average January daily high temperature is only 56 degrees.

Northern Cities Where Snow on the Ground Is Rare

These are not subtropical cities; they all lie north of 50 degrees North latitude. These cities have five or fewer days of snow on the ground per year on average.

1. Cork, Ireland
2. Dover, U.K.
3. Liverpool, U.K.
4. London, U.K. (within the urban heat island)
5. Plymouth, U.K.

Places in Cold Year-Round Climates That Have Never Recorded Zero-Degree Temperatures

Not all cold climates have seen sub-zero temperatures. A few locations, especially in oceanic areas, have stayed above zero, though they are often cold most of the time. To qualify for this list, a location's average annual temperature must be below 50 degrees F (so the milder sections of the British Isles, which have never seen zero, are otherwise just barely too warm, year-round).

1. La Paz, Bolivia
2. Punta Arenas, Chile
3. Stanley, Falkland Islands

Snowfall in Unexpected Places

Here are some occurrences of snow in places where it rarely falls (or at least is *perceived* to rarely fall).

1. Miami Beach, Florida and Freeport, Bahamas (Jan. 1977)

January 1977 was a rough month, weather-wise, for the eastern half of the United States. Snow flurries fell as far south as the Miami area (where Miami Beach recorded an all-time record low of 32 degrees) and even at Freeport in the Bahamas, though in neither place did snow accumulate. At one point during that month, all 48 contiguous states in the U.S. had snow covering at least a small part of each state.

2. Guadalajara, Mexico (Dec. 1997)

During El Niño of 1997–1998, much of the world from Southeast Asia to the Americas saw very unusual weather. This included an unusual cold snap over Mexico, which brought rare snowfall to Guadalajara (the first time since 1881). During the same time period, Monterrey saw its first snowfall in 30 years.

3. Southern California (Jan. 1949)

Many places in Southern California, even at sea level, had snow in January 1949, the coldest month ever for that region. This included accumulating snowfall at Malibu, Laguna Beach, Burbank and parts of Los Angeles. Six inches of snow were reported in one section of Riverside.

4. Fallbrook, California (Dec. 1967)

The avocado capital of the United States, in northern San Diego County, covered in three to four inches of snow after a storm in December 1967. Despite its elevation below 1000 feet, Fallbrook has had significant snowfall twice in the 20th century (similar amounts fell in January 1949).

5. Bakersfield, California (Jan. 1999)

A snowfall of three to six inches paralyzed Bakersfield at the southern end of the San Joaquin Valley. This was only the second time measurable snowfall had been reported there since 1932. Temperatures were near 32 degrees during this nocturnal storm.

6. Athens, Greece (Jan. 2002)

An Olympic-sized snowfall occurred over most of Greece during an unusually harsh winter in southeastern Europe. Two feet of snow fell in the outskirts, and four to six inches fell even in the city center.

7. Jerusalem, Israel (numerous times)

Every time snow falls in Jerusalem, at 2500 feet above sea level, it is deemed to be a rare event. However, snowfalls of a foot or more occur regularly, including in February 1992, January 2000 and January 2002. However, in Tel Aviv, at sea level, snow is very rare.

8. Amman, Jordan (Feb. 1992, Feb. 2003)

Two feet of snow fell in parts of Amman, both during storms in 1992 and 2003. Amman is at 3000 feet above sea level, so like Jerusalem, it receives occasional heavy snowfall, despite being in the Middle East.

9. Las Vegas, Nevada (Jan. 1974)

Las Vegas received nine inches of snow in 24 hours during January 1974. However, snow is not that rare; in fact, the average annual snowfall is 1.2 inches per year (though not distributed very evenly among years as many winters have no snow and others have frequent snow).

10. El Paso, Texas (Dec. 1987)

El Paso, on the Mexican border, received an astounding 22 inches of snow from a storm in December 1987! Snow is even more frequent here than in Las Vegas; the average annual snowfall is 5.3 inches.

Climates with Strong Seasons

Here are some places with extremely strong differences between winter and summer temperatures. Places that have strong seasonal temperature differences usually have them because of bitterly cold winters (versus hot summers).

Listed is the difference between the average temperature in the warmest month and the coldest month of the year. For example, in Verkhoyansk, Siberia, July temperatures average a full 107 degrees higher than January temperatures!

City, Country	Temperature Difference Between Warmest & Coldest Months
1. Verkhoyansk, Russia	107
2. Yakutsk, Russia	104
3. Usu, China	75
4. Harbin, China	73
5. Fairbanks, Alaska, U.S.A.	70
6. Vostok, Antarctica	67
7. Omsk, Russia	66
7. Ulaanbaatar, Mongolia	66
7. Winnipeg, Manitoba, Canada	66
10. Fargo, North Dakota, U.S.A.	65
10. Regina, Saskatchewan, Canada	65
10. Urumqi, China	65

Numerous other small towns, especially in Siberia, would also rank high on this list.

U.S. Climates with Strong Seasons

Here are some of the places in the United States with the strongest differences between average temperatures in the warmest month versus coldest month. Not surprisingly, these places are all in the North, and most are far from any large (moderating) bodies of water.

City, Country	Temperature Difference Between Warmest & Coldest Months
1. Fairbanks, Alaska	70
2. Fargo, North Dakota	65
3. International Falls, Minnesota	64
4. Bismarck, North Dakota	62
4. St. Cloud, Minnesota	62
6. Minneapolis, Minnesota	59
7. Sioux Falls, South Dakota	59
9. Duluth, Minnesota	58
9. La Crosse, Wisconsin	58

Non-Tropical Climates (More Than 30 Degrees Latitude from the Equator) with Very Little Seasonal Change in Temperature

Most equatorial climates have little change in temperature between seasons. However, few climates outside the tropics or subtropics have small differences between the average temperatures of the warmest month versus coldest month of the year. All of the places listed here are either islands or coastal locations.

City, Country	Temperature Difference Between Warmest & Coldest Months
1. Evangelistas Island, Chile	7
1. Macquarie Island (New Zealand poss.)	7
3. Campbell Island, New Zealand	8
3. Langebaanweg, South Africa	8
3. Marion Island (South Africa poss.)	8
6. Crozet Island (French poss./Indian O.)	9

6. Gough Island (South Africa poss.)   9
6. Half Moon Bay, California, U.S.A.   9
6. Morro Bay, California, U.S.A.   9
10. Eureka, California, U.S.A.   10
10. Kerguelen Isl. (French poss./Indian O.) 10
10. St. Paul Island (French poss./Indian O.) 10
10. San Nicholas Island, California, U.S.A. 10

And If You Go More Than 60 Degrees Latitude from the Equator...

1. Thorshavn, Faroe Islands (Denmark)   14
2. Lerwick, Shetland Islands (U.K.)   15
3. Angissoq, Greenland (south tip)   16
3. Vestmannaeyjar, Iceland   16
5. Deception Island, New Zealand (near Antarctica) 18

Climates Within 30 Degrees Latitude of the Equator with the Strongest Seasons

As one gets closer to the equator, the seasonal variation in temperature gets smaller. However, some places at subtropical latitudes still have relatively strong differences between average temperatures in the warmest month versus the coolest month, especially in southeastern China, which is strongly influenced by high pressure over Siberia in winter, and the deserts of the Middle East, which have unbearably hot summers (but somewhat cool winters). All locations on this list are in the Northern Hemisphere, since the Southern Hemisphere (with the moderating effects of its larger oceanic area) has less pronounced seasons.

City, Country	Temperature Difference Between Warmest & Coldest Months
1. Jiujiang, China	47
2. Kuwait City, Kuwait	45
3. Changsha, China	44
3. Hafar Al Batin, Saudi Arabia	44
5. Nanchang, China	43
5. Zahedan, Iran	43
7. In Salat, Algeria	42

8. Chongqing, China	39
8. Riyadh, Saudi Arabia	39
10. Dhahran, Saudi Arabia	37

Weather Stations (at Low Elevations) Closest to the Equator That Have Recorded Freezing Temperatures

City	Latitude	Lowest Temperature Recorded (°F)
1. N'Guigmi, Niger	14 deg. N.	32
2. Chicoa, Mozambique	16 deg. S.	32
3. Vientiane, Laos	18 deg. N.	32
4. Robore, Bolivia	18 deg. S.	32
5. Zhanjiang, China	21 deg. N.	32
6. Wadi Halfa, Sudan	22 deg. N.	28
7. Lan Song, Vietnam	22 deg. N.	30
8. Mariscal, Paraguay	22 deg. S.	23
9. Tampico, Mexico	22 deg. N.	27
10. Baroda, India	22 deg. N.	30

Only weather stations below 1,000 feet above sea level are listed here, as many higher elevation cities in the tropics (including Quito, Ecuador near the equator) have recorded temperatures at or below freezing. One station is listed per country (the station nearest to the equator which is below 1,000 feet).

Overblown: Windiest Cities in the United States

The Great Plains, northern Rockies and some coastal (or lakeside) parts of the Northeast have the windiest cities in the United States. These figures are based on the average annual wind speed.

City, State	Average Annual Wind Speed (MPH)
1. Dodge City, KS	13.8
2. Amarillo, TX	13.3
3. Cheyenne, WY	13.0
4. Casper, WY	12.9
5. Boston, MA	12.5
6. Great Falls, MT	12.4

7. Wichita, KS	12.3
8. Fargo, ND	12.2
9. Grand Island, NE	11.8
10. Buffalo, NY	11.6

U.S. Cities That Have Strong Winds Most Often

This is a list of cities in which the highest percentage of time has winds of 25 miles per hour or more. This happens most frequently in areas just east of the northern Rockies, which are prone to Chinook winds that blow down the slope from west to east.

City, State	Annual Percentage of Time When Wind Speeds Are Greater Than 25 MPH
1. Casper, WY	7.3
1. Cheyenne, WY	7.3
3. Great Falls, MT	7.2
4. Rapid City, SD	5.9
5. Dodge City, KS	5.7

Least Windy Cities in the United States

Valley locations in the western U.S. (and parts of coastal Southern California) are sheltered from the wind most of the time (though not always). However, in some of these locations, the air can become stagnant and pollution can be quite an issue.

Due to the complex terrain in the West, winds can vary significantly. While Santa Barbara typically enjoys light winds, nearby Point Conception is often quite windy, due to its exposure to the ocean.

City, State	Average Annual Wind Speed (MPH)
1. Medford, OR	4.8
2. Fairbanks, AK	5.3
3. Santa Barbara, CA	5.6
4. Elko, NV	5.9
5. Lewiston, ID	6.2
5. Long Beach, CA	6.2
5. Missoula, MT	6.2
5. Phoenix, AZ	6.2
9. Fresno, CA	6.3
10. Bakersfield, CA	6.4

Coldest Night of the Winter

Proximity to a coastline and latitude are the two keys to how cold the coldest night of the year (as measured from July 1 through June 30 to prevent splitting a winter) will be. Cities along the East Coast and (especially) West Coast will be much milder than their inland counterparts.

Data below are for a 30-year period ending in the winter of 2002–2003. In a few cases, the lowest temperature of the winter season occurred in late fall or even early spring. In many locations (especially along the East Coast), the winters were milder in the 1990s (and early 2000s) than they were in previous decades, and the average coldest night has become warmer.

City, State	Average Lowest Temp. (°F) of the Year
Fairbanks, AK	-46
Great Falls, MT	-25
Minneapolis, MN	-20
Anchorage, AK	-16
Chicago, IL	-11
Denver, CO	-10
Topeka, KS	-8
Cincinnati, OH	-6
Detroit, MI	-6
Pittsburgh, PA	-4
St. Louis, MO	-3
Boston, MA	1
Salt Lake City, UT	1
Nashville, TN	4
Philadelphia, PA	6
New York, NY (Central Park)	7
Raleigh, NC	8
Albuquerque, NM	9
Washington, D.C.	10
Atlanta, GA	11
El Paso, TX	14
Dallas, TX	15
Norfolk, VA	15
Portland, OR	19
Seattle, WA	19
Jacksonville, FL	21
Houston, TX	22

Las Vegas, NV	22
Orlando, FL	28
Phoenix, AZ	32
San Francisco, CA	33
Los Angeles, CA (airport)	38
Miami, FL	39
San Diego, CA	40
Honolulu, HI	57

Elsewhere around the World...

City, State	Average Lowest Temp. (°F) of the Year
Moscow, Russia	-20
Toronto, Ontario, Canada	-10
Munich, Germany	0
Beijing, China	7
Paris, France	18
Vancouver, British Columbia, Canada	18
Tehran, Iran	20
Madrid, Spain	21
Shanghai, China	22
London, U.K.	22
Buenos Aires, Argentina	26 *
Rome, Italy	26
Baghdad, Iraq	27
Johannesburg, South Africa	27 *
Tokyo, Japan	28
Athens, Greece	32
Melbourne, Australia	32 *
Mexico City, Mexico	32
Auckland, New Zealand	35 *
Lisbon, Portugal	35
Tel Aviv, Israel	36
Sydney, Australia	38 *
Cairo, Egypt	39
Delhi, India	39
San Juan, Puerto Rico	66

* For Southern Hemisphere locations, the average lowest temperature in a winter is based on a calendar year, versus July 1–June 30.

Dreaming of a White Christmas?

In Vermont, a white Christmas is far more likely than a mild day in December. Historically, across all of Vermont, December 25 has had at least one inch of snow on the ground more than 60 percent of the time (with some part of the state, especially in the north and over higher elevations, having had that occurrence more than 90 percent of the time).

In the well-known movie "White Christmas," the temperature was 69 degrees when Bob Wallace (played by Bing Crosby) and Phil Davis (played by Danny Kaye) arrived in Vermont. Seem impossible? Not quite; it can get that warm in Vermont in December, albeit very seldom. The temperature reached 72 degrees in Springfield, Vermont on December 7, 1998. At that time of year, a maximum temperature of 72 would even be above normal in places like San Diego, Corpus Christi and Tallahassee.

Mild January Days in Fairbanks

Fairbanks is almost always cold in January. The key word here is "almost." On January 15, 1981, Fairbanks had a high temperature of 50, its highest ever recorded in January. A few locations in the Lower 48 have not even achieved 50 in January; they include Duluth, Minnesota (only reached 47 in January), International Falls, Minnesota (48) and Sault Ste. Marie, Michigan (45).

Windiest Cities in the United States during January

Back on page 165, we saw the cities with the highest average annual wind speeds. However, the coldest month of the year (for most of the United States), January, is when the wind is most noticeable, due to the wind chill. The cities with the highest average wind speeds in January are (unfortunately) in colder climates than the cities with the highest average wind speeds during other months.

City, State	Average January Wind Speed (MPH)
1. Casper, WY	16.7
2. Cheyenne, WY	15.2
3. Great Falls, MT	14.6
4. Buffalo, NY	13.9

5. Boston, MA	13.8
6. Dodge City, KS	13.3
7. Erie, PA	13.1
8. Billings, MT	13.0
9. Amarillo, TX	12.8
10. Fargo, ND	12.7

Hottest Day of the Summer

Here is a list of cities and their average highest temperatures of the year. Generally, the cities with long, hot summers will rank high, but there are some exceptions. Portland, Oregon has cool summers compared with most of the U.S. (average July daily high temperature is only 80), yet strong, high pressure aloft and compressional heating due to downsloping winds off the Cascades will make Portland very hot for a few days of the year. Portland's average hottest day of the year is 100 degrees. In contrast, Miami, a location known for being hot and muggy for half the year, has an average hottest day with a temperature of only 95 degrees, five degrees cooler than its northern counterpart.

Data below are for a 30-year period ending in 2002. Unlike with the coldest temperatures of the year, the highest temperatures of the year have had little or no increase in the past 30 years in most locations.

City, State	Average Highest Temp. (°F) of the Year
Phoenix, AZ	115
Las Vegas, NV	113
El Paso, TX	106
Dallas, TX	104
Salt Lake City, UT	102
Topeka, KS	102
Albuquerque, NM	101
Houston, TX	100
Portland, OR	100
St. Louis, MO	100
Denver, CO	99
Great Falls, MT	99
Jacksonville, FL	99
Washington, D.C.	99
Nashville, TN	98
New York, NY (Central Park)	98

Norfolk, VA	98
Philadelphia, PA	98
Raleigh, NC	98
Atlanta, GA	97
Boston, MA	97
Chicago, IL	97
Minneapolis, MN	97
Orlando, FL	97
Detroit, MI	96
Los Angeles, CA (airport)	96
San Francisco, CA	96
Cincinnati, OH	95
Miami, FL	95
San Diego, CA	94
Pittsburgh, PA	93
Seattle, WA	93
Honolulu, HI	92
Fairbanks, AK	88
Anchorage, AK	77

Elsewhere around the World...

City, State	Average Highest Temp. (°F) of the Year
Kuwait City, Kuwait	121
Baghdad, Iraq	119
Delhi, India	111
Cairo, Egypt	108
Tehran, Iran	105
Melbourne, Australia	104 *
Tel Aviv, Israel	104
Madrid, Spain	102
Sydney, Australia	102 *
Athens, Greece	100
Beijing, China	100
Lisbon, Portugal	100
Shanghai, China	99
Buenos Aires, Argentina	98 *
San Juan, Puerto Rico	95
Tokyo, Japan	94

Rome, Italy	93
Toronto, Ontario, Canada	93
Paris, France	92
Munich, Germany	89
Johannesburg, South Africa	88 *
Mexico City, Mexico	88
Moscow, Russia	87
Vancouver, British Columbia, Canada	86
London, U.K.	85
Auckland, New Zealand	81 *

* For Southern Hemisphere locations, the average highest temperature in a summer is based on the period from July 1 through June 30.

How Many Mild Days Do Places Experience in January?

Here is a list of the average number of days per January in which the temperatures in various places reach 60 or even 70 degrees. Some northern cities will see fewer than one day in an average January with a temperature of 60 degrees or higher.

During the 1990s and early 2000s, most cities saw an increase in the number of mild days. This was especially the case along the East Coast of the United States but also strongly occurred in Las Vegas due to its expanding heat island, associated with its rapid growth. The data below show the long-term values covering (in most cases) over 50 years (up through 2003).

City, State	Number of 60° (or Warmer) Days in January	Number of 70° (or Warmer) Days in January
Miami, FL	30	26
Orlando, FL	28	19
San Diego, CA	27	7
Brownsville, TX	26	19
Phoenix, AZ	25	10
Los Angeles, CA (downtown)	23	10
Houston, TX	19	10
Monterey, CA	16	2–3
El Paso, TX	15	2–3

Dallas, TX	13	5
Las Vegas, NV	12	1
Atlanta, GA	9	2
San Francisco, CA (airport)	7	once every 3–4 years
Raleigh, NC	7	2
Norfolk, VA	7	1–2
Oklahoma City, OK	6	1
Washington, D.C.	3–4	once every 1–2 years
Denver, CO	3	once every 6 years
Albuquerque, NM	3	0
Philadelphia, PA	2	once every 6 years
Kansas City, MO	2	once every 10 years
Cincinnati, OH	1–2	once every 15 years
New York, NY (La Guardia)	once every 1–2 years	0
Boston, MA	once every 2 years	once every 40 years
Portland, OR	once every 2 years	0
Chicago, IL	once every 5 years	0
Seattle, WA	once every 6 years	0
Detroit, MI	once every 7 years	0
Salt Lake City, UT	once every 9 years	0
Minneapolis, MN	0	0

Overseas...

Most international data cover the time period from 1973 through 2003.

City, State	Number of 60° (or Warmer) Days in January	Number of 70° (or Warmer) Days in January
Hong Kong, China	28	11
Cairo, Egypt	28	5
Tel Aviv, Israel	23	4
Lisbon, Portugal	8	once every 10 years
Athens, Greece	8	once every 30 years
Rome, Italy	5	once every 30 years
Madrid, Spain	1 to 2	once every 30 years

Shanghai, China	1	once every 10 years
Tokyo, Japan	1	once every 30 years
Tehran, Iran	1	0
Paris, France	once every 8 years	0
London, U.K.	once every 15 years	0
Munich, Germany	once every 30 years	0
Beijing, China	0	0
Moscow, Russia	0	0

The United States has more variation in its winter weather than in most countries. Therefore, the number of mild days is larger, relative to the severity of the winters, than in other parts of the world.

Like much of the United States, during the 1990s and early 2000s, a majority of cities in Europe and the Middle East saw an increase in the number of mild days during winter.

Severity of Winter: How Long Between Mild or Warm Spells?

There are many ways to define the severity of winter, including average temperatures, coldest night of the year, or the length of the intervals between mild spells. In this case, we will look at the latter—more specifically, the longest period each winter (on average) where a location remains below a certain temperature—be it 70 degrees, 50 degrees or 32 degrees.

Average Longest Period in a Winter When the Temperature Stays Below 70 Degrees

In most mild climates, 70 degrees is not a difficult achievement during winter. However, in colder climates (or in some cases, marine climates where temperatures vary less from day to day), there may be periods of many months where the temperature never reaches 70 degrees. If you ever ask "When *was* the last time it hit 70?" then this is the list for you! In the statistics below, the "winter" period can include parts of autumn or spring.

City, State	Average Longest Period (Days) to Remain Below 70°F
Honolulu, Hawaii	almost 0
Miami, Florida	4

Jacksonville, Florida	13
Houston, Texas	17
Phoenix, Arizona	17
San Diego, California	24
Los Angeles, California (airport)	29
Dallas, Texas	30
El Paso, Texas	48
Atlanta, Georgia	59
Las Vegas, Nevada	64
Nashville, Tennessee	69
Washington, D.C.	82
St. Louis, Missouri	87
Topeka, Kansas	97
Cincinnati, Ohio	108
Denver, Colorado	108
San Francisco, California	110
Philadelphia, Pennsylvania	122
Pittsburgh, Pennsylvania	122
New York, New York (Central Park)	132
Chicago, Illinois	136
Boston, Massachusetts	143
Salt Lake City, Utah	154
Great Falls, Montana	163
Minneapolis, Minnesota	167
Seattle, Washington	185
Anchorage, Alaska	254
Fairbanks, Alaska	256

Average Longest Period in a Winter When the Temperature Stays Below 50 Degrees

This list really distinguishes between North and South. Most northern climates see at least one period of at least a month where temperatures fail to reach 50 degrees, while mild climates often will only have a small handful of days—if any—that stay below 50. Also, the otherwise cooler marine climates begin to be shifted towards the "mild" end of the list. For example, San Francisco was nearly tied with Cincinnati in the 70-degree list but is nearly tied with much more southerly Houston and Jacksonville in this list.

City, State	Average Longest Period (Days) to Remain Below 50°F
Honolulu, Hawaii	0
Los Angeles, California	almost 0
Miami, Florida	almost 0
San Diego, California	almost 0
Phoenix, Arizona	1
Jacksonville, Florida	2
San Francisco, California	3
El Paso, Texas	5
Las Vegas, Nevada	5
Dallas, Texas	8
Atlanta, Georgia	9
Denver, Colorado	16
Nashville, Tennessee	16
Seattle, Washington	20
Washington, D.C.	20
Cincinnati, Ohio	26
Philadelphia, Pennsylvania	26
St. Louis, Missouri	27
New York, New York (Central Park)	29
Topeka, Kansas	30
Boston, Massachusetts	33
Pittsburgh, Pennsylvania	36
Great Falls, Montana	38
Salt Lake City, Utah	50
Chicago, Illinois	57
Minneapolis, Minnesota	104
Fairbanks, Alaska	180
Anchorage, Alaska	181

Average Longest Period in a Winter When the Temperature Stays Below 32 Degrees

In most parts of the country, if the daily high temperature falls below freezing, it usually only remains there for a few days. In parts of the northern United States, temperatures can stay below freezing for weeks in average winters and months in harsh winters.

City, State	Average Longest Period (Days) to Remain Below 32°F
Honolulu, Hawaii	must we ask?
Los Angeles, California	0
Miami, Florida	0
Phoenix, Arizona	0
San Diego, California	0
San Francisco, California	0
Houston, Texas	almost 0
Jacksonville, Florida	almost 0 **
Las Vegas, Nevada	almost 0 **
El Paso, Texas	about ½
Atlanta, Georgia	1
Dallas, Texas	2
Seattle, Washington	2
Nashville, Tennessee	3
Washington, D.C.	3
Denver, Colorado	5
New York, New York (Central Park)	5
Philadelphia, Pennsylvania	5
Cincinnati, Ohio	6
Boston, Massachusetts	7
St. Louis, Missouri	8
Salt Lake City, Utah	8
Topeka, Kansas	9
Pittsburgh, Pennsylvania	10
Great Falls, Montana	11
Chicago, Illinois	14
Minneapolis, Minnesota	23
Anchorage, Alaska	28
Fairbanks, Alaska	73

** Believe it or not, Jacksonville, Florida has had occasions where the high temperature failed to even hit 32. That is extremely rare in Florida and has only occurred in the far northern areas, such as around Jacksonville. Possibly even more impressive is that Las Vegas, Nevada has had daily high temperatures below 32 degrees (including 29 on Jan. 12, 1963).

Two Places That Have Recorded Their Highest Temperature Ever Around the Winter Solstice

Except within 1,000 miles (14 degrees of latitude) of the equator, it is very rare for a location to have recorded its all-time highest temperature when the day length is shortest. Both locations below are between 1,000 and 2,000 miles from the equator; places further than 2,000 miles from the equator (29 degrees of latitude) will have too large of a difference in solar radiation between summer and winter for this to occur.

1. Walvis Bay, Namibia

Walvis Bay, at 23 degrees South Latitude, has reached 100 degrees during the months of June and July (of course, that would be during winter in the Southern Hemisphere), when dry east-to-west flow from the land can descend down from the mountains and compress, much like the Santa Ana winds of Southern California. In contrast, the cold current along the "Skeleton Coast" and common summer fog has resulted in Walvis Bay never climbing above the upper 80s during January or February.

2. Hawaii Volcanoes National Park, Hawaii

At the headquarters of this national park, at 19 degrees North Latitude, and at nearly 4,000 feet above sea level, the all-time record high of 89 was set on December 15, 2000. The highest summer temperature ever recorded there was 87.

Places with Very Frequent Thunderstorms

Here are 10 cities and towns with a very large average number of days with thunderstorms per year. Most of these places are in or near tropical rainforests.

City, Country	No. of Days with T-Storms per Year
1. Bunia, Congo (Dem. Rep.)	229
2. Kamembe, Rwanda	221
3. Bandung, Indonesia	218
4. Kuala Lumpur, Malaysia	209
5. Kisangani, Congo (Dem. Rep.)	197
6. Douala, Cameroon	191
7. Niamtougou, Togo	189
8. Kitale, Kenya	185

9. Bandar Seri Begawan, Brunei   184
10. Penang, Malaysia   182

Honorable Mentions:

City, Country	No. of Days with T-Storms per Year
Palmerola, Honduras	163
Singapore, Singapore	159
Bangui, Central African Republic	157
Colón, Panama	149

Dry Climates with Frequent Thunderstorms

Most places with abundant thunderstorms receive a lot of rain. Conversely, lower annual rainfall generally means that thunderstorms will be less common. However, some places with dry climates, especially in or near mountains with hot, humid summers, receive a lot of thunderstorms, though not enough to rank in the top thunderstorm locations in the world. In this list, a dry climate is defined as a place receiving 20 inches of rain per year or less.

Tucson, Arizona is a dry area known for its summer thunderstorms. In fact, because of the good visibility (partly because the rain shaft is smaller than in thunderstorms in the Eastern United States), Tucson is an excellent place for lightning photography. However, enough other arid and semi-arid locations (including some that are drier than Tucson) have more days with thunderstorms per year, so Tucson would only rank No. 14 on this list!

City, Country	No. of Days with Annual T-Storms per Year	Rainfall (In.)
1. Maracaibo, Venezuela	93	20
2. Xigaze, Tibet (China)	91	15
3. Santa Marta, Colombia	79	13
4. Lhasa, Tibet (China)	79	16
5. Kohat, Pakistan	76	14
6. Silver City, New Mexico, U.S.A.	60	11
7. El Obeid, Sudan	60	15

8. Nogales, Mexico	59	17
9. Nema, Mauritania	54	11
10. Douglas, Arizona, U.S.A.	52	12

A Few Places Receiving Less Than 10 Inches of Annual Precipitation...

City, Country	No. of Days with Annual T-Storms per Year	Rainfall (In.)
Alamogordo, New Mexico, U.S.A.	49	9
Truth or Consequences, NM, U.S.A.	48	7
Columbus, New Mexico, U.S.A.	45	9
Twentynine Palms, California, U.S.A.	30	4

Most Thunderstorms in the United States

Here are the 10 cities in the United States with the largest average number of days with thunderstorms per year. All except one are in Florida.

City, State	No. of Days with T-Storms per Year
1. Fort Myers, Florida	92
2. Orlando, Florida	87
3. Tampa, Florida	86
4. Tallahassee, Florida	83
5. West Palm Beach, Florida	79
6. Apalachacola, Florida	78
6. Daytona Beach, Florida	78
6. Gainesville, Florida	78
6. Mobile, Florida	78
10. Lake Charles, Louisiana	77

Wet and Dry Seasons: The Most Extreme Locations

Tropical savannas are monsoonal climates with very wet summers and very dry winters. They can be found on all continents except Antarctica and Europe and are most prevalent around the latitudes of 15 degrees North and South, well within reach of the wet "Intertropical

Convergence Zone" during summer, but too close to the equator for the jet streams to bring storms during winter.

The locations listed below are the most extreme of the monsoonal climates, where little or no rain will fall in some months, but enormous rainfall averages of up to one to two inches per *day* occur during other months. All of the most extreme locations are on southwest coasts in Africa or Asia.

Place	Driest Month's Av. Rainfall (In.)	Wettest Month's Av. Rainfall (In.)
Sandoway, Burma	0.02 (Feb.)	56.85 (Jul.)
Conakry, Guinea	0.04 (Jan.)	52.64 (Jul.)
Cubi Point, Philippines	0.10 (Jan., Feb.)	42.90 (Aug.)
Freetown, Sierra Leone	0.30 (Feb.)	36.57 (Aug.)
Cox's Bazar, Bangladesh	0.14 (Jan.)	35.52 (Jul.)
Bissau, Guinea-Bissau	0.02 (Jan., Mar.)	26.87 (Aug.)
Mumbai (Bombay), India	0.05 (Dec.–Apr.)	25.60 (Jul.)

States with the Most Tornadoes per 10,000 Square Miles per Year

The Plains states are well-known for having a lot of tornadoes. However, when calculated per 10,000 square miles (1950–1995), Florida actually has more than even states like Oklahoma or Kansas. However, Florida's tornadoes are usually smaller. The fewest tornadoes are in the West.

State	Tornadoes per 10,000 Sq. Mi. per Year
1. Florida	8.4
2. Oklahoma	7.5
3. Delaware	6.1
4. Kansas	5.8
5. Louisiana	5.6
6. Iowa	5.5
7. Indiana	5.4
8. Mississippi	5.0
9. Nebraska	4.8
10. Illinois	4.7
10. Texas	4.7

States with the Fewest Tornadoes per 10,000 Square Miles per Year

State	Tornadoes per 10,000 Sq. Mi. per Year
1. Alaska	0.0
2. Nevada	0.1
2. Oregon	0.1
4. Utah	0.2
4. Washington	0.2
6. Arizona	0.3
6. California	0.3
6. Idaho	0.3
9. Montana	0.4
10. Maine	0.6

States with the Most Violent Tornadoes (Rated "F2" or Higher) per 10,000 Square Miles per Year

The strength of tornadoes is rated using the Fujita Scale, where an "F0" tornado is the weakest, and an "F5" tornado is the strongest. When the weaker "F0" and "F1" tornadoes are eliminated from statistics, Oklahoma clearly stands out as the number one tornado state (based on annual tornadoes per 10,000 square miles between 1950 and 1995).

State	Strong Tornadoes per 10,000 Sq. Mi. per Year
1. Oklahoma	2.4
2. Indiana	2.0
3. Iowa	1.9
3. Mississippi	1.9
5. Alabama	1.8
6. Arkansas	1.7
7. Louisiana	1.6
8. Illinois	1.5
9. Kansas	1.4
10. Delaware	1.3

Good Visibility: 10 Cities in the United States with the Highest Percentage of Time When Visibility Is 10 Miles or More

Visibility is generally best in the Rocky Mountain states where the air is dry and (relatively) clean and cities are widely spaced. However, rapid growth in many of these cities threatens the previously high visibility.

City, State	Percentage of Time When Vis. Is 10 Mi. or More
1. Tucson, Arizona	99.4
2. Las Vegas, Nevada	99.1
3. Honolulu, Hawaii	98.6
4. Albuquerque, New Mexico	98.2
5. Phoenix, Arizona	98.1
6. Grand Junction, Colorado	96.3
7. El Paso, Texas	95.9
8. Helena, Montana	94.8
9. Pueblo, Colorado	94.2
10. Casper, Wyoming	93.5

Bad Visibility: 10 Cities in the United States with the Highest Percentage of Time When Visibility Is 1/4 Mile or Less

These are cities where (at least at the airport) visibility of a quarter mile or less is most likely to occur (based on percentage of time annually). When this visibility occurs, fog is the most likely reason, though heavy rain or snow can also be a cause. Dense fog is also most likely at night, because the relative humidity is usually highest then.

The most common areas for dense fog are in mountain valleys of the Appalachians and in New England, and in valleys inland from the Pacific Coast. People in these areas are more likely to encounter hazardous conditions when driving a car or flying (and especially landing) an airplane (even a model airplane!).

City, State	Percentage of Time When Vis. Is 1/4 Mi. or More
1. Worcester, Massachusetts	5.5
2. Charleston, West Virginia	4.2
3. Olympia, Washington	4.2

4. Medford, Oregon	3.4
5. Eugene, Oregon	3.1
6. Stockton, California	2.8
7. Duluth, Minnesota	2.7
8. Asheville, North Carolina	2.6
9. Fresno, California	2.5
10. Huntington, West Virginia	2.3

Worst Visibility: 10 Cities in the World with the Highest Percentage of Time When Visibility Is ¼ Mile or Less

This is based on the city's airport.

City, Country	Percentage of Time When Vis. Is ¼ Mi. or More
1. Vladivostok, Russia	9.3
2. Milan, Italy	7.6
3. Walvis Bay, Namibia *	7.4
4. St. John's, Newfoundland, Canada	5.6
5. Bucharest (Otopeni), Romania	5.1
6. Luxembourg, Luxembourg	5.0
7. Venice, Italy	4.9
8. Ljubljana, Slovenia	4.8
9. Zagreb, Croatia	4.3
10. Dnipropetrovs'k, Ukraine	4.1

* Hardly a large city, Walvis Bay is used in this list since it typifies the foggy coastline of the "Skeleton Coast" of Namibia (where the water is unusually cold for a subtropical latitude).

Chapter Note:

Most data used for the lists in this chapter are from the National Climatic Data Center (Asheville, NC), the *International Station Meteorological Climate Summary* (1996, available through the National Climatic Data Center), Western Region Climate Center (Reno, NV) or a combination of these three sources.

CHAPTER SIX
Demographic Geography

Previous chapters dealt with geographic features such as climate, mountains and the roads (including some names of the roads). This chapter will deal with none of that. This chapter is specifically about people. Nobody's name will be listed; instead we will view lists about characteristics of people in various locations. This chapter explores where people are from and where certain races, languages, religions and even genders are common (or, in some cases, exceedingly rare).

Locals Only: U.S. Cities Where People Born in the City's State Make up the Highest Percentage of the Population

These are cities with few outsiders, whether they originally come from other states or other countries. Such cities are most prevalent in the South and Appalachian states, though a few places near New York City are overwhelmingly full of native New Yorkers.

City, State	Percentage of the Population Born "In-State"
1. West Mifflin, Pennsylvania	92.5
2. Opelousas, Louisiana	92.4

3. West Seneca, New York	90.3
4. Altoona, Pennsylvania	90.0
5. Bessemer, Alabama	89.3
6. Massapequa, New York	89.2
7. McKeesport, Pennsylvania	89.0
7. West Islip, New York	89.0
9. Prichard, Alabama	88.8
10. Johnstown, Pennsylvania	88.6

Cities listed have at least 20,000 people.

Source: 2000 U.S. Census.

Larger U.S. Cities Where People Born in the City's State Make up the Highest Percentage of the Population

Some of these cities lie near state borders (such as Louisville, Philadelphia or Cincinnati), yet they still have fewer people from out of state than most other large cities.

City, State	Percentage of the Population Born "In-State"
1. Pittsburgh, Pennsylvania	78.1
2. Buffalo, New York	77.4
2. New Orleans, Louisiana	77.4
2. Toledo, Ohio	77.4
5. Louisville, Kentucky	75.6
6. Corpus Christi, Texas	73.5
7. Philadelphia, Pennsylvania	71.7
8. Cincinnati, Ohio	71.6
9. Baltimore, Maryland	71.2
9. Cleveland, Ohio	71.2

Cities listed have at least 250,000 people.

Source: 2000 U.S. Census.

U.S. Cities Where People Born in the City's State Make up the Lowest Percentage of the Population

Most of these cities filled with transplants from other states (or other countries) are either retirement cities or military centers.

City, State	Percentage of the Population Born "In-State"
1. Sun City West, Arizona	0.7
2. Sun City, Arizona	2.4
3. Aventura, Florida	9.5
4. Bethesda, Maryland	11.2
5. Fort Bragg, North Carolina	11.7
5. Naples, Florida	11.7
7. Fountain Hills, Arizona	11.9
8. Lake Havasu City, Arizona	12.4
9. Boca Del Mar, Florida	12.6
10. Bullhead City, Arizona	12.7
10. Fortuna Foothills, Arizona	12.7

Cities listed have at least 20,000 people.

Source: 2000 U.S. Census.

Larger U.S. Cities Where People Born in the City's State Make up the Lowest Percentage of the Population

Among the larger cities, there are a variety of reasons for most of the residents being from out of state. Some cities (such as Las Vegas or Colorado Springs) are fast-growing cities in lower-population states, while others have large numbers of immigrants (Miami).

City, State	Percentage of the Population Born "In-State"
1. Las Vegas, Nevada	19.7
2. Miami, Florida	26.6
3. Colorado Springs, Colorado	29.6
4. Anchorage, Alaska	32.1
5. Mesa, Arizona	33.0
6. Aurora, Colorado	33.9

7. Phoenix, Arizona	34.6
7. San Francisco, California	34.6
9. Virginia Beach, Virginia	37.7
10. Tucson, Arizona	38.2

Cities listed have at least 250,000 people.

Source: 2000 U.S. Census.

U.S. Cities (outside the Northeast) with the Most People Born in the Northeast (as a Percentage of the Population)

Florida retirement communities have more northeasterners (as a percentage of population) than any other cities outside of the Northeast. The only exception in this list is Newark, Delaware, which is just a few miles from the Pennsylvania border.

City, State	Percentage of the Population Born in the Northeastern U.S.
1. Boca Del Mar, Florida	47.7
2. Palm Coast, Florida	47.0
3. Tamarac, Florida	46.9
4. Spring Hill, Florida	46.7
5. Bayonet Point, Florida	42.3
6. Palm City, Florida	42.0
7. Coconut Creek, Florida	41.3
8. Newark, Delaware	40.8
9. Jupiter, Florida	40.1
10. Aventura, Florida	39.4
10. Port St. Lucie, Florida	39.4

The Northeast consists of Connecticut, Maine, Massachusetts, New Hampshire, New Jersey, New York, Pennsylvania, Rhode Island, and Vermont.

Cities listed have at least 20,000 people.

Source: 2000 U.S. Census.

Larger U.S. Cities (outside the Northeast) with the Most People Born in the Northeast as a Percentage of the Population)

Most of these cities are in climates with mild winters. However, few other similarities exist between these larger cities containing a sizable number of northeasterners.

City, State	Percentage of the Population Born in the Northeastern U.S.
1. Virginia Beach, Virginia	17.8
2. Raleigh, North Carolina	13.2
3. Charlotte, North Carolina	12.4
4. Tampa, Florida	12.1
5. Washington, D.C.	11.9
6. Las Vegas, Nevada	10.3
7. Jacksonville, Florida	10.1
8. San Francisco, California	8.8
9. Tucson, Arizona	8.5
10. Colorado Springs, Colorado	8.4

Cities listed have at least 250,000 people.

Source: 2000 U.S. Census.

U.S. Cities (outside the Midwest) with the Most People Born in the Midwest (as a Percentage of the Population)

Cities with the most Midwesterners (outside of the Midwest) are retirement communities. While most (but not all) of the Florida communities ranking at the top of the northeastern list (the 20,000-population-or-more cities) were on the east coast of that state, all three of the Florida places listed below are on the west coast of Southern Florida.

City, State	Percentage of the Population Born in the Midwestern U.S.
1. Sun City, Arizona	58.3

2. Sun City West, Arizona   55.0
3. Fountain Hills, Arizona   41.0
4. Apache Junction, Arizona   34.5
5. North Fort Myers, Florida   34.0
6. Bonita Springs, Florida   33.4
7. Naples, Florida   32.6
8. Scottsdale, Arizona   31.3
9. Oro Valley, Arizona   30.6
10. South Bradenton, Florida   28.0

The Midwest consists of Illinois, Indiana, Iowa, Kansas, Michigan, Minnesota, Missouri, Nebraska, North Dakota, Ohio, South Dakota and Wisconsin.

Cities listed have at least 20,000 people.

Larger U.S. Cities (outside the Midwest) with the Most People Born in the Midwest (as a Percentage of the Population)

Most of these cities are in the West, except for two cities which are within 100 miles of a Midwestern state (Tulsa and Lexington).

City, State	Percentage of the Population Born in the Midwestern U.S.
1. Mesa, Arizona	23.0
2. Colorado Springs, Colorado	21.7
3. Aurora, Colorado	18.4
4. Phoenix, Arizona	16.9
5. Tucson, Arizona	16.3
6. Denver, Colorado	16.2
7. Las Vegas, Nevada	14.9
8. Anchorage, Alaska	14.5
9. Tulsa, Oklahoma	13.4
10. Lexington-Fayette, Kentucky	13.0

Cities listed have at least 250,000 people.

Source for Both Lists: 2000 U.S. Census.

U.S. Cities (outside the South) with the Most People Born in the South (as a Percentage of the Population)

Most cities outside the South (except for the Chicago area) that have a large number of southerners are near the border of a southern state.

City, State	Percentage of the Population Born in the Southern U.S.
1. Clarksville, Indiana	42.3
2. Jeffersonville, Indiana	42.0
3. Hobbs, New Mexico	35.5
4. New Albany, Indiana	32.6
5. Carlsbad, New Mexico	24.4
6. Clovis, New Mexico	24.0
6. North Chicago, Illinois	24.0
8. Maywood, Illinois	23.5
9. Alamogordo, New Mexico	22.8
10. Gary, Indiana	22.1

The South consists of Alabama, Arkansas, Delaware, Florida, Georgia, Kentucky, Louisiana, Maryland, Mississippi, North Carolina, Oklahoma, South Carolina, Tennessee, Texas, Virginia and West Virginia, plus the District of Columbia.

Cities listed have at least 20,000 people.

Larger U.S. Cities (outside the South) with the Most People Born in the South (as a Percentage of the Population)

City, State	Percentage of the Population Born in the Southern U.S.
1. Detroit, Michigan	18.3
2. Colorado Springs, Colorado	16.0
3. Cincinnati, Ohio	14.5
4. Cleveland, Ohio	13.9
5. Anchorage, Alaska	13.7
6. Wichita, Kansas	13.3

7. Albuquerque, New Mexico	12.3
8. Columbus, Ohio	12.1
9. Indianapolis, Indiana	12.0
9. Newark, New Jersey	12.0
9. Oakland, California	12.0
9. St. Louis, Missouri	12.0

Cities listed have at least 250,000 people.

Source for Both Lists: 2000 U.S. Census.

U.S. Cities (outside the West) with the Most People Born in the West (as a Percentage of the Population)

Since migration has been more toward the West than from it, westerners fill a lower percentage of non-western cities' populations, versus northeasterners, midwesterners and southerners outside of their areas. Some of these cities have military installations.

City, State	Percentage of the Population Born in the Western U.S.
1. Fort Bragg, North Carolina	15.1
2. Fort Hood, Texas	15.0
3. Leavenworth, Kansas	11.8
4. Rapid City, South Dakota	11.7
5. Southlake, Texas	11.3
6. North Chicago, Illinois	11.0
7. Copperas Cove, Texas	10.8
7. Rogers, Arkansas	10.8
9. North Platte, Nebraska	10.4
10. Springdale, Arkansas	10.3

The West consists of Alaska, Arizona, California, Colorado, Hawaii, Idaho, Montana, Nevada, New Mexico, Oregon, Utah, Washington and Wyoming.

Cities listed have at least 20,000 people.

Larger U.S. Cities (outside the West) with the Most People Born in the West (as a Percentage of the Population)

Most of these cities are in the Plains States, not too far from the West.

City, State	Percentage of the Population Born in the Western U.S.
1. El Paso, Texas	7.3
2. Tulsa, Oklahoma	6.4
3. Oklahoma City, Oklahoma	6.3
4. Arlington, Texas	6.1
5. Virginia Beach, Virginia	5.9
6. Austin, Texas	5.8
7. Washington, D.C.	5.6
8. Wichita, Kansas	5.5
9. Omaha, Nebraska	5.1
10. Fort Worth, Texas	4.5

Cities listed have at least 250,000 people.

Source for Both Lists: 2000 U.S. Census.

Cities in the United States with the Highest Percentage of People Having Been Born in Selected Countries (Plus the "Runner-Up")

On the following two pages are the cities where immigrants from specific countries are the highest percentage of their total populations (children of immigrants do not count if they were born in the U.S., of course). The "runner-up" cities are also listed for each nationality.

Most of the cities with the highest concentrations in the U.S. of immigrants from various countries are suburbs, especially of New York, Los Angeles, Miami (though Miami itself has the most Hondurans, as a percentage of its total population) and Washington, D.C. In most cases, the core cities have too large of an overall population (and often with people from numerous countries, versus a concentration of one or two countries) to make this list. Percentages are quite variable; some nations that send many people to the United States, such as Mexico or the Philippines, have large concentrations in the cities listed below (and many cities not listed, too), while others that send few people to the U.S., such as South Africa or Sweden, will only be concentrated in small parts of cities, if even that.

Cities in California win the contest for highest concentrations of people from most of East Asia and Mexico (and L.A. suburbs give California several former Soviet nations), while cities close to New York City and Miami share the Caribbean and Central and South American honors. A few peculiarities are noted; Aventura and Hallandale, both in Florida, have the largest concentrations of people who were born in Austria. These cities have large senior populations; not incidentally, the peak decade in recent history of immigration from Austria to the United States was the 1950s (the immigration rate has only been about a third since then). People who were born in Germany are most concentrated in cities near military bases (especially Air Force bases) as many of these people are children (born during a German tour of duty) or spouses (met during a German tour of duty) of Americans in the armed forces. People from Britain and France are most concentrated in upscale communities. Suburban Detroit has a large population of people born in the Middle East (which started during the early 20th century due to recruitment to the auto industry).

Country	City with Highest Concentration	% of City Pop.	City with Second Highest Concentration	% of City Pop.
Afghanistan	Springfield, VA	1.80	Fremont, CA	1.39
Argentina	Miami Beach, FL	4.39	Aventura, FL	2.11
Armenia	Glendale, CA	8.90	Burbank, CA	2.79
Australia	Brookline, MA	0.41	Foster City, CA	0.36
Austria	Aventura, FL	0.38	Hallandale, FL	0.36
Bangladesh	Hamtramck, MI	8.23	Atlantic City, NJ	1.78
Barbados	Mount Vernon, NY	0.67	Elmont, NY	0.66
Belarus	West Hollywood, CA	1.69	Pikesville, MD	1.22
Bolivia	Bailey's Crossrds., VA	3.01	Annandale, VA	2.90
Bosnia & Herz.	Hamtramck, MI	9.38	Utica, NY	4.28
Brazil	Framingham, MA	6.59	Danbury, CT	5.56
Cambodia	Lowell, MA	5.21	White Center, WA	3.33
Canada	Hallandale, FL	4.67	Gardner, MA	3.84
Chile	Doral, FL	1.83	Fountainbleau, FL	1.36
China*	Arcadia, CA	24.50	Monterey Park, CA	24.50
Colombia	Kendall West, FL	11.92	The Hammocks, FL	11.63

Costa Rica	Summit City, NJ	3.24	Trenton, NJ	1.00
Cuba	Westchester, FL	55.81	Hialeah, FL	53.48
Czechoslov.**	Key West, FL	1.04	Linden, NJ	0.67
Dominican Rep.	Lawrence, MA	21.43	Perth Amboy, NJ	16.41
Ecuador	Ossining, NY	10.12	North Plainfield, NJ	7.77
Egypt	Bayonne, NJ	2.66	Jersey City, NJ	1.86
El Salvador	Brentwood, NY	12.91	Hempstead, NY	12.28
Ethiopia	North Atlanta, GA	2.07	Silver Spring, MD	1.95
France	North Bethesda, MD	1.00	Palo Alto, CA	0.98
Germany	Alamogordo, NM	4.33	Security-Widefield, CO	3.00
Ghana	Mount Vernon, VA	2.17	Groveton, VA	1.87
Greece	Tarpon Springs, FL	3.18	Holiday, FL	2.10
Guatemala	San Rafael, CA	5.37	Spring Valley, NY	4.75
Guyana	Orange, NJ	2.86	Irvington, NJ	2.42
Haiti	North Miami, FL	24.37	Golden Glades, FL	3.73
Honduras	Miami, FL	4.45	Chelsea, MA	4.18
Hungary	Hallandale, FL	1.08	North Port, FL	0.61
India	Edison, NJ	12.92	Sunnyvale, CA	7.96
Indonesia	Walnut, CA	2.18	San Gabriel, CA	1.10
Iran	Beverly Hills, CA	15.43	Glendale, CA	12.37
Iraq	Oak Park, MI	6.01	Rancho San Diego, CA	4.39
Ireland	Milton, MA	1.98	Yonkers, NY	1.52
Israel	Fair Lawn, NJ	3.09	Aventura, FL	1.67
Italy	Franklin Square, NY	5.64	Glen Cove, NY	5.00
Jamaica	Norland, FL	18.50	Lauderdale Lakes, FL	16.75
Japan	Fort Lee, NJ	4.91	Rcho. Palos Verdes, CA	4.22
Jordan	Burbank, IL	0.86	Oak Lawn, IL	0.71
Korea	Fort Lee, NJ	13.53	Cerritos, CA	12.06
Laos	Parkway-South Sacramento, CA	5.12	Merced, CA	4.43
Lebanon	Dearborn, MI	10.49	Dearborn Heights, MI	2.47
Malaysia	Stillwater, OK	0.85	West Lafayette, IN	0.69
Mexico	Calexico, CA	49.69	Coachella, CA	46.01
Micronesia***	Springdale, AR	1.19	Waipahu, HI	1.13
Netherlands	Forest Hills, MI	0.59	Holland, MI	0.52

Nicaragua	Fountainbleau, FL	12.17	Miami, FL	7.18
Nigeria	Chillum, MD	2.50	Greenbelt, MD	2.26
Pakistan	Herndon, VA	2.91	Groveton, VA	1.92
Panama	Doral, FL	1.09	Kendall West, FL	0.89
Peru	Paterson, NJ	5.32	The Hammocks, FL	4.66
Philippines	Waipahu, HI	32.66	Daly City, CA	23.19
Poland	Garfield, NJ	14.33	Elmwood Park, IL	10.81
Portugal	Fall River, MA	15.66	New Bedford, MA	13.86
Romania	Hallandale, FL	2.51	Parma Heights, OH	1.39
Russia	West Hollywood, CA	5.31	Fair Lawn, NJ	4.73
Sierra Leone	Chillum, MD	1.55	Greenbelt, MD	1.08
South Africa	Irvine, CA	0.65	Cave Spring, VA	0.56
Spain	Kearny, NJ	1.81	Westchester, FL	1.32
Sweden	Winchester, MA	0.34	Westport, CT	0.29
Syria	Allentown, PA	1.15	Watertown, MA	1.07
Thailand	Wausau, WI	2.30	Parkway-South Sacramento, CA	2.15
Trinidad & Tobago	Orange, NJ	2.36	Chillum, MD	1.89
Turkey	Cliffside Park, NJ	2.20	Watertown, MA	1.21
Ukraine	West Hollywood, CA	7.83	Pikesville, MD	4.43
U.K.	Santa Monica, CA	2.15	Los Gatos, CA	1.81
Venezuela	Fountainbleau, FL	4.20	Weston, FL	4.03
Vietnam	Westminster, CA	24.98	Rosemead, CA	20.32
Yugoslavia	Niles, IL	1.76	Schererville, IN	1.55

* Includes Hong Kong and Taiwan.
** Includes both Czech Republic and Slovakia.
*** Includes Federated States of Micronesia, Marshall Islands and Palau.

Cities listed have at least 20,000 people.

Source: 2000 U.S. Census.

Larger Cities in the United States with the Highest Percentage of People Born in Selected Countries

New York City clearly leads this list; when compared with other cities of 250,000 people or more, New York is No. 1 for highest percentage of its population represented by immigrants from 16 of the 73 nations listed here. However, California has 23 nationalities represented among its various larger cities. While California, New York and Florida have the most cities on this list, 10 other states (and the District of Columbia) have cities represented here.

Country	City	Percentage of City's Population Comprised of Immigrants from the Listed Nation
Afghanistan	San Diego, CA	0.12
Argentina	Miami, FL	0.59
Armenia	Los Angeles, CA	0.79
Australia	San Francisco, CA	0.14
Austria	New York, NY	0.08
Bangladesh	New York, NY	0.54
Barbados	Boston, MA	0.41
Belarus	San Francisco, CA	0.14
Bolivia	Santa Ana, CA	0.10
Bosnia & Herz.	St. Louis, MO	1.40
Brazil	Newark, NJ	2.45
Cambodia	Long Beach, CA	2.40
Canada	Seattle, WA	0.94
Chile	Miami, FL	0.32
China*	San Francisco, CA	12.43
Colombia	Miami, FL	1.88
Costa Rica	Miami, FL	0.30
Cuba	Miami, FL	30.31
Czechoslovakia**	New York, NY	0.11
Dominican Rep.	New York, NY	4.61
Ecuador	Newark, NJ	3.56
Egypt	New York, NY	0.19
El Salvador	Los Angeles, CA	4.61
Ethiopia	Minneapolis, MN	0.51
France	San Francisco, CA	0.32
Germany	Colorado Springs, CO	0.94

Ghana	Newark, NJ	0.48
Greece	New York, NY	0.37
Guatemala	Los Angeles, CA	2.73
Guyana	New York, NY	1.63
Haiti	Miami, FL	3.89
Honduras	Miami, FL	4.45
Hungary	New York, NY	0.14
India	San Jose, CA	2.00
Indonesia	San Francisco, CA	0.23
Iran	Los Angeles, CA	1.17
Iraq	Detroit, MI	0.39
Ireland	Boston, MA	0.84
Israel	Los Angeles, CA	0.29
Italy	New York, NY	0.90
Jamaica	New York, NY	2.23
Japan	Honolulu, HI	3.47
Jordan	Anaheim, CA	0.11
Korea	Honolulu, HI	3.13
Laos	St. Paul, MN	4.26
Lebanon	Los Angeles, CA	0.21
Malaysia	San Francisco, CA	0.11
Mexico	Santa Ana, CA	41.93
Micronesia***	Honolulu, HI	0.79
Netherlands	San Jose, CA	0.09
Nicaragua	Miami, FL	7.18
Nigeria	Newark, NJ	0.45
Pakistan	New York, NY	0.49
Panama	Miami, FL	0.30
Peru	Miami, FL	0.88
Philippines	Honolulu, HI	7.64
Poland	Chicago, IL	2.40
Portugal	Newark, NJ	4.45
Romania	Portland, OR	0.37
Russia	New York, NY	1.02
Sierra Leone	Washington, D.C.	0.10
South Africa	San Diego, CA	0.15
Spain	Newark, NJ	0.54
Sweden	Honolulu, HI	0.10
Syria	Los Angeles, CA	0.13
Thailand	St. Paul, MN	1.63
Trinidad & Tobago	New York, NY	1.11
Turkey	New York, NY	0.11

Ukraine	New York, NY	0.87
United Kingdom	San Francisco, CA	0.68
Venezuela	Miami, FL	0.59
Vietnam	San Jose, CA	7.53
Yugoslavia	New York, NY	0.24

* Includes Hong Kong and Taiwan.
** Includes both Czech Republic and Slovakia.
*** Includes Federated States of Micronesia, Marshall Islands and Palau.

Cities listed have at least 250,000 people.

Source: 2000 U.S. Census.

Largest Numbers of Immigrants from Certain Countries in Any One U.S. City

This is a very simple list containing the cities with the largest number of immigrants for a given nationality. Thus, the largest city in the United States, New York (which also happens to have the largest number of immigrants), has the largest number of many specific immigrant groups.

Country	City	Total Number or Immigrants in City
Afghanistan	New York, NY	4,833
Argentina	New York, NY	11,677
Armenia	Los Angeles, CA	29,068
Australia	New York, NY	3,860
Austria	New York, NY	6,700
Bangladesh	New York, NY	42,865
Barbados	New York, NY	27,065
Belarus	New York, NY	11,187
Bolivia	Arlington, VA	5,264
Bosnia & Herz.	Chicago, IL	6,714
Brazil	New York, NY	14,241
Cambodia	Long Beach, CA	11,091
Canada	New York, NY	17,318
Chile	New York, NY	6,780
China*	New York, NY	261,551
Colombia	New York, NY	84,404

Costa Rica	New York, NY	5,819
Cuba	Hialeah, FL	121,084
Czechoslovakia**	New York, NY	8,628
Dominican Rep.	New York, NY	369,186
Ecuador	New York, NY	114,944
Egypt	New York, NY	15,231
El Salvador	Los Angeles, CA	170,313
Ethiopia	Seattle, WA	2,777
France	New York, NY	12,386
Germany	New York, NY	27,708
Ghana	New York, NY	14,915
Greece	New York, NY	29,805
Guatemala	Los Angeles, CA	100,786
Guyana	New York, NY	130,647
Haiti	New York, NY	95,580
Honduras	New York, NY	32,358
Hungary	New York, NY	11,144
India	New York, NY	68,263
Indonesia	Los Angeles, CA	3,170
Iran	Los Angeles, CA	43,175
Iraq	Chicago, IL	5,133
Ireland	New York, NY	22,604
Israel	New York, NY	21,288
Italy	New York, NY	72,481
Jamaica	New York, NY	178,922
Japan	New York, NY	19,415
Jordan	Chicago, IL	1,484
Korea	Los Angeles, CA	73,666
Laos	St. Paul, MN	12,237
Lebanon	Dearborn, MI	10,258
Malaysia	New York, NY	7,618
Mexico	Los Angeles, CA	625,504
Micronesia***	Honolulu, HI	2,940
Netherlands	New York, NY	2,455
Nicaragua	Miami, FL	26,026
Nigeria	New York, NY	15,689
Pakistan	New York, NY	39,165
Panama	New York, NY	23,118
Peru	New York, NY	27,278
Philippines	Los Angeles, CA	80,632
Poland	Chicago, IL	69,501
Portugal	Fall River, MA	14,397

Romania	New York, NY	19,280
Russia	New York, NY	81,408
Sierra Leone	New York, NY	1,599
South Africa	Los Angeles, CA	2,656
Spain	New York, NY	7,836
Sweden	New York, NY	2,421
Syria	New York, NY	5,191
Thailand	Los Angeles, CA	9,399
Trinidad & Tobago	New York, NY	88,794
Turkey	New York, NY	9,026
Ukraine	New York, NY	69,727
United Kingdom	New York, NY	28,996
Venezuela	New York, NY	8,181
Vietnam	San Jose, CA	67,375
Yugoslavia	New York, NY	19,535

* Includes Hong Kong and Taiwan.
** Includes both Czech Republic and Slovakia.
*** Includes Federated States of Micronesia, Marshall Islands and Palau.

Source: 2000 U.S. Census.

Countries from Which the Most Immigrants Came to the United States (1991–2000)

Mexico, by far, was the origination point for more immigrants to the U.S. than any other country between 1991 and 2000. The Pacific Rim contributed many immigrants (especially to the West Coast) as well as the Caribbean (mainly to the East Coast).

Country	Immigrants to U.S. from 1991 to 2000
1. Mexico	2,249,421
2. China	525,893 *
3. Philippines	503,945
4. India	363,060
5. Dominican Republic	335,251
6. Vietnam	286,145
7. El Salvador	213,539
8. Canada	191,987

9. Haiti	179,644
10. Cuba	169,322

* Includes China, Hong Kong and Taiwan.

Source: Immigration and Naturalization Service, 2001, based on immigrants admitted (legally) for permanent residence.

Countries from Which the Fewest Immigrants Came to the United States (1991–2000)

Over 9 million people officially immigrated to the United States between 1991 and 2000. However, some nations were not well represented, so there probably won't be a "Little San Marino" or "Little Funafuti" in the U.S. anytime soon.

The common factor is that these countries all have low populations (and thus simply cannot send very many people to the United States).

Country	Immigrants to U.S. from 1991 to 2000
1. Vatican City	0
2. Maldives	8
2. San Marino	8
2. Tuvalu	8
5. Liechtenstein	14
5. Nauru	14
5. Vanuatu	14
8. Comoros	17
9. Andorra	20
10. Equatorial Guinea	26

Source: Immigration and Naturalization Service, 2001, based on immigrants admitted (legally) for permanent residence.

Exodus: Countries in Which the Highest Percentage of Their Populations Emigrated to the U.S. (1991–2000)

Except for Guyana, all of these are island nations, and only one is outside the Caribbean region. Most of these countries are predominantly English-speaking.

Country	Percentage of the Country's Population that Immigrated to the U.S. from 1991 to 2000
1. St. Kitts & Nevis	12.48
2. Guyana	10.60
3. Grenada	8.24
4. Dominica	7.82
5. Antigua & Barbuda	7.33
6. Jamaica	6.51
7. Trinidad & Tobago	5.98
8. Tonga	4.81
9. St. Vincent & The Grenadines	4.80
10. Dominican Republic	3.91

Source: Immigration and Naturalization Service, 2001, based on immigrants admitted (legally) for permanent residence.

Countries in Which the Lowest Percentage of Their Populations Emigrated to the U.S. (1991–2000)

These are countries far from the United States, mostly in Africa or in the Indian Ocean. Only 0.0014 percent of Burkina Faso's or Chad's populations immigrated to the United States; this is equivalent to one out of every 70,000 people.

Country	Percentage of the Country's Population that Immigrated to the U.S. from 1991 to 2000
1. Vatican City	0
2. Burkina Faso	0.0014
2. Chad	0.0014
4. Bhutan	0.0018
5. Madagascar	0.0021
6. Central African Republic	0.0025
7. Maldives	0.0026
7. Mozambique	0.0026
9. Comoros	0.0029
10. Papua New Guinea	0.0033

Source: Immigration and Naturalization Service, 2001, based on immigrants admitted (legally) for permanent residence.

Cities in the United States with the Greatest Immigrant Diversity

Below are the cities with the most nations represented by immigrants and the number of nations (of the 73 listed in the previous two lists). In order for a nation to qualify in a city, immigrants from that nation must make up at least 0.5 percent of the population of the city (or one out of every 200 people).

City, State	Number of Immigrant Nationalities Composing at Least 0.5% of City Population
1. Cliffside Park, New Jersey	22
2. North Bethesda, Maryland	21
2. Wheaton-Glenmont, Maryland	21
4. Aventura, Florida	20
4. Miami Beach, Florida	20
6. Bailey's Crossroads, Virginia	19
6. Jersey City, New Jersey	19
6. The Crossings, Florida	19
9. Doral, Florida	18
9. Hallandale, Florida	18

Cities listed have at least 20,000 people.

Source: 2000 U.S. Census.

Larger Cities in the United States with the Greatest Immigrant Diversity

City, State	Number of Immigrant Nationalities Composing at Least 0.5% of City Population
1. New York, New York	17
2. Miami, Florida	13
3. San Francisco, California	12
4. Boston, Massachusetts	11
4. Newark, New Jersey	11
6. Los Angeles, California	10
7. Anaheim, California	8

7. Sacramento, California	8
9. Houston, Texas	7
9. Long Beach, California	7
9. San Jose, California	7
9. Seattle, Washington	7

Cities listed have at least 250,000 people.

Source: 2000 U.S. Census.

Cities in the United States Where People Born in the U.S. Make Up the Highest Percentage of the Population

These cities are quite the opposite of the cities featured in the previous lists and contain very few immigrants (from anywhere). They are most prominent in the Midwest, South and Appalachians.

City, State	Percentage of City Population Born in U.S.
1. East St. Louis, Illinois	99.75
2. Opelousas, Louisiana	99.62
3. Paragould, Arkansas	99.34
4. Meridian, Mississippi	99.33
5. Prichard, Alabama	99.29
6. Aberdeen, South Dakota	99.26
7. Greenville, Mississippi	99.25
8. West Mifflin, Pennsylvania	99.19
9. Ashland, Kentucky	99.16
9. Pekin, Illinois	99.16

People from U.S. territories and dependencies, such as Puerto Rico and Guam, are included, since they are automatically granted U.S. citizenship at birth.

Cities listed have at least 20,000 people.

Source: 2000 U.S. Census.

Larger Cities in the United States Where People Born in the U.S. Make Up the Highest Percentage of the Population

City, State	Percentage of City Population Born in U.S.
1. Toledo, Ohio	96.98
2. Louisville, Kentucky	96.24
3. Cincinnati, Ohio	96.23
4. Memphis, Tennessee	95.99
5. New Orleans, Louisiana	95.75
6. Buffalo, New York	95.61
7. Cleveland, Ohio	95.53
8. Baltimore, Maryland	95.45
9. Indianapolis, Indiana	95.39
10. Detroit, Michigan	95.21

People from U.S. territories and dependencies, such as Puerto Rico and Guam, are included, since they are automatically granted U.S. citizenship at birth.

Cities listed have at least 250,000 people.

Source: 2000 U.S. Census.

Most Populous U.S. Cities with Populations More Than 90 Percent White

These are the largest overwhelmingly Caucasian cities in the United States. In general, the Midwest, Northeast and parts of the West lead this list (as well as the next one).

1. Scottsdale, AZ (202,705)
2. Boise, ID (185,787)
3. Springfield, MO (151,580)
4. Overland Park, KS (149,080)
5. Warren, MI (138,247)
6. Sterling Heights, MI (124,471)
7. Sioux Falls, SD (123,975)
8. Cedar Rapids, IA (120,758)

9. Independence, MO (113,288)
10. Manchester, NH (107,006)

Total population (of all races) is in parentheses.

Source: 2000 U.S. Census.

Most Populous U.S. Towns with Populations More Than 99 Percent White

1. Kiryas Joel, NY (13,138)
2. Old Forge, PA (8,798)
3. Longboat Key, FL (7,603)
4. Wolfeboro, NH (6,083)
5. Pana, IL (5,614)
6. Swoyersville, PA (5,157)
7. Monticello, IL (5,138)
8. West Pittston, PA (5,072)
9. Montoursville, PA (4,777)
10. Villages of Oriole, FL (4,758)

Total population (of all races) is in parentheses.

Source: 2000 U.S. Census.

Most Populous U.S. Cities and Towns with Populations Less Than 5 Percent White

Most of these places are located near large cities. Except for Waipahu, Hawaii, the inhabitants are primarily African American.

1. East Orange, NJ (69,824)
2. Suitland-Silver Hill, MD (33,515)
3. Waipahu, HI (33,108)
4. East St. Louis, IL (31,542)
5. Candler-McAfee, GA (28,294)
6. East Cleveland, OH (27,217)
7. Greater Landover, MD (22,900)
8. Highland Park, MI (16,746)
9. Hillcrest Heights, MD (16,359)
10. Tuskegee, AL (11,846)

Total population (of all races) is in parentheses.

Source: 2000 U.S. Census.

Most Populous U.S. Towns with Populations Less Than 1 Percent White

All of these places have fewer than 10,000 people.

1. Glenarden, MD (6,318)
2. Lincoln Heights, OH (4,113)
3. Santo Domingo Pueblo, NM (2,550)
4. Mound Bayou, MS (2,102)
5. San Felipe Pueblo, NM (2,080)

Total population (of all races) is in parentheses.

Source: 2000 U.S. Census.

Most Populous U.S. Cities and Towns with Populations More Than 10 Percent American Indian (Including Alaska Natives)

1. Rapid City, SD (59,607)
2. Muskogee, OK (38,310)
3. Farmington, NM (37,844)
4. Juneau, AK (30,711)
5. Shawnee, OK (28,692)
6. Lumberton, NC (20,795)
7. Gallup, NM (20,209)
8. McAlester, OK (17,783)
9. Sault Ste. Marie, MI (16,542)
10. Claremore, OK (15,873)

Of the places listed above, Gallup has the highest percentage of its population being American Indian at 36.6 percent.
Total population (of all races) is in parentheses.

Source: 2000 U.S. Census.

Most Populous U.S. Cities and Towns (outside of Hawaii) with Populations More Than 2 Percent Native Hawaiian or Other Pacific Islander

1. West Valley City, UT (108,896)
2. Carson, CA (89,730)
3. San Bruno, CA (40,165)
4. Kearns, UT (33,659)
5. East Palo Alto, CA (29,506)

All of these cities, except for East Palo Alto, have Hawaiian/Pacific Islander populations of 2 to 3 percent. East Palo Alto has a Hawaiian/Pacific Islander population of 7.6 percent, the highest in the U.S. outside of Hawaii.

Total population (of all races) is in parentheses.

Source: 2000 U.S. Census.

Most Populous U.S. Cities and Towns with Populations More Than 90 Percent Latino

1. Hialeah, FL (226,419)
2. Laredo, TX (176,576)
3. Brownsville, TX (139,722)
4. East Los Angeles, CA (124,283)
5. South Gate, CA (96,375)
6. Huntington Park, CA (61,348)
7. Pharr, TX (46,660)
8. Bell Gardens, CA (44,054)
9. Bell, CA (36,664)
10. Maywood, CA (28,083)

Of the places listed above, East Los Angeles has the highest percentage of its population being Latino, at 96.8 percent.

Total population (of all races) is in parentheses.

Source: 2000 U.S. Census.

Most Populous U.S. Cities and Towns with Populations Less Than 1 Percent Latino

1. Jackson, MS (184,256)
2. Cheektowaga, NY (79,988)
3. Bismarck, ND (55,532)
4. Pine Bluff, AR (55,085)
5. Charleston, WV (53,421)
6. Middletown, OH (51,605)
7. Huntington, WV (51,475)
8. Mentor, OH (50,278)
9. Altoona, PA (49,523)
10. Cuyahoga Falls, OH (49,374)

Total population (of all races) is in parentheses.

Source: 2000 U.S. Census.

Most Populous U.S. Cities and Towns with Populations More Than 80 Percent African American

1. Detroit, MI (951,270)
2. Gary, IN (102,746)
3. East Orange, NJ (69,824)
4. Irvington, NJ (60,695)
5. Oxon Hill-Glassmanor, MD (35,355)
6. Redan, GA (33,841)
7. Suitland-Silver Hill, MD (33,515)
8. East St. Louis, IL (31,542)
9. Prichard, AL (28,633)
10. Candler-McAfee, GA (28,294)
Total population (of all races) is in parentheses.

Source: 2000 U.S. Census.

Most Populous U.S. Cities and Towns with Populations Less Than 1 Percent African American

1. Huntington Beach, CA (189,594)
2. Boise, ID (185,787)
3. Laredo, TX (176,576)
4. Brownsville, TX (139,722)
5. East Los Angeles, CA (124,283)
6. El Monte, CA (115,965)
7. McAllen, TX (106,414)
8. Provo, UT (105,166)
9. Arvada, CO (102,153)
10. Livonia, MI (100,545)

Total population (of all races) is in parentheses.

Source: 2000 U.S. Census.

Most Populous U.S. Cities and Towns with Populations More Than 50 Percent Asian

1. Honolulu, HI (371,657)
2. Daly City, CA (103,621)
3. Milpitas, CA (62,698)
4. Monterey Park, CA (60,051)
5. Cerritos, CA (51,488)
6. Rowland Heights, CA (48,553)
7. Waipahu, HI (33,108)
8. Pearl City, HI (30,976)
9. Walnut, CA (30,004)
10. Waimalu, HI (29,371)

Total population (of all races) is in parentheses.

Source: 2000 U.S. Census.

Most Populous U.S. Cities and Towns with Populations Less Than 1 Percent Asian

1. Detroit, MI (951,270)
2. Miami, FL (362,470)
3. Birmingham, AL (242,820)
4. Hialeah, FL (226,419)
5. Shreveport, LA (200,145)
6. Jackson, MS (184,256)
7. Laredo, TX (176,576)
8. Dayton, OH (166,179)
9. Brownsville, TX (139,722)
10. Flint, MI (124,943)

Total population (of all races) is in parentheses.

Source: 2000 U.S. Census.

U.S. Cities with the Highest Percentage of Their Population Speaking Only English at Home

Most of these places are in the Midwest and the Appalachian Range.

City, State	Percentage of Population That Only Speaks English at Home
1. Sun City West, Arizona	95.4
2. Sun City, Arizona	94.2
3. Chillicothe, Ohio	92.8
4. Cumberland, Maryland	92.4
4. East Peoria, Illinois	92.4
4. Parkersburg, West Virginia	92.4
7. Ashland, Kentucky	92.2
7. Pleasure Ridge Park, Kentucky	92.2
9. Huntington, West Virginia	91.9
10. Bristol, Tennessee	91.7

Cities listed have at least 20,000 people.

Source: 2000 U.S. Census.

Larger U.S. Cities with the Highest Percentage of Their Populations Speaking Only English at Home

City, State	Percentage of Population That Only Speaks English at Home
1. Louisville, Kentucky	87.7
2. Cincinnati, Ohio	86.5
3. Baltimore, Maryland	86.3
4. Lexington-Fayette, Kentucky	86.0
4. Pittsburgh, Pennsylvania	86.0
4. Toledo, Ohio	86.0

Cities listed have at least 250,000 people.

Source: 2000 U.S. Census.

Ten Most Spoken Languages in the World

This is based on primary (first) languages and is given as a percentage of the total world population.

Language	Percentage of the World's Population Speaking the Language as a Primary Language
1. Mandarin Chinese	14.37
2. Hindi	6.02
3. English	5.61
4. Spanish	5.59
5. Bengali (Bangla)	3.40
6. Russian	2.75
7. Portuguese	2.63
8. Japanese	2.06
9. German (Standard)	1.64
10. Korean	1.28

Despite the fact that French is one of the two working languages of the United Nations and is spoken (at least somewhat frequently) in about 50 countries, it ranks only No. 11 at 1.27 percent.

Source: CIA World Factbook, 2003 (based on 2000 data).

Most Spoken Languages That Are Not the Number One Primary Language in Any Nation

Mandarin Chinese, the foremost language in China, is also the most spoken language in the world, with nearly 900 million primary speakers. The number one language in India is Hindi, though only 180 million of the billion people there speak it as a primary (first) language (with almost as many speaking it as a secondary language). India has nearly 400 native languages, some of which are completely unrelated to each other.

Language	Primary Speakers (All Nations)
1. Wu Chinese (China)	77 million
2. Telugu (India)	75 million
3. Yue Chinese (China)	71 million *
4. Marathi (India)	68 million
5. Tamil (India)	66 million
6. Urdu (India & Pakistan)	60 million **
7. Gujarati (India)	46 million
8. Min Nan Chinese (China)	45 million
9. Xiang Chinese (China)	36 million
10. Malayalam (India)	35 million

And the highest outside of China or India:

Sunda (Indonesia)	27 million ***

* Also referred to as Cantonese.

** While Urdu (with many secondary speakers) is generally more visible than Sindhi in Pakistan, Sindhi has more primary speakers in that country.

*** Estimates for primary Indonesian speakers range from 17 million to 30 million. If the upper end of the range were in fact true, then Indonesian would be the largest in this list outside of China and India, as Javanese is the No. 1 primary language of Indonesia.

Source: www.ethnologue.com, SIL International, 2003.

Ten Most Common Languages Spoken at Home in the United States (Other Than English)

Spanish is by far the most common language spoken in the United States (other than English). However, large numbers of Chinese immigrants have moved their language from fourth to second place on the list from 1990 to 2000 (relatively few recent immigrants are from French- or German-speaking countries).

Language	Percentage (6 Years or Older) Who Speak the Language at Home	1990 Rank
1. Spanish (or Spanish Creole)	10.71	1
2. Chinese*	0.77	4
3. French**	0.63	2
4. German	0.53	3
5. Tagalog	0.47	6
6. Italian	0.38	5
6. Vietnamese	0.38	9
8. Korean	0.34	8
9. Russian	0.27	14
10. Polish	0.25	7

* Includes Chinese languages.
** Includes Patois and Cajun.

Source: 2000 U.S. Census.

Ten States with the Highest Percentage of People Who Speak Spanish at Home

It should be no surprise that the four states with the highest percentage of people who speak Spanish at home are along the Mexican border. While Southwestern states attract mostly Spanish speakers from Mexico, states on the East Coast (Florida, New York, New Jersey) attract Spanish speakers from many other locations, such as the Caribbean and South America.

State	Percentage (6 Years or Older) Who Speak Spanish at Home
1. New Mexico	28.74
2. Texas	27.00
3. California	25.80
4. Arizona	19.51
5. Florida	16.46
6. Nevada	16.18
7. New York	13.61
8. New Jersey	12.32
9. Illinois	10.86
10. Colorado	10.53

Source: 2000 U.S. Census.

Ten States with the Lowest Percentage of People Who Speak Spanish at Home

Rural states bordering Canada rank lowest; they are both far from Mexico (or the Caribbean) and have relatively few immigrants (from any country). Some rural Appalachian and southern states also rank low. Hawaii, while receiving many immigrants, attracts mainly Asians.

State	Percentage (6 Years or Older) Who Speak Spanish at Home
1. Maine	0.80
2. Vermont	1.01
3. West Virginia	1.03
4. North Dakota	1.37
5. South Dakota	1.43
6. Montana	1.53
7. New Hampshire	1.61
8. Hawaii	1.66
9. Kentucky	1.86
10. Mississippi	1.91

Source: 2000 U.S. Census.

A Sampling of Other Languages In Various States

Arabic:

State	Percentage (6 Years or Older) Who Speak Arabic at Home
1. Michigan	0.81
2. New Jersey	0.60
(District of Columbia	0.39)
3. New York	0.39
3. Virginia	0.39
5. California	0.34
50. Montana	0.02

Chinese:

State	Percentage (6 Years or Older) Who Speak Chinese at Home
1. California	2.60
2. Hawaii	2.59
3. New York	2.11
4. New Jersey	1.07
5. Washington	0.88
50. Montana	0.06

French (including Patois, Cajun):

State	Percentage (6 Years or Older) Who Speak French at Home
1. Maine	5.28
2. Louisiana	4.68
3. New Hampshire	3.41
4. Vermont	2.54
5. Rhode Island	1.97
50. South Dakota	0.18

German:

State	Percentage (6 Years or Older) Who Speak German at Home
1. North Dakota	2.48
2. South Dakota	1.91
3. Montana	1.11
4. Wisconsin	0.96
5. Indiana	0.78
50. Louisiana	0.19

Hebrew:

State	Percentage (6 Years or Older) Who Speak Hebrew at Home
1. New York	0.38
2. New Jersey	0.19
3. Maryland	0.13
4. California	0.11
4. Massachusetts	0.11
50. South Dakota	0*

Hindi:

State	Percentage (6 Years or Older) Who Speak Hindi at Home
1. New Jersey	0.40
2. California	0.24
3. Maryland	0.23
3. New York	0.23
5. Virginia	0.18
50. Montana	0.01

Korean:

State	Percentage (6 Years or Older) Who Speak Korean at Home
1. Hawaii	1.62
2. California	0.94

3. Alaska	0.75
4. Washington	0.72
5. New Jersey	0.70
50. Maine	0.03

Navajo:

State	Percentage (6 Years or Older) Who Speak Navajo at Home
1. New Mexico	4.07
2. Arizona	1.89
3. Utah	0.46
4. Colorado	0.06
5. Wyoming	0.04

Persian (Farsi):

State	Percentage (6 Years or Older) Who Speak Persian at Home
1. California	0.49
2. Virginia	0.29
3. Maryland	0.24
4. New York	0.15
5. Nevada	0.12
50. Wyoming	0**

Tagalog (Filipino):

State	Percentage (6 Years or Older) Who Speak Tagalog at Home
1. Hawaii	5.37
2. California	1.99
3. Nevada	1.59
4. Alaska	1.54
5. New Jersey	0.85
50. Vermont	0.02

Vietnamese:

State	Percentage (6 Years or Older) Who Speak Vietnamese at Home
1. California	1.30
2. Hawaii	0.73
3. Washington	0.72
4. Texas	0.64
5. Louisiana	0.56
5. Oregon	0.56
50. Wyoming	0.01

* South Dakota was the only state where the U.S. Census found no speakers of Hebrew. However, not all residents of South Dakota were surveyed for the language spoken at home.

** Wyoming was the only state where the U.S. Census found no speakers of Persian. However, not all residents of Wyoming were surveyed for the language spoken at home.

Source: 2000 U.S. Census.

Ten Countries with the Most Living Languages

A language that is living, of course, implies that it is in use. However, a number of languages in the nations listed below are nearly extinct, so that these numbers will likely decrease in the next few decades, especially with factors such as migration into cities, development of native lands, aging (and deaths) of remaining speakers, and increased communication between speakers of rare languages and the outside world (which is usually done using the more dominant language of the outside world). Of course, one way to save some of these languages is for people to learn languages such as Taloki, Aimele, Beezen, Itzá and Achumawi, all of which have fewer than 1,000 primary speakers (Where are these languages spoken? Answers to follow!), though a lot of people would find it more practical to learn languages such as Spanish or Mandarin Chinese!

Countries that have a lot of languages are often those with large, diverse populations. Some less-populated nations, such as Papua New Guinea, are extremely diverse too, as they have many isolated native cultures with their own languages. A large number of Native American languages are still living, both in the United States and other countries in the Americas.

Country	Number of Living Languages
1. Papua New Guinea	823
2. Indonesia	726
3. Nigeria	505
4. India	387
5. Mexico	288
6. Cameroon	279
7. Australia	235
8. Congo (Dem. Rep.)	218
9. China	201
10. Brazil	192

The United States ranks No. 11 with 176 (not including most immigrant languages, such as Korean or Vietnamese).

The rare languages listed in the previous list are in the following countries:

Taloki—Indonesia
Aimele—Papua New Guinea
Beezen—Cameroon
Itzá—Guatemala
Achumawi—United States (California)

Source: www.ethnologue.com, SIL International, 2003.

Countries with the Most Official Languages

Some countries (including the United States) have no "official" languages, though most have at least one. Official languages are listed alphabetically.

1. India, 16

Assamese, Bengali, English*, Gujurati, Hindi, Kannada, Kashmiri, Malayalam, Marathi, Oriya, Punjabi, Sanskrit, Sindhi, Tamil, Telugu, Urdu

* English is an "associate official" language.

2. South Africa, 11
Afrikaans, English, Ndebele, Pedi, Sotho, Swazi, Tsonga, Tswana, Venda, Xhosa, Zulu

3. Palau, 6
Anguar, English, Japanese, Palauan, Sonsorolese, Tobi

4. Singapore, 4
Chinese, English, Malay, Tamil

5. Bolivia, 3
Aymara, Quechua, Spanish

5. Rwanda, 3
English, French, Kinyarwanda

5. Switzerland, 3
French, German, Italian

Source: CIA World Factbook, 2003.

U.S. Cities with the Highest Percentage of Females

The United States has more females than males (50.9 percent to 49.1 percent). Most areas in the United States are within a few percentage points of these numbers for men and women, though the percentage of women is above average in most of the states in the East and below average in most of the states in the West. Urban areas tend to have more women as well as retirement communities. Military towns, agricultural areas and mountain resort communities tend to have more men. University towns can swing either way—some, like Huntsville, Texas (Sam Houston State) and West Lafayette, Indiana (Purdue) are strongly male, while others, like Northampton and Wellesley, Massachusetts are strongly female (they have Smith College and Wellesley College, respectively, which are all-woman colleges).

City, State	Percentage of Females
1. Sun City, Arizona	58.9
2. Northampton, Massachusetts	56.9
3. Wellesley, Massachusetts	56.2
4. Seal Beach, California	56.1

4. Selma, Alabama   56.1
6. Suitland-Silver Hill, Maryland   55.9
7. East Cleveland, Ohio   55.7
7. Spartanburg, South Carolina   55.7
9. Macon, Georgia   55.6
10. Aventura, Florida   55.5

Cities listed have at least 20,000 people.

Source: 2000 U.S. Census.

Larger U.S. Cities with the Highest Percentage of Females

City, State	Percentage of Females
1. Philadelphia, Pennsylvania	53.5
2. Baltimore, Maryland	53.3
3. New Orleans, Louisiana	53.1
4. Buffalo, New York	53.0
4. St. Louis, Missouri	53.0
6. Detroit, Michigan	52.9
6. Washington, D.C.	52.9
8. Cincinnati, Ohio	52.8
9. Louisville, Kentucky	52.7
9. Memphis, Tennessee	52.7

Cities listed have at least 250,000 people.

Source: 2000 U.S. Census.

U.S. Cities with the Lowest Percentage of Females

City, State	Percentage of Females
1. Fort Bragg, North Carolina	31.5
2. Wasco, California	35.3
3. Fort Hood, Texas	38.0
4. Jacksonville, North Carolina	39.0
4. North Chicago, Illinois	39.0
6. Huntsville, Texas	39.5

7. Coronado, California	41.7
8. Havelock, North Carolina	42.8
8. Marina, California	42.8
8. West Lafayette, Indiana	42.8

Cities listed have at least 20,000 people.

Source: 2000 U.S. Census.

Larger U.S. Cities with the Lowest Percentage of Females

City, State	Percentage of Females
1. Santa Ana, California	48.1
2. Austin, Texas	48.6
3. Phoenix, Arizona	49.1
4. Las Vegas, Nevada	49.2
4. San Francisco, California	49.2
4. San Jose, California	49.2
7. Anchorage, Alaska	49.4
8. Denver, Colorado	49.5
9. Dallas, Texas	49.6
9. San Diego, California	49.6

Cities listed have at least 250,000 people.

Source: 2000 U.S. Census.

Dating Dearth for Men: Men Versus Women in the Wild, Wild West

While most U.S. locations today are relatively balanced between men and women, that was certainly not the case back during the westward expansion in the 19th century. Here are statistics from the infancies of a few states, back when "Sure, I'd love to" was an exceedingly rare response from a woman to a man's request for a date (simply because there were so few available women).

For every woman, there were about:

6 men in Nevada in 1860
12 men in California in 1850
16 men in Colorado in 1860

Source: U.S. Census.

Countries with the Highest Percentage of Females

With the largest disparities between male and female life expectancies (with female life expectancies being over 10 years higher, in some cases), the former Soviet bloc countries have the highest percentages of their populations being female.

Country	Percentage of Females
1. Latvia	54.1
2. Ukraine	53.8
3. Estonia	53.7
4. Belarus	53.2
4. Lithuania	53.2
4. Russia	53.2
7. Moldova	52.5
8. Georgia	52.4
8. Hungary	52.4
8. Monaco	52.4

If the U.S. Virgin Islands and Northern Mariana Islands were independent countries, they would each rank in this list, with 53.5 and 52.4 percent females, respectively.

Source: CIA World Factbook, 2003.

Countries with the Lowest Percentage of Females

The oil-rich Persian Gulf countries rank highest as many foreign male workers from further east in Asia (and some from the United States) have immigrated to the Persian Gulf, at least temporarily.

Country	Percentage of Females
1. Qatar	34.5
2. Kuwait	39.7
3. United Arab Emirates	40.5

4. Samoa	41.8
5. Bahrain	43.9
5. Oman	43.9
7. Saudi Arabia	45.1
8. Palau	46.8
9. Brunei	47.7
10. Jordan	47.6

If Greenland and French Guiana were independent countries, they would each rank in this list, with 47.0 and 47.1 percent females, respectively.

Source of Data: CIA World Factbook, 2003.

Countries with the Highest Percentage of Their Populations Being Elderly

These countries have a combination of people living long lives and low birth rates. While some in this age group might disagree, "old" is defined as 65 years or greater.

Country	Percentage of People over 65
1. Monaco	22.4
2. Italy	18.6
3. Greece	18.1
4. Japan	18.0
5. Spain	17.4
6. Sweden	17.3
7. Belgium	17.1
8. Germany	17.0
9. Bulgaria	16.9
10. San Marino	16.4

Vatican City had no data, but it would likely rank high.

Source: CIA World Factbook, 2003.

Countries with the Lowest Percentage of Their Populations Being Elderly

These countries either have a low life expectancy or a high birth rate (or a combination of the two), or they have an extremely high immigration rate (such as in the Middle East with its oil industry). Again, "old" is defined as 65 years or greater.

Country	Percentage of People over 65
1. Nauru	1.7
2. Marshall Islands	2.0
3. Uganda	2.1
4. Cote d'Ivoire	2.2
4. Mauritania	2.2
4. Sudan	2.2
7. Benin	2.3
7. Niger	2.3
9. Oman	2.4
10. Congo (Dem. Rep.)	2.5
10. Gambia	2.5
10. Kuwait	2.5
10. Togo	2.5
10. Zambia	2.5

If Mayotte were an independent nation, it would be tied for No. 1 at 1.7.

Source: CIA World Factbook, 2003.

Nations with the Highest Percentage of Their Populations Being Muslim, outside of Asia (Including the Middle East), the Former Soviet Union, Africa, and the Indian Ocean *

These are nations outside of the heart of Islam. In comparison, some Middle Eastern and North African nations, such as Saudi Arabia and Mauritania, are nearly 100 percent Muslim.

Country	Percentage of Population That Is Muslim
1. Albania	70
2. Bosnia & Herzegovina	40
3. Macedonia	30
4. Suriname	20
5. Serbia & Montenegro	19

6. Bulgaria — 12
7. Guyana — 10
8. Fiji — 8
9. Trinidad & Tobago — 6
10. Netherlands — 4

* On this list, Asia includes island nations nearby, such as Indonesia, the Philippines and Cyprus.

Source: CIA World Factbook, 2003.

Nations with the Highest Percentage of Their Populations Being Hindu, outside of Asia

Nepal and India have the highest percentage of their populations being Hindu at 86 and 81 percent, respectively. However, numerous nations outside of South Asia have sizable Hindu populations, all due to past Indian migrations.

Country	Percentage of Population That Is Hindu
1. Mauritius	52
2. Fiji	38
3. Guyana	35
4. Suriname	27
5. Trinidad & Tobago	24

Source: CIA World Factbook, 2003.

Nations with the Highest Percentage of Their Populations Being Catholic, outside of Europe and the Americas

A majority of Catholics reside in either Latin America or Europe, and some nations in those areas are over 90 percent Catholic. However, Catholicism is the majority religion in some countries in other parts of the world, especially island nations, many of which were once owned by predominantly Catholic nations such as Portugal, Spain and France.

Country	Percentage of Population That Is Roman Catholic
1. Cape Verde	over 90
2. East Timor	90
3. Seychelles	87
4. Philippines	83
5. Equatorial Guinea	81
6. Sao Tome & Principe	80
7. Burundi	62
8. Rwanda	57
9. Kiribati	52
10. Congo, Dem. Rep.	50
10. Micronesia, Fed. States of	50

Source: CIA World Factbook, 2003, except for numbers for Cape Verde, Equatorial Guinea and Sao Tome & Principe, which are Department of State estimates.

CHAPTER SEVEN

Money Geography

I t is an understatement to say that economies vary around the world. Some of the richest countries in the world have a per capita income (based on gross domestic product) of nearly 100 times that of some of the very poorest. Sometimes countries with very widely different incomes border each other! Even in the United States, the very richest towns have per capita incomes of more than 30 times that of the very poorest towns.

While the United States has become much more homogenized with the national chain stores in malls and strip malls, there are still many regional chain stores (even if they are not always exactly unique), where just seeing one in a picture can tell you immediately whether the picture is from the South, Northeast or West. Some of the regional chains will be explored in this chapter.

Countries That Use the United States Dollar as Their Official Currency

In addition to the United States and its territories and dependencies, these countries use either the U.S. dollar or a currency directly pegged to the U.S. dollar (one-for-one) in value.

There are a variety of reasons that these countries use the U.S. dollar as their currency. The Bahamas derives much of its income from tourists, especially nearby Americans. The Marshall Islands, Micronesia and Palau were administered by the U.S. after World War II and never developed their own currencies after independence in the 1990s. After a period of severe inflation, Ecuador replaced its sucre with the U.S. dollar.

1. Bahamas *
2. East Timor
3. Ecuador
4. El Salvador **
5. Guatemala **
6. Liberia *
7. Marshall Islands
8. Micronesia, Fed. States of
9. Palau
10. Panama *

Bermuda (a dependency of the U.K.) has its own dollar, which is pegged one-for-one to the value of the U.S. dollar (and not the British pound). The Turks and Caicos Islands (also a dependency of the U.K.) and the British Virgin Islands use the U.S. dollar as their currency.

Some other nations, including China and Saudi Arabia, link the exchange rates of their currencies to the U.S. dollar, but not at one-for-one.

* The currency is directly linked one-for-one to the value of the U.S. dollar.
** Both a national currency and the U.S. currency are official.

Data current as of 2003.

Stark Relief: Bordering Nations with Vastly Differing Incomes

The border between the United States and Mexico is often considered to be where the developed nations and developing nations meet. Based on strict differences in income, these countries have the largest arithmetic difference between incomes of any two bordering nations. The United States has a per capita income, based on GDP (gross domestic product), of four times what Mexico has. When multiples like that are used, many bordering nations have greater disparities between their incomes than the United States and Mexico.

Highest Ratios of Incomes between Bordering Nations

The numbers seen below for each pair of nations are simply the per capita GDP of the first (richer) nation divided by that of the second (poorer) nation. Thus, one could say that South Korea is 19 times richer than bordering North Korea.

Richer Country – Poorer Country	Ratio of Higher Per Capita GDP to Lower Per Capita GDP
1. South Korea-North Korea	19.4
2. Saudi Arabia-Yemen	12.9
3. South Africa-Mozambique	10.4
4. Oman-Yemen	10.0
5. Libya-Niger	9.3
6. Iran-Afghanistan	8.8
7. Libya-Chad	7.4
8. Gabon-Congo (Rep.)	6.1
9. Indonesia-East Timor	6.0
9. Kuwait-Iraq	6.0

Only independent nations were listed. However, if the Gaza Strip were considered as an independent nation, Israel would have a per capita GDP of 30 times that of the Gaza Strip.

Source: CIA World Factbook, 2003 (using mostly 2002 data).

Specific Dollar Differences in GDPs of Bordering Nations

This is simply the richer nation's GDP (gross domestic product) minus the poorer nation's. While this is a good indicator of disparity of income, this arithmetic method will ignore extreme contrasts between moderate-income and very low-income neighbors (versus high- and low-income neighbors) and excessively highlight differences in income between the very richest country in the world (Luxembourg) and its (still rich) neighbors.

Richer Country – Poorer Country	Difference in Per Capita GDP
1. U.S.-Mexico	$27,300
2. Norway-Russia	$23,000

3. Luxembourg-France	$18,300
4. Finland-Russia	$17,400
4. Luxembourg-Germany	$17,400
6. Germany-Poland	$17,100
7. Israel-Syria	$15,800
8. Austria-Slovakia	$15,500
9. Israel-Egypt	$15,300
10. Luxembourg-Belgium	$15,000

Source: CIA World Factbook, 2003 (using mostly 2002 data).

How Evenly Is Income Distributed between Rich and Poor in Various Nations?

Most countries have a large difference between income of the rich and poor. The largest differences are in parts of Africa and Latin America, where the wages of workers are kept low by various forces, both public and private. In European nations, the difference is not quite so large; however, there are some developing nations with relatively small differences, such as India and Ghana. Compared with other well-developed nations, the ratio between income of the rich and poor in the United States is large.

How Much Do You Multiply the Poor's Income to Get the Rich's Income?

Here is a listing of selected nations that shows how many times more money the top 10 percent of households earn compared with the bottom 10 percent of households. A higher value obviously means that there is a larger difference in the money that rich households earn versus the poor households. At the other extreme, an idealistic value of one would mean that every household makes exactly the same amount of money—not one cent more or less, unless somebody mistakes his paycheck for fireplace kindling!

Country	How Much Poorest 10% of Income Is Multiplied to Get Richest 10%
Sierra Leone	87
Guinea-Bissau	85
Panama	85

Guatemala	78
Paraguay	67
Brazil	60
Colombia	46
Kenya	40
South Africa	34
Mexico	20
United States	19
China	14
Algeria	10
Australia	10
France	10
Switzerland	10
United Kingdom	10
Canada	9
Netherlands	9
Ghana	8
Egypt	7
Russia	7
Denmark	6
India	6
Sweden	5.4
Norway	5.2
Finland	5.1
Ukraine	5.1
Belarus	4.0
Slovakia	3.6

Source: CIA World Factbook, using most recent data (always from 1989 or later).

How Much Do the Richest Earn?

Here are selected countries listed by percent of the total national income earned by the top 10 percent of households. A higher percentage value means that income is less evenly distributed so that the gap between rich and poor is larger (at the extreme, 100 percent would mean that all income is earned by the top 10 percent of households). An idealistic lower extreme value of 10 percent (the lowest mathematically possible) would mean that income is the same among all households.

Country	Percentage of National Income Earned by Top 10% of Households
Brazil	47.9
Kenya	47.7
South Africa	47.3
Zimbabwe	46.9
Paraguay	46.6
Colombia	46.0
Sierra Leone	43.6
Panama	42.5
Mexico	36.6
China	30.9
United States	28.5
India	25.0
United Kingdom	24.7
Canada	23.8
Russia	22.2
Norway	21.2
Denmark	20.5
Belgium	20.2
Romania	20.2
Sweden	20.1
Belarus	19.4
Slovakia	18.2

Source: CIA World Factbook, using most recent data (always from 1989 or later).

How Much (or Little) Do the Poorest Earn?

Here are selected countries listed by percent of total income earned by the bottom 10 percent of households. A higher percentage value generally means that income is more evenly distributed so that the gap between rich and poor is smaller. Just as in the previous list, the idealistic perfect value of 10 percent (the highest mathematically possible) would mean that income is the same among all households in the nation. Of course, since we're looking at the households and not individuals, you could theoretically have a sister who brags to her brother about how she earns a higher allowance in that idealistic nation!

Country	Percentage of National Income Earned by Bottom 10% of Households
Slovakia	5.1
Belarus	4.9
Czech Republic	4.6
Finland	4.2
India	4.1
Norway	4.1
Ukraine	4.1
Sweden	3.7
Russia	3.0
Switzerland	2.9
Canada	2.8
United Kingdom	2.4
China	2.2
Mexico	1.8
Sri Lanka	1.8
Zimbabwe	1.8
Papua New Guinea	1.7
United States	1.5
Zambia	1.5
South Africa	1.4
Nigeria	1.3
Kenya	1.2
Colombia	1.0
Brazil	0.8
Paraguay	0.7
Guatemala	0.6
Guinea-Bissau	0.5
Panama	0.5
Sierra Leone	0.5

Source: CIA World Factbook, using most recent data (always from 1989 or later).

Disparity Between Rich and Poor Towns in the United States

In each state, towns, cities and suburbs with at least 1,000 people were analyzed for the differences between those with higher versus lower incomes. For this list, towns with a 90th percentile per capita income (where exactly 10 percent of other towns within the same state were richer) were compared with towns with a 10th percentile per capita income (where exactly 10 percent of other towns within the same state were poorer). These lists show the states where that "10th-percentile town" has the highest percentage of the income of the "90th-percentile town" (most equitable, least discrepancy) and the lowest percentage (least equitable, most discrepancy). High percentages are typical in more homogeneous regions of the country, like the northern and central Plains. To get a low percentage, there must either be a large number of rich towns or (especially) suburbs, a large number of poor towns or (certainly the case in California) both.

Top 10 (Most Equity between Rich and Poor Towns):

State	Percentage of 90th-Percentile Town's Income That the 10th-Percentile Town Has
1. Nebraska	74.8
2. Iowa	74.6
3. Kansas	70.4
4. Alaska	68.1
4. North Dakota	67.6
6. Montana	65.7
7. Vermont	63.9
8. New Hampshire	62.6
9. South Dakota	61.4
10. Wisconsin	61.2

Bottom 10 (Least Equity between Rich and Poor Towns):

State	Percentage of 90th-Percentile Town's Income That the 10th-Percentile Town Has
1. California	26.9
2. Texas	30.3
3. Arizona	31.4
4. Florida	33.7
5. New Mexico	35.4
6. New York	37.2

7. Colorado	39.0
8. New Jersey	41.3
9. Virginia	42.5
10. Kentucky	44.0

Source: 2000 U.S. Census.

Ten Richest and Poorest States in the U.S. in 1929 versus 2002

Things change a lot over 73 years. However, one thing has not changed all that much—many of the richest and poorest states in 1929 (right before the Great Depression) remained so in 2002. Six of the 10 richest states in the U.S. at the beginning of the Great Depression remained in the top 10 a year before the end of the 20th century. Of the states on the 1929 rich list, all but Michigan still had per capita incomes above the national average in 2002. Five of the 10 poorest states in the U.S. in 1929 were still on the list in 2002, and all 10 from the 1929 list had 2002 per capita incomes still below the national average. Throughout the years, the richest states mostly have been in the Northeast, and the poorest states mostly have been in the Southeast. The following lists are the 10 richest and poorest states in 1929 and 2002, based on per capita income (not adjusted for inflation):

The 10 Richest States in 1929 and 2002, Based on Per Capita Income:

1929:

1. New York	$1,152
2. Delaware	$1,032
3. Connecticut	$1,024
4. California	$991
5. Illinois	$948
6. New Jersey	$918
7. Massachusetts	$906
8. Rhode Island	$874
9. Nevada	$868
10. Michigan	$790
(Dist. of Columbia	$1,269)

2002:

1. Connecticut	$42,706
2. New Jersey	$39,453
3. Massachusetts	$39,244
4. Maryland	$36,298
5. New York	$36,043
6. New Hampshire	$34,334
7. Minnesota	$34,071
8. Illinois	$33,404
9. Colorado	$33,276
10. California	$32,996
(Dist. of Columbia	$42,120)

Here Are the 10 Poorest States in 1929 and 2003, Based on Per Capita Income:

1929:

1. South Carolina	$271
2. Mississippi	$286
3. Arkansas	$310
4. Alabama	$323
5. North Carolina	$332
6. Georgia	$347
7. Tennessee	$378
8. North Dakota	$382
9. Kentucky	$393
10. New Mexico	$410

2002:

1. Mississippi	$22,372
2. Arkansas	$23,512
3. West Virginia	$23,688
4. New Mexico	$23,941
5. Utah	$24,306
6. Montana	$25,020
7. Idaho	$25,057
8. Alabama	$25,128
9. South Carolina	$25,400
10. Louisiana	$25,446

Source: Regional Economic Measurement Division, Dept. of Commerce, 2003.

Five States Whose Per Capita Incomes Dropped the Most from 1929 to the Heart of the Great Depression

From 1929 through 1933, in the early part of the Great Depression, the per capita income of the United States decreased by almost half, or 47 percent, from $700 to $373 (not adjusted for inflation—or in the case of 1929 through 1933, deflation, as what cost $700 in 1929 actually cost, on average, $558, or about 20 percent less, in 1933). Some states saw their per capita incomes drop faster than others, with farm states generally suffering the most. Listed below are the five states that dropped the most (with percent loss from the 1929 per capita income to the lowest year's income, in all cases either 1932 or 1933, with deflation not factored in):

State	Percentage Drop in Per Capita Income from 1929 to the Peak of the Great Depression
1. South Dakota	70
2. North Dakota	62
3. Nebraska	57
4. Iowa	56
5. Michigan	56

Five States Whose Per Capita Incomes Dropped the Least from 1929 to the Heart of the Great Depression

All states (and the District of Columbia) were hit hard by the Great Depression. However, some states, primarily those on the East Coast, saw less of an effect on their per capita incomes, percentage-wise. Here are the five that dropped the least (with, again, percent loss from the 1929 per capita income to the lowest year's income, in all cases either 1932 or 1933):

State	Percentage Drop in Per Capita Income from 1929 to the Peak of the Great Depression
1. Virginia	35
2. Rhode Island	36
3. Maine	38
3. Massachusetts	38
5. Maryland	39
(Dist. of Columbia	29)

Source: Regional Economic Measurement Division, Dept. of Commerce, 2003.

Countries That Spend the Highest Percentage of Their GDPs on Military Expenditures

Not surprisingly, most of the countries that spend the highest percentage of their GDPs (gross domestic products) on the military are either in the Middle East or are directly engaged in a war (including civil war).

Country	Percentage of GDP Spent on Military Expenditures
1. North Korea	31.3
2. Angola	22
3. Eritrea	19.8
4. Saudi Arabia	13
5. Ethiopia	12.6
6. Oman	12.2
7. Qatar	10
8. Israel	8.75
9. Jordan	8.6
9. Maldives	8.6

Source: CIA World Factbook, 2003 (using data mostly between 1999 and 2002). Figures were unavailable for a few nations, including Afghanistan and Iraq, which have had large military expenditures (relative to their GDP) in recent years.

Countries with the Highest Amount of External Debt, Relative to Their GDPs

While the United States has the highest amount of external debt in the world (public or private debt owed to foreign entities), the debt amounts to less than 10 percent of the gross domestic product. Here are some countries where the external debt makes up a large percentage of the GDP (in some cases *greater* than the GDP).

Country	Debt as a Percentage of GDP
1. Congo (Rep.)	200
2. Sao Tome & Principe	134
3. Cuba	115*
4. Iraq	105
5. Qatar	80
6. Angola	78

6. Guinea-Bissau   78
8. Marshall Islands   75
9. Zambia   68
10. Somalia   63

* Includes estimated debt to Russia.

Two dependencies would score high on this list: Cook Islands (134) and French Guiana (120).

Source: CIA World Factbook, 2003 (using data mostly between 1999 and 2002).

Most Agrarian Societies: Nations with the Highest Percentage of Their Labor Force in Agriculture

These countries are overwhelmingly poor, and in many cases, the agriculture is subsistence (Bhutan isn't exactly Asia's "breadbasket").

Country	Percentage of Labor Force in Agriculture
1. Bhutan	93
2. Burkina Faso	90
2. Niger	90
2. Rwanda	90
5. Lesotho	86
5. Malawi	86
7. Angola	85
7. Chad	85
7. Papua New Guinea	85
7. Zambia	85

Source: CIA World Factbook, 2003, with data mostly from the 1990s or 2000.

Nuclear Nations: Countries in Which the Highest Percentage of Electricity Produced Is from Nuclear Power

Nuclear power is biggest in Europe, though some European nations, such as Austria, Denmark, Italy and Norway, produce no nuclear power.

Country	Percentage of Electricity Produced by Nuclear Power
1. France	77
1. Lithuania	77
3. Belgium	58
4. Slovakia	48
5. Bulgaria	44
6. Ukraine	43
7. Hungary	40
8. South Korea	38
9. Sweden	37
9. Switzerland	37

Source: CIA World Factbook, 2003 (using mostly 2000 data).

Countries in Which More Than 99 Percent of Electricity Produced Is from Fossil Fuels

Many of these 45 nations produce large amounts of oil, are island (or flat) nations with no access to hydroelectric power, or are poor nations with few opportunities to develop other sources of electricity (including renewable). Some of these countries (such as Israel, with wind power) have unrealized potential to develop other sources of energy.

1. Algeria	11. Cyprus
2. Antigua and Barbuda	12. Djibouti
3. Bahamas	13. East Timor
4. Bahrain	14. Eritrea
5. Barbados	15. Estonia
6. Belarus	16. The Gambia
7. Botswana	17. Grenada
8. Brunei	18. Guinea-Bissau
9. Cape Verde	19. Israel
10. Chad	20. Kiribati

21. Kuwait
22. Liberia
23. Libya
24. Maldives
25. Malta
26. Mongolia
27. Nauru
28. Niger
29. Oman
30. Qatar
31. St. Kitts and Nevis
32. St. Lucia
33. Saudi Arabia

34. Senegal
35. Seychelles
36. Sierra Leone
37. Singapore
38. Solomon Islands
39. Somalia
40. Tonga
41. Trinidad and Tobago
42. Turkmenistan
43. United Arab Emirates
44. Vanuatu
45. Yemen

Source: CIA World Factbook, 2003 (using mostly 2000 data).

Countries in Which the Lowest Percentage of Electricity Produced Is from Fossil Fuels

Most of these countries use their hydroelectric resources for most of their power. Paraguay, a mostly flat nation, is on this list? Yes, the Parana River (along the borders with Brazil and Argentina, in and near the hillier parts of Paraguay as well as Iguacu Falls along the Brazil-Argentina border) supplies significant amounts of hydroelectric power, making Paraguay a net exporter of electricity.

Country	Percentage of Electricity Produced by Fossil Fuels
1. Bhutan	0.05
2. Iceland	0.07
2. Paraguay	0.07
4. Zambia	0.55
5. Norway	0.63
6. Congo (Rep.)	0.66
7. Burundi	0.71
8. Uganda	0.98
9. Tajikistan	1.90
10. Namibia	2.00

Source: CIA World Factbook, 2003 (using mostly 1999 data).

Countries in Which the Highest Percentage of Electricity Produced Is from Alternative Sources

This includes (among others), geothermal, solar, wind and biomass (any source other than fossil fuels, hydroelectric or nuclear power). The countries that rank highest (including the Philippines) produce large amounts of geothermal power. Denmark has extensive wind-driven electricity production.

Country	Percentage of Electricity Produced by Alternative Sources
1. Philippines	23
2. El Salvador	22
3. Iceland	17
3. Luxembourg	17
5. Costa Rica	16
5. Denmark	16
7. Finland	12
8. Nicaragua	9
9. Kenya	8
10. Jamaica	7
10. New Zealand	7

Source: CIA World Factbook, 2003 (using mostly 2000 data).

Five Territories (Etc.) That Have Higher Per Capita Incomes Than Their Parent Nations

This is a list of all territories, dependencies and special administrative regions that have higher per capita incomes, based on gross domestic products (GDPs) than the administering nations (ranked by percentage of parent nations' per capita GDPs).

Territory	Per Capita GDP	(Percentage of Parent Nation)
1. Hong Kong	$25,000	(543% of China's)
2. Macau	$17,600	(383% of China's)
3. Bermuda	$34,800	(138% of United Kingdom's)
4. Cayman Islands	$30000	(119% of United Kingdom's)
5. Aruba	$28,000	(104% of Netherlands')

Source: CIA World Factbook, 2003 (using mostly 2002 data).

Territories (Etc.) That Are the Poorest Relative to Their Parent Nations

These are the territories, dependencies, administrative divisions and free associations with the lowest per capita GDPs, relative (by percent) to the administering nations.

Territory	Per Capita GDP	(Percentage of Parent Nation)
1. Mayotte	$600	(2% of France's)
2. Gaza Strip	$625	(3% of Israel's)
3. Tokelau	$1,000	(5% of New Zealand's)
3. West Bank	$1,000	(5% of Israel's)
5. Wallis & Futuna	$2,000	(8% of France's)
6. Montserrat	$2,400	(9% of United Kingdom's)
7. St. Helena	$2,500	(10% of United Kingdom's)
8. Niue	$3,600	(18% of New Zealand's)
9. Reunion	$4,800	(19% of France's)
10. French Polynesia	$5,000	(19% of France's)

American Samoa is the poorest territory of the United States. Its per capita GDP of $8,000 is 22 percent of that of the U.S., which would place it at No. 11 on this list.

Source: CIA World Factbook, 2003 (using data mostly from 2002).

Ten Most Populous Countries without a McDonald's Restaurant

Travelers (as of 2003) who wish to see a country devoid of McDonald's can consider these (mostly African, Asian and some small island nations). McDonald's reported its presence in 118 countries (including some territories) around the world, though that is down from 121 in 2001.

1. Bangladesh
2. Nigeria
3. Vietnam
4. Iran
5. Ethiopia
6. Congo (Dem. Rep.)
7. Burma

8. Tanzania
9. Sudan
10. Algeria

Countries with the Highest Amount of Government Spending per Person

The United States is quite well-known for having the largest government budget in the world. However, per capita, the United States ranks only No. 19 among independent nations in national government spending. All of the countries that rank higher than the United States are in Europe, except for Kuwait and Brunei.

Country	Govt. Spending Per Capita
1. Vatican City	$220,600 *
2. Monaco	$16,700
3. San Marino	$14,400
4. Norway	$12,700
5. Liechtenstein	$12,600
6. Sweden	$12,400
7. Luxembourg	$12,200
8. Iceland	$11,800
9. Belgium	$10,300
10. Germany	$9,900

* Vatican City's figure is artificially inflated, as it has high costs, but only 900 people reside there.

Source: CIA World Factbook, 2003 (most data from 1999–2001).

Countries with the Lowest Amount of Government Spending per Person

These countries spend very little money per person (often because of the inability to raise any revenue from the impoverished populace). Given that some of these countries are at war (especially civil war), one must wonder where their militaries (one government expenditure) really receive their money.

Country	Govt. Spending Per Capita
1. Congo (Dem. Rep.)	$4
2. Chad	$24
3. Burkina Faso	$25 *
4. Burundi	$28
4. Ethiopia	$28
4. Liberia	$28
4. Nigeria	$28
8. Tajikistan	$29
9. Niger	$30
10. Lesotho	$36

* Based on government revenues.

Source: CIA World Factbook, 2003 (most data from 2000–2001). Data were unavailable for Afghanistan and Somalia.

Steal This Book: Countries without Copyright Relations with the United States

Various countries have set up copyright relations with the United States (and other countries) that set guidelines on the protection of various writings, music and other works. Other nations have not, though some writings may still have some protection in these countries (so, just because you make photocopies of this book and sell them in Muscat, Oman, doesn't necessarily mean you're legally off the hook!).

1. Afghanistan
2. Bhutan
3. Comoros
4. Eritrea
5. Ethiopia
6. Iran
7. Iraq
8. Jordan
9. Kiribati
10. Nauru
11. Nepal
12. North Korea
13. Oman
14. Palau

15. Samoa
16. San Marino
17. Sao Tome and Principe
18. Seychelles
19. Somalia
20. Sudan
21. Syria
22. Tonga
23. Tuvalu
24. Vanuatu
25. Yemen

Source: U.S. Copyright Office, 1999.

Gasoline: Cheapest Countries in the World

Most of the countries with the cheapest gasoline are large oil producers but have low wages, though some nations with cheap gasoline subsidize their oil. Some of these countries have high year-to-year volatility (for example, Turkenistan's price fell about 75 percent from 1998 to 2000, and Iraq's price rose rapidly after 2000).

Country	Price per Gallon
1. Turkmenistan	$0.08
2. Iraq	$0.11
3. Iran	$0.19
4. Venezuela	$0.45
5. Uzbekistan	$0.53
6. Qatar	$0.61
7. Indonesia	$0.64
8. Ghana	$0.76
9. Kuwait	$0.79
9. Yemen	$0.79

Price shown is usually for "super gasoline" (unleaded).

Source: German Agency for Technical Cooperation and World Bank, "Fuel Prices and Vehicle Taxation" (2001) with primarily 2000 data.

Gasoline: Most Expensive Countries in the World

These countries (plus Hong Kong and Palestinian Territories) with the most expensive gasoline (usually due to high gasoline taxation) are found in many parts of the world. Not only are they in Europe but also in parts of Asia, South America and Africa.

Country	Price per Gallon
1. Hong Kong	$5.53
2. Norway	$4.50
2. Uruguay	$4.50
4. United Kingdom	$4.43
5. Israel	$4.31
6. Palestinian Territories	$4.09
7. Argentina	$4.05
8. Finland	$4.01
8. Japan	$4.01
10. Djibouti	$3.97
10. Iceland	$3.97

Price shown is usually for "super gasoline" (unleaded).

Source: German Agency for Technical Cooperation and World Bank, "Fuel Prices and Vehicle Taxation" (2001) with primarily 2000 data.

Gasoline: Cheapest Countries in the World Based on How Much the Populace Can Afford

This is more reflective of how expensive gasoline is to the people who live in a given nation. Here, the price of gasoline for a nation is multiplied by how much higher the income (gross domestic product per capita) is in the United States than in that nation.

As an example, Jamaica has about 1/10 the per capita income of the U.S., so the $2.35 per gallon cost of gasoline might be perceived by the average Jamaican as what an American would think of $23.50 per gallon.

Thus, given the income of the United States, gasoline is extremely cheap (even with this survey, showing U.S. data from November 2000, when gasoline prices were near a peak). In most countries with similar incomes (such as in western Europe), gasoline is much more expensive, yet it would still seem cheap relative to gasoline in poor nations (where most of the populace use gasoline purchased by others, e.g., public transportation).

Country	"Apparent" Price per Gallon to an Average Resident of the Country
1. Iran	$0.26
2. Turkmenistan	$0.58
3. Qatar	$1.04
4. United Arab Emirates	$1.63
5. Iraq	$1.65
6. United States	$1.78
7. Kuwait	$1.91
8. Luxembourg	$2.34
9. Brunei	$2.36
10. Venezuela	$2.70

Price shown is usually for "super gasoline" (unleaded).

Source: German Agency for Technical Cooperation and World Bank, "Fuel Prices and Vehicle Taxation" (2001) with primarily 2000 data and the CIA World Factbook.

Gasoline: Most Expensive Countries in the World Based on How Much the Populace Can Afford

The same formula applies here. Nearly all of these countries are in Africa, which has both the poorest nations and many nations with expensive gasoline.

To a resident of the Democratic Republic of Congo, the gasoline would be perceived as costing what an American would think of $233 per gallon in U.S. money. In fact, 156 gallons of gasoline would equal the gross domestic product per person of the Democratic Republic of Congo!

Country	"Apparent" Price per Gallon to an Average Resident of the Country
1. Congo (Dem. Rep.)	$233
2. Burundi	$231
3. Palestinian Territories	$171
4. Tanzania	$169
5. Sierra Leone	$168
6. Malawi	$144

7. Rwanda	$122
8. Madagascar	$120
9. Mali	$114
9. Niger	$114

Price shown is usually for "super gasoline" (unleaded).

Source: German Agency for Technical Cooperation and World Bank, "Fuel Prices and Vehicle Taxation" (2001) with primarily 2000 data and CIA World Factbook.

U.S. Cities with the Largest Discrepancies between Male Income and Female Income

Here is a listing of cities with at least 250,000 people, where women earn the least relative to what men earn. The numbers listed are the percentages of income that the average female resident earns compared to the income that the average male resident earns. Only full-time, year-round workers are considered here.

Despite the fact that these are the lowest ranking cities with more than 250,000 people, they are still close to the national average of 73.4 percent, as cities have more equitable incomes between the genders than rural areas.

City, State	Average Amount That Women Earn as a Percentage of What Men Earn
1. Toledo, Ohio	70.7
2. Wichita, Kansas	70.9
3. Corpus Christi, Texas	71.0
4. Colorado Springs, Colorado	71.8
5. El Paso, Texas	74.3

Cities listed have at least 250,000 people.

Source: 2000 U.S. Census.

U.S. Cities with the Smallest Discrepancies between Male Income and Female Income

In few places (and no large cities) in the U.S. do women make as much money as men. However, there are cities where the differences between male and female incomes are smaller, with cities in large metropolitan areas generally being more equitable than those in smaller metro areas.

As with the case in the previous list, the numbers listed are the percentages of income that the average female resident earns compared to the income that the average male resident earns. Only full-time, year-round workers are considered here.

City, State	Average Amount That Women Earn as a Percentage of What Men Earn
1. Los Angeles, California	94.7
2. Oakland, California	93.7
3. Dallas, Texas	90.6
4. Denver, Colorado	89.9
5. Washington, D.C.	89.8

Cities listed have at least 250,000 people.

Source: 2000 U.S. Census.

Currency Quiz

Some countries don't use typical names, like dollar, peso or pound, for their currencies. Which countries have these currencies?

1. Birr
2. Dong
3. Gourde
4. Kroon
5. Lempira
6. Metical
7. Pa'anga
8. Pula
9. Ringgit
10. Tugrik

Answers are at the bottom of page 263 and continue on page 264. A few of these currencies will appear in the next list.

Currencies with the Least Value per Unit

Here's one way people can become millionaires: Trade U.S. dollars for Turkish liras. Actually, it will only require one dollar, since that is worth about 1,400,000 liras. Of course, in Turkey, trillionaire (or Turkish "trilyoner") might be a more meaningful word than millionaire.

Below are currencies that require the largest amount to equal one U.S. dollar.

Country	Currency	How Many Are Needed for U.S. $1
1. Turkey	Lira	1,405,000
2. Romania	Leu	32,900
3. Mozambique	Metical	23,500
4. Somalia	Shilling	20,000
5. Vietnam	Dong	15,521
6. Sao Tome & P.	Dobre	8,700
7. Ghana	Cedi	8,652
8. Indonesia	Rupiah	8,568
9. Iran	Rial	7,900
10. Laos	Kip	7,602

Currencies with the Most Value per Unit

Country	Currency	How Many Are Needed for U.S. $1
1. Kuwait	Dinar	0.30
2. Bahrain	Dinar	0.38
3. Oman	Rial	0.38
4. Malta	Lira	0.40
5. Cyprus	Pound	0.52
6. Latvia	Lats	0.57
7. U.K.	Pound	0.62
8. Jordan	Dinar	0.71
9. Cayman Is.	Dollar	0.82
10. (numerous)	Euro	0.88

Both of the above lists are based on market rates in August 2003.

U.S. Metropolitan Areas with the Highest Sales at Book Stores and News Dealers Per Capita

The entire top 10 list in this category is comprised of (mostly small) metropolitan areas dominated by a university town. Not surprisingly, students (and professors) buy a lot of books (including expensive textbooks). The average person in the United States spent around $50 at book stores and news dealers in 1997.

Metropolitan Area	Annual Sales Per Capita*
1. State College, PA	$265
2. Bryan-College Station, TX	$235
3. Lawrence, KS	$187
4. Bloomington, IN	$178
5. Lafayette, IN	$148
6. Tallahassee, FL	$147
7. Bloomington-Normal, IL	$142**
8. Madison, WI	$141
9. Ann Arbor, MI	$138
10. Boston, MA-NH	$129
10. Lexington, KY	$129

* Includes all sales from book stores and news dealers.
** Estimated data due to U.S. Census disclosure rules.

Source: U.S. Census, data from 1997.

States with the Most Wal-Marts per Million People

Wal-Mart's first store was opened in 1962 in Rogers, Arkansas, and Wal-Mart slowly and steadily expanded from that area (the first five states to have Wal-Marts were Arkansas, Missouri, Oklahoma, Kansas and Louisiana). All of those first five states are still in the top 10 states with the most Wal-Marts per million people, and most of the other states in the top 10 have low costs of living (thus wages and land to build those large stores and parking lots are cheaper).

New Hampshire is a slight oddity on this list, far removed from the other states (one contributing factor is that opposition to building Wal-Marts in Vermont resulted in stores being built immediately across the state line in New Hampshire).

State	Wal-Marts per Million People
1. Arkansas	32.3
2. Oklahoma	28.5
3. Mississippi	23.6
4. New Hampshire	22.5
5. Missouri	22.4
6. Wyoming	21.9
7. Kansas	21.3
8. Alabama	20.9
8. Louisiana	20.9
10. Iowa	19.7

Data current as of 2003. Includes Discount Stores, Supercenters, Sam's Clubs and Neighborhood Markets.

States with the Fewest Wal-Marts per Million People

Most of these states are on the Pacific Coast or in the Northeast, far from the starting point of Rogers, Arkansas. Many of the most expensive cities in the United States can be found in these states. In nine of these 10 states, Wal-Mart had no stores until the 1990s.

State	Wal-Marts per Million People
1. New Jersey	4.4
2. California	4.6
3. New York	4.8
4. Hawaii	5.6
5. Washington	6.0
6. Vermont	6.5
7. Massachusetts	7.0
8. Oregon	7.6
9. Michigan	8.3
10. Rhode Island	8.4

Data current as of 2003. Includes Discount Stores, Supercenters, Sam's Clubs and Neighborhood Markets.

States Where the Number of Target Stores Exceeds the Number of Wal-Mart Stores*

Target is headquartered in Minnesota, while Wal-Mart is No. 49 out of 50 states in stores per million people in California.

1. California
2. Minnesota

* Includes Discount Stores, Supercenters, Sam's Clubs and Neighborhood Markets.

States Where the Number of Kmart Stores Exceeds the Number of Wal-Mart Stores*

Kmart is headquartered in Michigan, while Wal-Mart is No. 50 out of 50 states in stores per million people in New Jersey.

1. Michigan
2. New Jersey

* Includes Discount Stores, Supercenters, Sam's Clubs and Neighborhood Markets.

Regional Stores: Furthest North, East, South or West Locations

Many chain retailers in the United States are not nationwide, but regional. In some cases, regional retailers will be owned by a chain from a different region (such as Safeway, based in Northern California, owning Vons, based in Southern California). Here are a few examples of the furthest north, east, south or west of various retailers' locations (with approximate latitudes or longitudes).

I. Service (Gasoline) Stations

Gulf

Furthest south: Ironton, Ohio (39° N)
Furthest west: Upper Sandusky, Ohio (83° W)

Gulf, based in Massachusetts, is common in the Northeast.

Phillips 66

Furthest east: Bethel (Perquimans County), North Carolina (76° W)
Furthest west: Ontario, Oregon (117° W)

There is only one service station named Phillips 66 in a state that borders the Pacific—the one in Ontario, Oregon (which happens to be along the eastern border with Idaho). Phillips 66, based in Oklahoma, is found most commonly in the Plains states. In addition to the Pacific Coast, Phillips 66 has yet to expand to the Northeast under that brand name.

Only service stations along roads or highways are included; aviation or marina stations are not.

Sinclair

Furthest east: Racine, Wisconsin (88° W)
Furthest west: Hines, Oregon (119° W)

Sinclair, based in Salt Lake City, is found mostly in the Rocky Mountain States and the Midwest.

2. Grocery Stores

Food Lion

Furthest north: Hamburg, Pennsylvania (41° N)
Furthest west: Hopkinsville, Kentucky (88° W)

Food Lion, based in North Carolina, is found from Florida to southeastern Pennsylvania and west into Tennessee and Kentucky.

H-E-B

Furthest north: Plano, Texas (33° N)
Furthest south: Tampico, Veracruz, Mexico (22° N)

H-E-B is found across parts of Texas and northeastern Mexico.

Hyvee

Furthest east: Peru, Illinois (89° W)
Furthest north: Watertown, South Dakota (45° N)
Furthest south: Jefferson City, Missouri (39° N)
Furthest west: Yankton, South Dakota (97° W)

Hyvee is very common in Iowa and extends into parts of other nearby states.

Publix

Furthest north: Hendersonville, Tennessee (36° N)

Publix is found in five southeastern states. It is based in Lakeland, Florida.

Vons

Furthest east: Boulder City, Nevada (115° W)
Furthest north: Mammoth Lakes, California (38° N)

Vons is found in Southern and Central California and Southern Nevada.

Wegman's

Furthest south: Downingtown, Pennsylvania (40° N)

Wegman's is found in parts of Upstate New York (its base is in Rochester), Pennsylvania and New Jersey.

Weis

Furthest north: Elmira, New York (42° N)
Furthest east: Newburgh, New York (74° W)
Furthest south: Manassas, Virginia (39° N)
Furthest west: Altoona, Pennsylvania (78° W)

The core area of Weis is in Central and Eastern Pennsylvania and Northern Maryland.

Winn-Dixie

Furthest north: Jeffersonville, Indiana (38° N)*
Furthest west: Pineville, Louisiana (94° W)

Winn-Dixie is primarily in the southeastern United States and the Bahamas.

* Not including Thriftway (Cincinnati area), which is owned by Winn-Dixie.

3. Restaurants

Rubio's

Furthest north: Portland, Oregon (46° N)
Furthest east: Highlands Ranch, Colorado (105° W)

This San Diego-based fast-food Mexican chain is found mostly in the Southwest.

Taco John's

Furthest south and East: Tavares, Florida (29° N, 82° W)
Furthest west: Fort Lewis, Washington (123° W)

Taco John's is primarily found in the north-central United States, especially in the area from Wyoming to Minnesota. However, there are a few renegade locations far away from that core region.

Taco Tico

Furthest east: Corbin, Kentucky (84° W)
Furthest north: Mason City, Iowa (43° N)
Furthest west: Guymon, Oklahoma (101° W)

This taco shop is based in Kansas and is found parts of in the central and south-central U.S. (except Texas).

Waffle House

Furthest north: Toledo, Ohio (42° N)
Furthest west: Goodyear, Arizona (112° W)

Waffle House is most common in the southeastern United States.

4. Retail

Gottschalks

Furthest east: Indio, California (116° W)
Furthest north: Fairbanks, Alaska (65° N)

Gottschalks, a department store based in Fresno, California, is found in all Pacific states except Hawaii. There are also a few locations in Idaho and Nevada, but none as far east as Indio, California.

Pamida

Furthest east: Columbiana, Ohio (81° W)
Furthest south: Somerville, Tennessee (35° N)
Furthest west: Libby, Montana (116° W)

Pamida is found mostly in small towns in the Midwest.

Shopko

Furthest east: Escanaba, Michigan (87° W)
Furthest south: Springfield, Illinois (40° N)

Shopko is based out of Green Bay, Wisconsin. This retail chain's domain extends from the Upper Midwest to the Pacific Northwest.

Data current as of 2003. No endorsement of any of the above companies is implied; they are listed strictly for educational and entertainment purposes.

Highest Elevations for Various Stores and Restaurants in the U.S.

These are the highest locations for various businesses. Many are in a cluster of towns (Dillon, Frisco, Silverthorne) near numerous major ski resorts in Colorado, though Leadville, at slightly over 10,000 feet, has three of the national chain businesses listed below. Hope the executives of Pizza Hut, Subway and Safeway can adjust to the altitude if they visit their Leadville locations!

Store	City	Elevation (Ft.)
Pizza Hut	Leadville, Colorado	10,200
Subway	Leadville, Colorado	10,150
Safeway	Leadville, Colorado	10,000
Starbucks	Breckenridge, Colorado	9,600
Taco Bell	Frisco, Colorado	9,100
Bed Bath & Beyond	Dillon, Colorado	9,050
Border's	Dillon, Colorado	9,050
McDonald's	Frisco, Colorado	9,050
Wal-mart	Frisco, Colorado	9,050
Burger King	Silverthorne, Colorado	8,750
Denny's	Silverthorne, Colorado	8,750
Target	Silverthorne, Colorado	8,750
Gap	Aspen, Colorado	7,900
Albertson's	Evergreen, Colorado	7,500
Home Depot	Avon, Colorado	7,500
AutoZone	Los Alamos, New Mexico	7,300
Kmart	Laramie, Wyoming	7,150
Radio Shack	Laramie, Wyoming	7,150
Barnes & Noble	Flagstaff, Arizona	6,900
JC Penney	Flagstaff, Arizona	6,800
Best Buy	Colorado Springs, Colorado	6,400
Nordstrom	Littleton, Colorado	5,850
Macy's	Albuquerque, New Mexico	5,300

Data current as of 2003. No endorsement of any of the above companies is implied; they are listed strictly for educational and entertainment purposes.

Answers for the currency quiz (page 254):

1. Birr—Ethiopia
2. Dong—Vietnam

3. Gourde—Haiti
4. Kroon—Estonia
5. Lempura—Honduras
6. Metical—Mozambique
7. Pa'anga—Tonga
8. Pula—Botswana
9. Ringgit—Malaysia
10. Tugrik—Mongolia

CHAPTER EIGHT
Recreation Geography

S tates vary widely as to the activities their people enjoy. Some states have a multitude of hunters; some are dominated by people who fish, while others have a populace who usually do neither. Some states are chock-full of golf courses; others have miniature golf courses. Some states like their skating rinks made for ice-skating; others prefer roller-skating. And then there are the states with plenty of chess players. This chapter looks at the geography of sports, games and recreation.

Largest Metropolitan Areas without Major League Sports Teams of Their Own

1. Norfolk-Virginia Beach-Newport News, Virginia-North Carolina
2. Las Vegas, Nevada
3. Greensboro-Winston Salem-High Point, North Carolina
4. Austin-San Marcos, Texas
5. Providence-Fall River-Warwick, Rhode Island-Massachusetts
6. Hartford, Connecticut
7. West Palm Beach-Boca Raton, Florida
8. Rochester, New York
9. Grand Rapids-Muskegon-Holland, Michigan
10. Oklahoma City, Oklahoma

Includes Major League Baseball, NBA, NFL and NHL. Metropolitan areas are defined by the U.S. Census.

Smallest Metropolitan Areas with at Least One Major League Sports Team

1. Green Bay, Wisconsin
2. Edmonton, Alberta
3. Calgary, Alberta
4. Ottawa-Hull, Ontario-Quebec
5. Jacksonville, Florida
6. Memphis, Tennessee
7. Buffalo, New York *
8. Raleigh-Durham-Chapel Hill, North Carolina
9. Nashville, Tennessee
10. Salt Lake City-Ogden, Utah

* Ranking does not include population in nearby Canadian cities/suburbs.

Includes Major League Baseball, NBA, NFL and NHL. Metropolitan areas are defined by the U.S. Census and Statistics Canada.

Check: States Where Chess Is Most Popular

Chess is most popular in the Southwest, the Northeast and some states near the Ohio Valley. This list is based on the number of people per million residents who have been rated with the U.S. Chess Federation.

State	Number of Rated Chess Players per Million People
1. Arizona	2,361
2. New Mexico	1,897
3. Kentucky	1,694
4. South Dakota	1,581
5. Nevada	1,511
6. Indiana	1,507
7. Vermont	1,493

8. Tennessee	1,487
9. Maine	1,454
10. New York	1,412

Source: U.S. Chess Federation Web site, 2003. www.uschess.org.

States Where Chess Is Least Popular

Chess is least popular in much of the Southeast (except the Tennessee Valley) and the northern Rockies.

State	Number of Rated Chess Players per Million People
1. Arkansas	327
2. Montana	329
3. Delaware	365
4. South Carolina	381
5. Wyoming	455
6. Hawaii	458
7. Mississippi	490
8. Louisiana	522
9. North Dakota	530
10. Wisconsin	550

Source: U.S. Chess Federation Web site, 2003. www.uschess.org.

Checkmate: States with the Best Chess Players

When only chess players who have been given a U.S. Chess Federation rating of 2,200 or higher (which is the Masters level, including Grandmasters) are considered, the Northeast and Southwest clearly dominate.

State	Number of Chess Players Rated at Least 2,200 per Million People
1. New York	23.0
2. Nevada	16.0
3. Vermont	14.8
4. Massachusetts	12.8

5. New Jersey	12.1
6. California	11.6
7. Maryland	10.6
8. New Hampshire	10.5
9. Rhode Island	10.5
10. Hawaii	9.9

Source: U.S. Chess Federation Web site, 2003. www.uschess.org.

Countries with the Most Master Chess Players per Million People*

Russia has the highest number of chess players with a FIDE (World Chess Federation) rating of 2,200 or higher (Masters and Grandmaster levels) and has long been famous for the performance of its people in chess matches. However, per capita, Russia only ranks No. 30 among independent nations.

Below are the countries with the highest number of chess players with the FIDE rating of 2,200 or higher (per million people). Very small European (and some mid-sized Eastern European) nations dominate this list.

Country	Number of Chess Players Rated at Least 2,200 per Million People
1. Iceland	315
2. Monaco	156
3. Serbia & Montenegro	93
4. Andorra	88
5. San Marino	72
6. Slovenia	70
7. Croatia	68
8. Liechtenstein	61
9. Hungary	58
10. Israel	48

* Some countries have fewer than a million people. If territories and dependencies were included, then the Faeroe Islands (239), British Virgin Islands (94) and Bermuda (63) would be in this list.

Ten Most Populous Countries Never to Win an Olympic Medal

1. Bangladesh **
2. Congo (Dem. Rep.)
3. Burma
4. Sudan
5. Afghanistan
6. Nepal
7. Yemen
8. Madagascar
9. Guatemala
10. Cambodia

This includes Summer and Winter Olympic medals (gold, silver and bronze).

** Since independence from Pakistan in 1971, Bangladesh has not won any Olympic medals. However, when Bangladesh was a part of Pakistan, Pakistan had won medals.

Five Least Populous Countries to Have Won an Olympic Medal

Despite having a population of only around 33,000, nine Olympic medals (all Winter Olympic medals) have been awarded to Liechtenstein.

1. Liechtenstein
2. Tonga
3. Barbados
4. Iceland
5. The Bahamas

If this list were to include dependencies and territories, Bermuda would be ranked between Liechtenstein and Tonga, while both the Virgin Islands and Netherlands Antilles would be between Tonga and Barbados.

This includes Summer and Winter Olympic medals (gold, silver and bronze).

States with the Highest Number of Bowling Alleys per Million People *

Bowling is a form of indoor recreation that can be done in almost any type of weather. That versatility shows on this list, as states with cold winters lead it. Also, states with smaller towns but few (or no) big cities rank higher as their bowling alleys tend to be smaller (and therefore serve fewer people).

State	Number of Bowling Alleys per Million People
1. South Dakota	82
2. North Dakota	72
3. Montana	63
4. Iowa	62
4. Wisconsin	62
6. Nebraska	57
7. Wyoming	56
8. Idaho	41
8. Minnesota	41
10. Kansas	38

* In some cases, the states have fewer than one million people.

States with the Lowest Number of Bowling Alleys per Million People

The Sun Belt has far fewer bowling alleys per capita than places further north.

State	Number of Bowling Alleys per Million People
1. Nevada	8
2. Alabama	9
2. California	9
2. Louisiana	9
5. Georgia	10
5. Mississippi	10
7. Florida	11
7. Texas	11
9. North Carolina	12
9. Tennessee	12

Source for last two lists: U.S. Census, Economic Census, 1997. Only establishments with a payroll are included.

Canadian Provinces with the Highest Number of Bowling Alleys per Million People *

Bowling alleys are about as common in Canada as they are in the northern Plains states of the United States.

Province	Number of Bowling Alleys per Million People
1. New Brunswick	82
2. Saskatchewan	73
3. Prince Edward Island	66
4. Nova Scotia	55
5. Quebec	46

Source: Canadian Internet directories (2003).

* In some cases, the provinces have fewer than one million people.

States with the Highest Number of Ice Skating Rinks per Million People *

Ice skating rinks are much more popular in the North than in other parts of the United States. A major sporting activity in ice rinks, hockey, has become more popular outside of the North in recent decades; however, the North is clearly its core area.

State	Number of Ice Skating Rinks per Million People
1. Montana	8.0
2. Vermont	6.8
3. Minnesota	5.3
4. Connecticut	5.2
5. Massachusetts	3.9
6. Delaware	3.8
7. North Dakota	3.1
8. South Dakota	2.7
9. New Hampshire	2.6
10. Maine	2.4

Source: U.S. Census, Economic Census, 1997. Only establishments with a payroll are included.

* In some cases, the states have fewer than one million people.

States with the Highest Number of Roller Skating Rinks per Million People *

The pattern of where roller skating rinks are most common is less clear than with other leisure activities. However, states in the central United States generally rank higher than in the East or the West (with Delaware being the glaring exception).

State	Number of Roller Skating Rinks per Million People
1. Delaware	13.2
2. Montana	12.5
3. Oklahoma	12.4
4. Wyoming	10.4
5. Iowa	10.2
6. Mississippi	9.9
7. South Carolina	9.8
8. Maine	9.6
8. Missouri	9.6
8. South Dakota	9.6

* In some cases, the states have fewer than one million people.

States with the Lowest Number of Roller Skating Rinks per Million People *

State	Number of Roller Skating Rinks per Million People
1. Nevada	1.8
2. New Hampshire	2.6
3. Arizona	2.9
4. California	3.0
5. North Dakota	3.1
6. Maryland	3.3
7. Hawaii	3.4
7. Vermont	3.4
9. New York	3.5

10. Massachusetts	3.9
10. Utah	3.9

Source for last two lists: U.S. Census, Economic Census, 1997. Only establishments with a payroll are included.

* In some cases, the states have fewer than one million people.

States with the Highest Number of Golf Courses per Million People *

Despite the long winters, there are more golf courses for every million people in the North than in the South.

State	Number of Golf Courses per Million People
1. Iowa	108
2. North Dakota	103
3. Nebraska	95
4. South Dakota	86
5. Minnesota	76
5. Montana	76
7. South Carolina	73
7. Vermont	73
9. Maine	72
10. Wisconsin	69
10. Wyoming	69

States with the Lowest Number of Golf Courses per Million People *

While the North has more golf courses than the South, if one goes *too* far north (such as to Alaska), the number of golf courses decreases substantially. Despite ranking second to last per capita, California has the most golf courses of any state (717).

State	Number of Golf Courses per Million People
1. Alaska	20
2. California	22

3. Utah	25
4. New Mexico	26
5. Maryland	28
5. New Jersey	28
7. Nevada	29
8. Louisiana	30
8. Texas	30
10. Virginia	34

Source for last two lists: U.S. Census, Economic Census, 1997. Only establishments with a payroll are included.

* In some cases, the states have fewer than one million people. This list includes golf courses and country clubs but not miniature golf courses.

States with the Highest Number of Miniature Golf Courses per Million People *

Like with golf, miniature golf courses are more common in the North than in the South, though the focus is more on the Northeast.

State	Number of Miniature Golf Courses per Million People
1. New Hampshire	18.8
2. Maine	12.8
3. Wyoming	10.4
4. Delaware	9.4
5. Vermont	8.5
6. Montana	8.0
7. South Carolina	7.7
8. Massachusetts	7.0
9. Wisconsin	6.9
10. New Jersey	6.1

* In some cases, the states have fewer than one million people.

States with the Lowest Number of Miniature Golf Courses per Million People

Many states that have fewer golf courses also have fewer miniature golf courses.

State	Number of Miniature Golf Courses per Million People
1. Utah	1.4
2. Louisiana	1.6
3. California	1.7
4. Mississippi	1.8
4. Nevada	1.8
6. Oregon	2.2
7. Georgia	2.3
8. Texas	2.4
9. Hawaii	2.5
9. Iowa	2.5

Source for the last two lists: U.S. Census, Economic Census, 1997. Only establishments with a payroll are included.

States with the Highest Number of Professional Golf Tournaments (2003)

States with mild winters (winter tournaments) and highly populated Northeast and Midwest states (summer tournaments) rank highest here.

State	Tournaments in 2003
1. California	18
2. Florida	14
3. Georgia	12
4. Texas	11
5. New York	10
5. Ohio	10
7. South Carolina	9
8. Illinois	8
8. Pennsylvania	8
10. North Carolina	7

This list includes the following tours: PGA, Champion's, Nationwide, European (yes, there are some U.S. stops!), Canadian, Ladies' European, NGA/Hooters, PGA of America and USGA.

States with the Most Ski Resorts

Colorado is probably the first state that comes to mind for most people when they think of skiing. However, is it number one on the list of states with the most ski resorts? No. Number one is actually New York, though most of the New York ski resorts are much smaller than those in Colorado. Despite the fact that Utah held the 2002 Winter Olympics, it was only No. 11 on this list.

State	Number of Ski Resorts
1. New York	34
2. Colorado	28
3. Michigan	26
4. California	25
5. Pennsylvania	20
6. Vermont	18
7. New Hampshire	17
7. Wisconsin	17
9. Maine	14
9. Oregon	14

Only downhill ski resorts with at least one lift are included.

Too Warm or Too Flat: States without Ski Resorts

1. Arkansas
2. Delaware
3. Florida
4. Hawaii
5. Kansas
6. Louisiana
7. Mississippi
8. Nebraska
9. Oklahoma
10. South Carolina
11. Texas

Some Exotic Ski Resorts Around the World

For skiers wanting something different, here are some unusual places (at least for most westerners) to ski.

1. Chacaltaya, Bolivia

This resort has the highest ski lift in the world, with the top of the lift (just a rope tow) reaching 17,785 feet above sea level. Interestingly, this ski resort is so high (and so cold) that it is open during the Bolivian summer but not winter. Don't count on a long descent to sea level; the total vertical drop is less than 1,000 feet.

2. Gulmarg, India (Kashmir)

In the middle of war-torn Kashmir is the Gulmarg ski resort, originally built in 1927 by the British. While this Himalayan resort has ski lifts, heli-skiing (as the term self-describes, where a helicopter is used instead of a ski lift) has been done elsewhere in Kashmir to achieve very high-altitude skiing.

3. Dizin, Iran

North of Tehran in the Alborz Mountains, the snow here has a much lower water content (a "dry snow") than in other parts of the world. Therefore, the quality of the snow is excellent for skiing. Tickets are also quite cheap—around the equivalent of $4 per person for a day.

4. Yabuli International, China

China's most popular ski resort is in the Lesser Hinggan Range of extreme northeastern China and is one of the colder ski resorts in the world. Average January high temperatures are around zero degrees Fahrenheit (with much colder nights)! Fortunately for the Chinese, who have only recently embraced skiing as an activity, numerous other ski resorts have opened, including some in milder winter climates.

5. Africa

Ski Africa? Certainly! In Africa, ski resorts exist in Algeria, Morocco, South Africa and Lesotho. Oxbow, at around 8,000 feet above sea level in Lesotho, a poor small mountainous enclave completely surrounded by South Africa, is not very developed and has only one part-time lift (when the lift is not operating, skiers must organize their own four-wheel-drive shuttle). In 2002, there were plans to modernize this ski area.

States Where There Are a Lot of Hunters

Primarily rural states are more likely to have a lot of hunters than more urbanized states. In the West, states that are further north have more hunters than those further south.

In the next two lists, the number of "hunting days" per resident (age 16 or higher) are listed. This number applies to whether the hunting was done in the resident's home state or elsewhere, which best displays the hunting habits of the population of each state.

State	Hunting Days per Year for Residents
1. Arkansas	4.43
2. West Virginia	3.84
3. Vermont	3.46
4. South Dakota	3.42
5. Mississippi	3.26
6. Idaho	3.08
7. Maine	2.74
8. Wyoming	2.60
9. Wisconsin	2.59
10. Michigan	2.45

Source: U.S. Fish and Wildlife Service, 1996.

States Where There Are Relatively Few Hunters

The animals don't need to hide quite as much, and "venison" is less of a household name in these states. Southwestern states and the urban corridor of the Northeast have the fewest number of hunting days per year among their residents who are 16 years or older.

State	Hunting Days per Year for Residents
1. Hawaii	0.29
2. Connecticut	0.35
3. California	0.36
4. Massachusetts	0.37
5. New Jersey	0.39
6. Maryland	0.44
7. Arizona	0.47
8. Florida	0.48
9. New Mexico	0.53
10. Rhode Island	0.58

Source: U.S. Fish and Wildlife Service, 1996.

States Where There Are a Lot of People Who Fish

As with the hunters, rural states are more likely to have people who fish often than urban states. The southeastern United States (more so than with hunters) and some far northern areas of the country have the heaviest concentration of anglers, while the dry Southwest and urbanized parts of the Northeast have the lowest.

Much like the "hunting days" lists, the next two lists have the number of "fishing days" per resident (age 16 or higher). This number applies to whether the fishing was done in the resident's home state or elsewhere and applies to both freshwater and saltwater fishing.

State	Fishing Days per Year for Residents
1. Alaska	7.32
2. Louisiana	6.40
3. Minnesota	5.98
4. Oklahoma	5.48
5. South Carolina	4.85
6. Alabama	4.63
7. Idaho	4.22
8. Arkansas	4.15
9. Maine	4.13
10. Delaware	4.12

States Where There Are Relatively Few People Who Fish

State	Fishing Days per Year for Residents
1. Arizona	1.41
2. California	1.63
3. New York	1.95
4. New Mexico	2.16
5. Ohio	2.25
6. Utah	2.27
7. Massachusetts	2.30
8. Nevada	2.36
9. Connecticut	2.39
10. Maryland	2.57

Source for the last two lists: U.S. Fish and Wildlife Service, 1996.

States That Have Greyhound Racetracks

Greyhound racing is a controversial sport. The Humane Society of the United States reports that thousands of dogs involved with racing have been killed, either due to injuries or because they are no longer competitive. Over-breeding of dogs (when there is a glut of dogs waiting for adoption) and limited human companionship for the dogs are also issues. Fifteen states still have operating greyhound racetracks (2003).

1. Alabama
2. Arizona
3. Arkansas
4. Colorado
5. Connecticut
6. Florida
7. Iowa
8. Kansas
9. Massachusetts
10. New Hampshire
11. Oregon
12. Rhode Island
13. Texas
14. West Virginia
15. Wisconsin

States Where Cockfighting Is Legal

Cockfighting is where two roosters fight each other in a pit, usually until one dies. Gambling is involved; spectators bet on which rooster they expect to win. Surviving roosters sometimes suffer severe injuries.

1. Louisiana
2. New Mexico

Since 1998, Arizona, Missouri and Oklahoma have banned cockfighting.

CHAPTER NINE
Travel Geography

This chapter focuses on where people go (or don't go), including (in a few cases) where they *can't* go. Chapter 3 ("Transportation Geography") has a large number of "travel geography" lists too, but they focus more on getting to the places listed in this chapter instead of actually being there.

Globetrotter Destinations: Countries and the Percentage of World Travelers Who Have Been There

World travelers (defined as those who have been in at least 20 different countries on at least two continents) were surveyed to determine which countries they had visited (including the country/countries in which they resided) at some point during their lives. Two surveys were conducted; the first included 150 people who live in various countries (including European countries, Australia, Japan, the United States and Canada, among others); the second included 100 people who live in the United States. In most cases, U.S. world travelers were more likely to have been in other North American or Caribbean countries but less likely to have been in various European countries than other world travelers. The surveys were conducted in 2001.

A = Percentage of World Travelers (20+ Countries, 2+ Continents) Who Have Been in the Given Country

B = Percentage of World Travelers (20+ Countries, 2+ Continents) Who Live in the U.S. Who Have Been in the Given Country

Country	A	B
Afghanistan	*	*
Albania	*	*
Algeria	6	*
Andorra	17	12
Angola	*	*
Antigua & Barbuda	7	8
Argentina	25	23
Armenia	*	*
Australia	37	38
Austria	74	64
Azerbaijan	*	*
Bahamas	25	26
Bahrain	5	6
Bangladesh	*	*
Barbados	13	15
Belarus	*	6
Belgium	67	59
Belize	5	18
Benin	*	*
Bhutan	*	*
Bolivia	7	13
Bosnia & Herz.	9	9
Botswana	7	10
Brazil	29	25
Brunei	5	5
Bulgaria	22	12
Burkina Faso	*	*
Burma	13	9
Burundi	*	*
Cambodia	9	12
Cameroon	*	*
Canada	64	85
Cape Verde	*	*
Central Afr. Rep.	*	*
Chad	*	*
Chile	18	19
China	52^	44^
Colombia	14	18
Comoros	*	*
Congo (Dem. Rep.)	*	*
Congo (Rep.)	*	*

Costa Rica	21	24
Cote d'Ivoire	*	5
Croatia	23	17
Cuba	15	14
Cyprus	24	9
Czech Rep.	51	51
Denmark	56	46
Djibouti	*	*
Dominica	*	6
Dominican Rep.	9	14
East Timor	*	*
Ecuador	14	15
Egypt	47	33
El Salvador	5	13
Equatorial Guinea	*	*
Eritrea	*	*
Estonia	15	15
Ethiopia	*	*
Fiji	11	10
Finland	35	25
France	96	97
Gabon	*	*
Gambia	*	*
Georgia	*	5
Germany	92	92
Ghana	*	5
Greece	63	55
Grenada	7	7
Guatemala	11	25
Guinea	*	*
Guinea-Bissau	*	*
Guyana	*	*
Haiti	5	11
Honduras	8	19
Hungary	44	36
Iceland	15	13
India	27	22
Indonesia	29	24
Iran	5	*
Iraq	*	*
Ireland	36	32
Israel	23	27

Italy	91	91
Jamaica	16	28
Japan	37	44
Jordan	16	19
Kazakhstan	5	5
Kenya	19	14
Kiribati	*	*
Kuwait	5	5
Kyrgyzstan	*	*
Laos	9	7
Latvia	9	10
Lebanon	9	7
Lesotho	*	5
Liberia	*	*
Libya	*	*
Liechtenstein	27	18
Lithuania	8	13
Luxembourg	36	30
Macedonia	9	10
Madagascar	*	*
Malawi	*	5
Malaysia	37	33
Maldives	6	*
Mali	*	*
Malta	14	8
Marshall Is.	*	*
Mauritania	*	*
Mauritius	5	*
Mexico	61	78
Micronesia	*	*
Moldova	*	*
Monaco	36	30
Mongolia	5	*
Morocco	35	32
Mozambique	*	6
Namibia	9	10
Nauru	*	*
Nepal	16	16
Netherlands	80	69
New Zealand	26	23
Nicaragua	7	9
Niger	*	*

Nigeria	5	*
North Korea	*	*
Norway	43	32
Oman	7	8
Pakistan	9	5
Palau	*	*
Panama	13	19
Papau New Guinea	*	*
Paraguay	9	7
Peru	21	24
Philippines	17	17
Poland	25	26
Portugal	41	31
Qatar	5	5
Romania	14	9
Russia	31	27
Rwanda	*	*
St. Kitts & Nevis	*	6
St. Lucia	13	9
St. Vincent & Gr.	*	*
Samoa	*	5
San Marino	17	10
Sao Tome & Prin.	*	*
Saudi Arabia	9	9
Senegal	5	5
Serbia & Mont.	24	15
Seychelles	7	*
Sierra Leone	*	*
Singapore	40	34
Slovakia	19	18
Slovenia	19	12
Solomon Islands	*	*
Somalia	*	*
South Africa	20	19
South Korea	15	24
Spain	78	69
Sri Lanka	9	6
Sudan	*	*
Suriname	*	*
Swaziland	5	7
Sweden	49	42
Switzerland	75	74

Syria	8	6
Taiwan	11	22
Tajikistan	*	*
Tanzania	10	8
Thailand	59	53
Togo	*	*
Tonga	*	*
Trinidad & Tobago	8	10
Tunisia	27	10
Turkey	49	40
Turkmenistan	*	*
Tuvalu	*	*
Uganda	*	6
Ukraine	10	11
UAE	16	12
U.K.	89	93
U.S.A.	91	100
Uruguay	10	10
Uzbekistan	5	6
Vanuatu	*	*
Vatican City	51	44
Venezuela	15	16
Vietnam	17	18
Yemen	*	*
Zambia	8	11
Zimbabwe	14	14

* Less than 5 percent.
^ Figures include trips to Hong Kong. If Hong Kong is excluded, then 27 percent of world travelers (and 28 percent of American world travelers) have been in China. These figures do not include Taiwan, which is listed separately.

Travel Agents' Staples: Countries with the Highest Number of International Tourists per Year

These are countries commonly visited, either by tourists in neighboring countries or those on the other side of the globe.

Country	Number of Tourists per Year
1. France	76.5 million
2. Spain	49.5 million
3. United States	45.5 million
4. Italy	39.0 million
5. China	33.2 million
6. United Kingdom	23.4 million
7. Russia	21.2 million
8. Mexico	19.8 million
9. Canada	19.7 million
10. Austria	18.2 million

Source: World Tourism Organization, 2002. Data are for the most recent year available (usually 2001).

Off the Beaten Path (or No Path at All): Countries with the Lowest Number of International Tourists per Year

Here is a "wish-list" for those who like to say "I've been to Rwanda, Bhutan and Tuvalu, among others; what are some of the countries *you* have been to?"

Country	Number of Tourists per Year
1. Kiribati	1,000
1. Tuvalu	1,000
3. Rwanda	2,000
4. Afghanistan	4,000
5. Sao Tome & Principe	5,000
5. Marshall Islands	5,000
7. Bhutan	7,000
8. Central African Republic	10,000
8. Sierra Leone	10,000
8. Somalia	10,000

Data were not available for Equatorial Guinea or Guinea-Bissau, two countries that would likely be on this list.

Source: World Tourism Organization, 2002. Data are for the most recent year available (usually during the late 1990s).

Countries That U.S. Citizens May Visit without Passports

While United States citizens may enter the following countries with just a certified birth certificate or naturalization certificate, the U.S. Department of State strongly recommends using a passport to visit these countries.

1. Antigua and Barbuda
2. Bahamas
3. Barbados
4. Canada
5. Dominica
6. Dominican Republic *
7. Federated States of Micronesia
8. Grenada
9. Jamaica
10. Mexico
11. Palau
12. Panama *
13. St. Kitts and Nevis
14. St. Lucia
15. St. Vincent and the Grenadines

In addition, U.S. citizens may go to the dependencies/territories of Anguilla, Aruba, Bermuda, British Virgin Islands, Cayman Islands, Montserrat, Netherlands Antilles, Turks and Caicos, and all U.S. territories without a passport. However, passports *are* required for the French West Indies islands of Guadeloupe and Martinique.

* While a passport is not technically required, travelers may experience difficulty entering or exiting the country without one (even with a certified birth certificate).

Source: U.S. Department of State, 2003. A certified birth certificate or other documentation is usually required if one has no passport.

Ten Most Populous Countries That Pope John Paul II Has Never Visited

From 1979 until 2003, Pope John Paul II had been in 129 independent nations (plus Guam, Puerto Rico and Reunion), including some where Catholics are a very small minority. That leaves 63 independent countries that the Pope had not yet visited, mostly in Asia, the former Soviet Union or on small islands.

1. China
2. Russia
3. Vietnam
4. Ethiopia
5. Iran
6. Burma
7. Algeria
8. Afghanistan
9. Nepal
10. Uzbekistan

Countries That Had the Highest Number of Visitors to the U.S. in 2002

Country	Arrivals from the Country (of Residence) to the U.S. in 2002
1. Canada	12,968,103
2. Mexico	9,807,000
3. United Kingdom	3,816,736
4. Japan	3,627,264
5. Germany	1,189,856
6. France	734,260
7. South Korea	638,697
8. Australia	407,130
9. Italy	406,160
10. Brazil	405,094

Visitors who came more than once were counted for each arrival.

Source: Department of Commerce (ITA Tourism Industries), 2003.

Countries That Had the Lowest Number of Visitors to the U.S. in 2002

Country	Arrivals from the Country (of Residence) to the U.S. in 2002
1. Vatican City	8
2. Comoros	19
3. Somalia	23
4. East Timor	27
5. North Korea	29
6. Guinea-Bissau	30
7. Sao Tome & Principe	33
8. Nauru	39
9. Tuvalu	41
10. Maldives	72

Visitors who came more than once are counted for each arrival (though that probably didn't happen often with these countries).

Source: Department of Commerce (ITA Tourism Industries), 2003.

Visitors to the U.S. Expressed as a Percentage of Their Populations: Countries with the Highest Percentages

Proximity to the United States is the biggest factor here as large percentages of the countries' populations are more likely to visit the U.S. (often multiple times). The only country outside of North America or the Caribbean region listed here is affluent Monaco.

Country	Arrivals to the U.S. Expressed as a Percentage of the Country's Population in 2002
1. Bahamas	87.3
2. Canada	40.6
3. Dominica	24.6
4. Antigua & Barbuda	24.2
5. St. Kitts & Nevis	20.4

6. Barbados	15.2
7. Monaco	12.0
8. Trinidad & Tobago	10.2
9. Mexico	9.5
10. Belize	8.5

In addition, six dependencies (all in the Caribbean or western Atlantic Ocean) would be on this list if they were independent nations: Cayman Islands, 96.7; British Virgin Islands, 68.2; Turks and Caicos Islands, 53.3; Anguilla, 24.5; Netherlands Antilles (plus Aruba), 20.4; Bermuda, 9.7.

Visitors who came more than once are counted for each arrival.

Source: Department of Commerce (ITA Tourism Industries), 2003.

Visitors to the U.S. Expressed as a Percentage of Their Populations: Countries with the Lowest Percentages

Most of these countries are overwhelmingly poor, and few residents have the means to travel to the United States (or almost anywhere else).

Country	Arrivals to the U.S. Expressed as a Percentage of the Country's Population in 2002
1. North Korea	0.00013
2. Congo (Dem. Rep.)	0.00015
3. Somalia	0.00030
4. Afghanistan	0.00049
5. Guinea-Bissau	0.0022
6. Comoros	0.0023
6. Iraq	0.0023
6. Sudan	0.0023
9. Yemen	0.0024
10. Chad	0.0025

Visitors who came more than once are counted for each arrival.

And the Lowest in the Americas:

1. Paraguay	0.21
2. Brazil	0.23
3. Cuba	0.24
4. Bolivia	0.30
5. Argentina	0.43

Source: Department of Commerce (ITA Tourism Industries), 2003.

What Percentage of Well-Traveled Americans Have Been to Certain States?

Here is a list of each state (and the District of Columbia) and what percentages of Americans (who have been in at least 20 states) have been there. One hundred people were included in the survey.

State	Percentage of Well-Traveled Americans Who Have Been in the Given State
Alabama	58
Alaska	19
Arizona	69
Arkansas	57
California	84
Colorado	72
Connecticut	54
Delaware	48
Florida	94
Georgia	81
Hawaii	33
Idaho	42
Illinois	83
Indiana	64
Iowa	41
Kansas	49
Kentucky	62
Louisiana	58
Maine	50
Maryland	66

Massachusetts	71
Michigan	58
Minnesota	47
Mississippi	56
Missouri	60
Montana	34
Nebraska	38
Nevada	75
New Hampshire	54
New Jersey	73
New Mexico	61
New York	92
North Carolina	77
North Dakota	22
Ohio	70
Oklahoma	56
Oregon	46
Pennsylvania	86
Rhode Island	53
South Carolina	67
South Dakota	28
Tennessee	74
Texas	84
Utah	60
Vermont	55
Virginia	86
Washington	57
West Virginia	58
Wisconsin	53
Wyoming	50

Since people from the East Coast are more likely to have traveled to more states (because the states are smaller, so more are nearby), the East Coast states have the advantage in this list. People from the West Coast must travel to at least one state in the eastern half of the United States in order to have been in 20 or more states. Meanwhile, a person from Washington, D.C. is within 600 miles of 21 states. The states that are remote from major population centers, including Alaska and Hawaii, rank low as even the well-traveled people usually visit the closer states first.

By the way, the "average person" in this survey has been to about 30 states.

States That Had the Most Overseas* Tourists in 2000

Los Angeles, San Francisco, Miami, New York City and Las Vegas are just a few of the destinations found in high-ranking states frequented by overseas tourists.

State	Number of Overseas Tourists in 2000
1. California	6,364,000
2. Florida	6,026,000
3. New York	5,922,000
4. Hawaii	2,727,000
5. Nevada	2,364,000
6. Massachusetts	1,429,000
7. Illinois	1,377,000
8. Texas	1,169,000
9. New Jersey	909,000
10. Arizona	883,000

* Overseas is defined as anywhere outside of the United States (and territories), Canada and Mexico.

Source: Department of Commerce (ITA Tourism Industries), 2001.

Largest Cities in the United States Not to Have an Embassy or Consulate of Mexico

There are 54 embassies and consulates (including honorary consulates) of Mexico in the United States. Mexico has more U.S. consulates than any other nation.

1. Indianapolis, Indiana
2. Jacksonville, Florida
3. Columbus, Ohio
4. Baltimore, Maryland
5. Memphis, Tennessee

Countries with No U.S. Embassies or Consulates Within Their Borders

Not all of these countries have no U.S. embassies within their borders because they are dangerous or have poor relations with the United States. Some do not simply because they are small or remote.

1. Andorra
2. Antigua and Barbuda
3. Bhutan
4. Central African Republic *
5. Comoros
6. Congo (Rep.) *
7. Cuba
8. Dominica
9. Guinea-Bissau *
10. Iran
11. Iraq
12. Kiribati
13. Libya
14. Liechtenstein
15. Maldives *
16. Monaco
17. Nauru
18. North Korea
19. Sao Tome & Principe
20. Seychelles *
21. Solomon Islands **
22. Somalia
23. St. Kitts & Nevis
24. St. Lucia
25. St. Vincent & the Grenadines
26. Tonga
27. Tuvalu
28. Vanuatu
29. Vatican City ***

* A previously used embassy closed after 1995.
** Has a U.S. Consulate but not an embassy.
*** The embassy serving Vatican City is in Rome, Italy.

Source: U.S. Department of State, 2003.

Places Where One Can Rent a Car and Drive It into Another Country

In some countries, one can rent a car and drive it into numerous other countries (either with or without special permission and extra insurance, based on the rental car company, of course). Here are some examples:

1. Germany (among other European Union countries)

Driving across borders in the European Union is quite easy, as there are no longer border controls. Many rental car companies allow customers to drive rented cars into numerous other European Union countries and sometimes into non-E.U. countries. If one wanted to take a driving trip around Europe using a rental car company in Germany, the trip could theoretically include countries such as Andorra, Austria, Belgium, Czech Republic, Denmark, Finland, France, Hungary, Italy, Liechtenstein, Luxembourg, Monaco, The Netherlands, Norway, Portugal, San Marino, Slovakia, Slovenia, Spain, Sweden, Switzerland and even the United Kingdom (if one didn't mind driving on the left in a car built for driving on the right).

2. Serbia and Montenegro

With permission by at least one rental car company, one can drive from Serbia and Montenegro to countries such as Russia and Ukraine (with proper visas, of course), as well as Greece, Bulgaria, Romania, Hungary plus numerous countries in central and western Europe. This is likely the most expansive area one can cover in a single rental car (if one, of course, chooses to "see the world by rental car").

3. South Africa

Since many neighboring countries have well-known tourist destinations (such as game parks in Botswana and Namibia or Victoria Falls on the Zimbabwe-Zambia border), rental car companies will often allow customers to cross into certain other countries with the rented car. One company with a liberal policy (which the author used) allowed (in 2002) customers, with permission, to use the car in Botswana, Lesotho, Malawi, Mozambique, Namibia, Swaziland, Zambia and Zimbabwe.

4. Kenya

Some rental car companies will allow travel with their vehicles into Tanzania and Uganda.

5. Chile & Argentina

Some rental car companies will allow travel between these two countries (usually with an additional charge). However, cross-border travel is difficult between most other South American countries with a rental car.

Nationalities That are Banned from Certain Countries

Citizens of the following nations are denied entry to some countries around the world (as of 2003).

Nationality	Countries That Ban Them
Iran	Algeria
Israel	Algeria, Bahrain, Bangladesh, Brunei, Iran, Iraq, Kuwait, Lebanon, Libya, Malaysia, Oman, Pakistan, Qatar, Saudi Arabia, Sudan, Syria, United Arab Emirates, Yemen
Malaysia	Serbia & Montenegro
Serbia & Montenegro	Malaysia
Taiwan	Croatia, Mauritius, Serbia & Montenegro
Vietnam	Algeria

CHAPTER TEN
Geography of Politics and Issues

In this chapter, we look at some of the laws and political issues that vary significantly in the United States and around the world. For example, in Arizona, it is legal to buy hard liquor in grocery stores but illegal to buy or use fireworks. In Alabama, one must buy liquor from a state-run liquor store, but a wide supply of fireworks can be bought in season (or, in South Carolina, even in the "off-season"). This chapter will also include some somber issues still affecting the world today, such as slavery or the death penalty.

Since this is the politics chapter, a few voting statistics are presented here. Those who thought the Florida vote was extremely close in the 2000 Presidential Election will be surprised to see some states where the margin of victory in past presidential elections was even smaller.

Left-Trenders: Counties That Were the Most Democratic in Presidential Elections from 1992 to 2000 That Went Republican in at Least Six of Seven Presidential Elections from 1948 to 1972

Parts of the West, Northeast, Midwest and Southern Florida, especially those with higher incomes or universities, have trended strongly Democratic in presidential elections in recent decades. Some areas that voted solidly Democratic between 1992 and 2000 in presidential elections voted solidly Republican 40 or 50 years ago.

Listed below are the number of Democratic votes (plus Ralph Nader votes) for every 100 Republican votes in the 1992, 1996 and 2000 presidential elections. (Thus, if 200 were the number listed, there would be twice as many Democratic votes as Republican votes.) All counties below had more Republican votes than Democratic votes in at least six of the seven presidential elections from 1948 through 1972 (most counties in the U.S. went for Johnson in 1964).

County, State	Number of Democratic Pres. Votes for Every 100 Republican Pres. Votes
1. Santa Cruz, California	251 (UC Santa Cruz)
2. Marin, California	237 (Suburban San Francisco)
3. Sonoma, California	207 (Santa Rosa)
4. Broward, Florida	205 * (Fort Lauderdale)
5. Tompkins, New York	194 (Ithaca/Cornell)
6. Windham, Vermont	193 ** (southeastern VT)
7. Arlington, Virginia	182 (D.C. area)
8. Washtenaw, Michigan	178 (Ann Arbor/U of Michigan)
9. Boulder, Colorado	171 (Boulder/U of Colorado)
10. San Juan, Washington	169 (San Juan Islands)
10. Washington, Vermont	169 ** (Montpelier)

Ralph Nader votes from the 2000 election were added to the Democratic votes in this list.

* Voted Republican in all seven presidential elections from 1948 through 1972.

** Votes are for 1996 and 2000 elections only.

Recent Left-Trenders: Counties That Were the Most Democratic in Presidential Elections from 1992 to 2000 That Went Republican in at Least 10 of 11 Presidential Elections from 1948 to 1988

These are the most recent converts to Democratic presidential voting. These counties voted Republican in at least 10 of the 11 presidential elections between 1948 and 1988 (with one having gone Republican in all 11). The same point system is used here as in the previous list.

County, State	Number of Democratic Pres. Votes for Every 100 Republican Pres. Votes
1. Palm Beach, Florida	164 * (West Palm Beach)
2. Monterey, California	156 (Monterey/Salinas)
3. Ingham, Michigan	148 (Lansing)
4. Westchester, New York	146 (North of NYC)
5. Union, New Jersey	145 (Southwest suburbs of NYC)

Vermont counties were not included due to incomplete data. Nader votes from the 2000 election were added to the Democratic votes in this list.

* Voted Republican in all 11 presidential elections from 1948 through 1988, then went Democratic in the three presidential elections from 1992 through 2000.

Right-Trenders: Counties That Were Most Republican in Presidential Elections from 1992 to 2000 That Went Democratic in Six of Seven Presidential Elections from 1948 to 1972

The counties on this list are all in Texas (especially central Texas) and voted overwhelmingly for George W. Bush in 2000. Many counties in rural areas and in the South have trended Republican in recent decades.

The numbers on this list represent the number of Republican votes for every 100 Democratic votes (plus Ralph Nader votes) in the 1992, 1996 and 2000 presidential elections. So, a number of 200 would mean that twice as many people voted for the Republican candidates versus Democratic candidates.

County, State	Number of Republican Pres. Votes for Every 100 Democratic Pres. Votes
1. Rockwall, Texas	297
2. King, Texas	260
3. Borden, Texas	251

4. Hockley, Texas	232
5. Garza, Texas	187
6. Llano, Texas	186
7. Archer, Texas	183
8. Callahan, Texas	181
9. Ellis, Texas	178
10. Williamson, Texas	174

Among counties where the Democratic presidential candidate received more votes than the Republican presidential candidate in *all* elections from 1948 through 1972 (even the Nixon landslide of 1972), Plumas County, California was the most Republican in presidential elections between 1992 and 2000 with 132 Republican votes for every 100 Democratic votes. Despite coastal California trending Democratic, parts of the interior of California (such as Plumas County) have trended Republican.

Ralph Nader votes from the 2000 election were added to the Democratic votes on this list.

States with the Smallest Margins Between Their Top Two Candidates in Presidential Elections in the Past 100 Years (1904–2000)

This list shows exactly why presidential candidates campaign heavily in the "swing states." Literally, just a handful of votes can decide the winner. In 1916, 1960 and 2000, the elections were not just close in the states listed but also at the national level.

State (Year)	State Winner	State Loser	Vote Difference
1. New Hampshire (1916)	Wilson	Hughes	56
2. Hawaii (1960)	JFK	Nixon	115
3. California (1912)	T.Roosevelt	Wilson	174
4. New Mexico (2000)	Gore	G.W.Bush	366
5. Nevada (1908)	Bryan	Taft	437
6. Florida (2000)	G.W.Bush	Gore	537
7. Maryland (1908)	Taft	Bryan	605
8. Missouri (1908)	Taft	Bryan	629
9. Kentucky (1952)	Stevenson	Eisenhower	700
10. Wyoming (1912)	Wilson	Taft	750

Elections were frequently even more tight in the 19th century, partly because there were fewer voters. In 1832, Henry Clay had exactly four more votes than Andrew Jackson in Maryland (though he lost big in the national vote count).

The Death Penalty

According to Amnesty International statistics, the death penalty is retained for ordinary crimes in 83 countries. This compares with 76 countries where the death penalty is not legal and not used, plus 21 countries where the death penalty is not used (though technically legal) and 15 countries that only use the death penalty under very unusual circumstances (such as military crimes).

Most of the countries that retain the death penalty are either in Asia (including, and especially the Middle East), the Caribbean or Africa. The more populous nations are more likely to have the death penalty than less populous nations; in fact, the death penalty is legal in all the 12 largest nations (though Russia has not used it in recent years). A disproportionate number of low-income nations have the death penalty. High-income nations are much less likely to have the death penalty, and it is illegal in all western European nations.

In 2002, China had the most known executions at 1060. Iran was in second place with 113 executions, while the United States was in third place at 71 (33 of them in Texas). These three countries accounted for 81 percent of all known executions by governments around the world.

Ten Most Populous Countries Where the Death Penalty Is Illegal in All Cases*

1. Germany
2. France
3. United Kingdom
4. Italy
5. Ukraine
6. South Africa
7. Colombia
8. Spain
9. Poland
10. Canada

* Including military crimes.

Source: Amnesty International, 2003.

Ten Richest Countries Where the Death Penalty Is Legal

Of the 35 richest countries in the world, only 10 have the death penalty.

1. United States
2. Japan
3. Singapore
4. United Arab Emirates
5. Qatar
6. South Korea
7. Greece *
8. Israel *
9. Brunei **
10. Taiwan

Based on gross domestic product (per capita).

* Death penalty used for only exceptional crimes, such as military crimes.
  ** Death penalty is legal but has not been used for at least 10 years.

Source: Amnesty International, 2003 and CIA World Factbook, 2003 (using economic data from 2002).

Ten Poorest Countries Where the Death Penalty Is Not Used

Among the 27 poorest nations in the world, the death penalty is illegal in only five (and has not been used for at least 10 years in five others).

1. East Timor
2. Madagascar *
3. Guinea-Bissau
4. Niger *
5. Kiribati
6. Mali *
7. Congo (Rep.) *
8. Mozambique

9. Burkina Faso *
10. Tuvalu

* Death penalty is legal but has not been used for at least 10 years.

Source: Amnesty International, 2003 and CIA World Factbook, 2003 (using economic data from 2002).

Seven Countries Known to Use the Death Penalty Against People under 18 Years Old at the Time of the Crime (1990–2003)

1. Congo (Dem. Rep.)
2. Iran
3. Nigeria
4. Pakistan*
5. Saudi Arabia
6. United States
7. Yemen

* Since its last execution (2001) of a person committing a capital crime as a minor, Pakistan made this practice illegal.

Source: Amnesty International, 2003.

Royal Nations: Which Countries Still Have Kings and Queens?

The following countries still have kings, queens, sultans or other royalty (based on heredity) as heads of state. In many cases, the monarch is little more than a figurehead and plays only a minor (or ceremonial) role in government.

1. Andorra
2. Antigua and Barbuda **B**
3. Australia **B**
4. Bahamas **B**
5. Bahrain *
6. Barbados **B**

7. Belgium
8. Belize **B**
9. Bhutan *
10. Brunei *
11. Cambodia *
12. Canada **B**
13. Denmark
14. Grenada **B**
15. Jamaica **B**
16. Japan
17. Jordan *
18. Kuwait *
19. Lesotho *
20. Liechtenstein
21. Luxembourg
22. Malaysia **
23. Monaco
24. Morocco *
25. Nepal
26. Netherlands
27. New Zealand **B**
28. Norway
29. Oman *
30. Papua New Guinea **B**
31. Qatar *
32. Saint Kitts and Nevis **B**
33. Saint Lucia **B**
34. Saint Vincent & the Grenadines **B**
35. Samoa
36. Saudi Arabia *
37. Solomon Islands **B**
38. Spain
39. Swaziland *
40. Sweden
41. Thailand
42. Tonga *
43. Tuvalu **B**
44. United Arab Emirates *
45. United Kingdom **B**

B British Commonwealth (Queen Elizabeth II is the Head of State).
* Countries with royalty still maintaining a great degree of power.

** Malaysia has the unusual circumstance where the "king" is elected every five years. Therefore, Malaysia is not a true monarchy in the hereditary sense.

Countries Where One Must Be 21 or Older to Vote

In a vast majority of world nations, the minimum voting age is 18. Until 1971, when the 26th Amendment was passed changing the voting age from 21 to 18, the United States would have also been on this list.

1. Bolivia *
2. Central African Republic
3. Fiji
4. Gabon
5. Kuwait **
6. Lebanon
7. Malaysia
8. Maldives
9. Monaco
10. Samoa
11. Singapore
12. Solomon Islands
13. Tonga

The only country with a minimum voting age above 21 is Italy (25), and that is only for senatorial elections.

* The minimum voting age is 21 for single people but 18 for married people.
** Only males who have lived in Kuwait since 1920 or have been naturalized for at least 30 years (and the male descendants of both groups) may vote in Kuwait.

Source: CIA World Factbook, 2003.

Countries Where People under 18 May Vote

No country has unrestricted voting by minors. However, some countries do have a voting age of less than 18. Minimum voting age is in parentheses.

1. Bosnia and Herzegovina (16)*
2. Brazil (16)
3. Croatia (16)*
4. Cuba (16)
5. East Timor (17)
6. Indonesia (17)**
7. Iran (15)
8. Nicaragua (16)
9. North Korea (17)
10. Serbia and Montenegro (16)*
11. Seychelles (17)
12. Slovenia (16)*
13. Sudan (17)

* 16 if employed, otherwise 18.
** Married people may vote regardless of age; otherwise, the voting age is 17 in Indonesia.

Source: CIA World Factbook, 2003.

Block the Vote: States That Never Ratified the 26th Amendment (Right to Vote at Age 18)

The 26th Amendment was ratified by 39 states (plus an additional three, Georgia, Virginia and Wyoming, after the amendment took effect July 7, 1971). The remaining eight states chose not to ratify the amendment granting the right to vote to people when they turn 18 (though, of course, the law went into effect in those states, too).

1. Florida
2. Kentucky
3. Mississippi
4. Nevada
5. New Mexico
6. North Dakota
7. South Dakota
8. Utah

States Where Spanking Is Still Legal in Public Schools

Twenty-two states in the South, Lower Midwest and the Rocky Mountains still do not have a law banning corporal punishment (spanking, paddling) in schools. In recent years, corporal punishment in schools has been rare, except in parts of the South.

1. Alabama
2. Arizona
3. Arkansas
4. Colorado
5. Delaware
6. Florida
7. Georgia
8. Idaho
9. Indiana
10. Kansas
11. Kentucky
12. Louisiana
13. Mississippi
14. Missouri
15. New Mexico
16. North Carolina
17. Ohio
18. Oklahoma
19. South Carolina
20. Tennessee
21. Texas
22. Wyoming

Data current as of 2004.

Countries Where Corporal Punishment Is Illegal in All Places (Including in the Home)

All corporal punishment of children (and, of course, adults), including spanking, is illegal in 11 countries, mostly in Europe. Sweden, in 1979, was the first country to make corporal punishment illegal, and spanking has been reported to have decreased there since then. Anti-corporal punishment legislation is pending in several additional countries not listed here, and many other nations prohibit this sort of punishment in schools and prisons.

1. Austria
2. Croatia
3. Cyprus
4. Denmark
5. Finland
6. Germany
7. Iceland
8. Israel
9. Latvia
10. Norway
11. Sweden

Source: Global Initiative to End All Corporate Punishment of Children Web site, 2004. www.endcorporalpunishment.org

States That Ban All Fireworks

Fireworks laws vary widely around the United States. Some states allow many fireworks to be sold (including a few that allow them to be sold year-round, such as South Carolina or Missouri), while the states listed here ban all fireworks, even sparklers. * In addition, many cities and counties (especially in California) in states not listed here ban fireworks.

1. Arizona
2. Delaware
3. Georgia
4. Massachusetts
5. New Jersey
6. New York
7. Rhode Island

* Missouri only allows fireworks sales to non-residents out of season.

Source: U.S. Consumer Product Safety Commission, 2002.

States That Ban Fireworks Except for Sparklers or Other Novelties

Essentially, nothing that goes "pop!" is allowed in these states.

1. Connecticut
2. Illinois
3. Iowa
4. Maine
5. Ohio
6. Pennsylvania
7. Vermont

Source: U.S. Consumer Product Safety Commission, 2002.

States That Did Not Ratify the Equal Rights Amendment

The Equal Rights Amendment was ratified by 35 states between 1972 and 1977. However, that was three states too few, and no other state ratified the E.R.A. between 1978 and the deadline on June 30, 1982.

1. Alabama
2. Arizona
3. Arkansas
4. Florida
5. Georgia
6. Illinois *
7. Louisiana
8. Mississippi
9. Missouri
10. Nevada
11. North Carolina
12. Oklahoma
13. South Carolina
14. Utah
15. Virginia

* On May 21, 2003, Illinois finally ratified the Equal Rights Amendment. However, this was long after the 1982 deadline.

Countries with the Highest Percentage of Female National Legislature Members

Scandinavia has the countries with the highest percentage of female parliament members, while many Arab nations and some Pacific Island nations have very few (or no) women in their legislatures.

Country	Percentage of Women in the National Legislature(s)
1. Sweden	45.3
2. Denmark	38.0
3. Finland	37.5
4. Norway	36.4
5. Cuba	36.0
6. Costa Rica	35.1
7. Belgium	34.4
8. Netherlands	33.3
9. Germany	31.4
10. Argentina	31.3

The United States ranks a distant No. 73 with 14.0 percent of the combined House and Senate members who are women.

Source: Inter-Parliamentary Union (IPU), 2003.

Countries with No Women in Their National Legislatures

1. Kuwait
2. Micronesia
3. Palau
4. Saudi Arabia
5. Solomon Islands
6. Tuvalu
7. United Arab Emirates

Data unavailable for the following Middle Eastern and Pacific nations: Kiribati, Libya, Nauru, Tonga.

Source: Inter-Parliamentary Union (IPU), 2003.

National Legislatures with the Longest Terms for Their Members

Nearly all national legislatures around the world have terms between three and six years for their members. Only seven countries have legislatures with terms longer than six years, and in each of those countries, the other national legislature (among the bicameral pair) has a shorter term. At the short end of the spectrum, four countries have national legislatures with terms of only two years (Federated States of Micronesia, Serbia & Montenegro, United Arab Emirates and the United States).

Country (Legislature)	Length of Term for Members
1. United Kingdom (House of Lords)	continuous *
2. Canada (Senate)	continuous **
3. France (Senate)	9
3. Liberia (Senate)	9
3. Morocco (Chamber of Counsels)	9
6. Brazil (Senate)	8
6. Chile (Senate)	8

* Members of the House of Lords have terms that can last for life after their appointments, much like U.S. Supreme Court Justices.

** Members of the Canadian Senate may keep their appointments until age 75.

Source: CIA World Factbook, 2003.

States Where There Are State-Run Liquor Stores

Some states have laws mandating that hard liquor can only be sold (for off-site consumption, meaning drunk somewhere other than where it is sold, e.g., in the home) in stores operated by the state (or its agents). In some cases, exceptions are allowed, mainly in rural areas. In some states, wine is also restricted to state liquor stores.

1. Alabama
2. Idaho *
3. Maine **
4. New Hampshire
5. North Carolina

6. Ohio
7. Oregon
8. Pennsylvania
9. Utah
10. Vermont
11. Virginia
12. Washington *

Montgomery County, Maryland only allows liquor to be sold through its county-run stores (though the rest of Maryland has private liquor stores). In Iowa, Michigan, Mississippi, Montana, West Virginia and Wyoming, the state runs wholesale operations of liquor, but the retail operations are private.

* Some private, non-agented liquor stores are allowed, mainly in rural areas.
** Maine used to be a state where liquor was only available from state stores. However, laws have changed so that liquor sales can also be conducted at other locations, even grocery stores, though some state liquor stores remain.

States Where Hard Liquor May Be Sold in Grocery Stores

Some states have few restrictions on where liquor can be sold. In stark contrast to the states that allow liquor to be sold (for off-site consumption) only in liquor stores (some state-run), these allow liquor to be sold in places like gas stations, convenience stores, drug stores and grocery stores.

1. Arizona
2. California
3. Hawaii *
4. Illinois
5. Iowa
6. Louisiana
7. Maine
8. Michigan
9. Missouri
10. Nebraska
11. Nevada

12. New Mexico
13. South Dakota
14. West Virginia
15. Wisconsin

In many other states, beer (and sometimes wine) can be sold in grocery stores.

* Liquor is sold at different cash registers from food items.

Nations That Forbid Alcohol

1. Afghanistan
2. Algeria *
3. Brunei
4. Iran **
5. Kuwait
6. Libya
7. Mauritania
8. Saudi Arabia
9. Sudan
10. Yemen

In addition, Sharjah, an emirate of the United Arab Emirates, and some northern sections of Nigeria forbid alcohol.

* Not available, though not technically illegal.
** Allowed only for non-Muslims with special permission.

Countries Where Slavery Still Exists

Unfortunately, most countries around the world (even the United States) are on this list. The American Anti-Slavery Group (www.iabolish.com) conservatively estimates 27 million people around the world are enslaved, more than at any time in history, but some other estimates have this number as high as 200 million. UNICEF (www.unicef.org) reports that hundreds of thousands of children are trafficked across borders and sold each year around the world (that does not even include those remaining in their home countries as slaves). However, statistics regarding slavery are difficult to determine, as slavery is very much underground (since it is illegal worldwide, though laws against slavery have often gone unenforced).

Slavery rears its ugly head in a number of forms, including debt bondage, forced labor, child labor and chattel slavery, which is where people are actually bought and sold as commodities (such as in the United States before 1865).

Below are 10 of the countries afflicted by slavery.

1. Mauritania

Mauritania is possibly the country in the world that has the highest percentage of the population being slaves. Estimates of the number of slaves in this desert nation in the northern part of West Africa range from 100,000 to one million (out of a total population of nearly 3 million). The slavery is based on race; the slave owners are the Arabs and Berbers, who are in control of the government, while the slaves are black Mauritanians.

Mauritania was the last country in the world to officially abolish slavery (in 1981).

2. Haiti

Haiti has a severe child slavery problem. UNICEF estimates 250,000 to 300,000 children are "restaveks," or servants. This is roughly 8 or 9 percent of Haiti's under-15 population (3.2 million). Poor families that are unable to provide for their children have "agents" that place their children (usually girls) in homes where they end up working long hours, sometimes 18 hours per day. Occasionally, the parents will receive money for their children's work (with the children going unpaid). The children are usually released onto the streets at age 15.

3. Sudan

Over 100,000 people are estimated to be enslaved today in Sudan. Most of the slaves are taken (in full-fledged slave raids) from the southern parts of Sudan (where the people are mostly black, unlike in the Arab northern parts) by both government-backed militias and rebel groups in the civil war. This includes people (mostly children) being forced to fight in the civil war or to become sex slaves, livestock herders or domestic workers, all without pay. The U.S. House of Representatives unanimously passed a resolution in 2003 condemning slavery in Sudan and recommended sanctions against that country.

4. Burma

Burma's military regime forces people into slavery. Estimates vary widely, but 800,000 to possibly over 8 million of Burma's 42 million people are forced to work for little or no pay. Due to the poor conditions for workers (whether as slaves or otherwise) in Burma, the International Confederation of Free Trade Unions has blacklisted 350 companies that do business with Burma (some of which are U.S. companies). This includes oil companies benefiting from a gas pipeline which the Burmese government used slave labor to build and operate.

To make matters worse, some of the slaves in Burma have had to provide their own food (despite being forced from their fields to work on the government projects, such as the pipeline or a railroad).

5. Pakistan

Debt bondage is a significant problem here, and the International Labor Organization of the United Nations estimates 20 million afflicted (of a population of 150 million)." About 14 million are children. As is the case in other countries, debt bondage is where people are forced into slave labor to pay off a family debt (usually children paying the parents' debt). The wages used to pay off the debt are usually so minimal that people remain slaves for many years.

6. India

Debt bondage is also a problem in neighboring India, with possibly millions (mainly children) working as slaves. The carpet industry is one culprit as children's small, nimble hands are considered ideal for making carpet. Like people in other poor countries, thousands of Indians have been trafficked to other countries (including in the Middle East).

7. Dominican Republic

Haitians are trafficked across the border to the Dominican Republic to perform forced labor in the sugar cane fields (which contribute to exports to the United States). Haitians who have entered the Dominican Republic willingly in search of work have also been forced to work in the fields, sometimes for 14 hours per day. The workers use machetes to cut the sugar cane, resulting in frequent and sometimes severe injuries.

8. United Arab Emirates

Jockeys (in races) are typically small, but in the United Arab Emirates, camel jockeys are sometimes extremely small and young (5 years old in one reported case). Pakistani, Bangladeshi and Indian boys have been trafficked to the United Arab Emirates, a rich nation due to oil and its status as a major Middle Eastern commercial center. While the camel owners make money when their camels win, the jockeys do not (and when the camels lose, jockeys are sometimes beaten). A recent ban on child camel jockeys will only help this problem if enforcement is applied.

The United Arab Emirates relies on foreign workers (a large majority of the population) as the backbone of its economy. Some of the low-skilled foreign workers have had passports and payment withheld, essentially placing them under slavery. As is too common elsewhere, sexual slavery exists here, mostly among women, trafficked from Eastern Europe and Central Asia, who were mendaciously promised legitimate jobs in the United Arab Emirates.

9. France
French police have estimated that 90 percent of approximately 15,000 prostitutes in France were trafficked and that 3,000 to 8,000 children are enslaved, including as prostitutes and beggars. There are other estimates of 3,000 household slaves in Paris alone. Most slaves in (or transiting through) France are from Africa, South America and Eastern and Southern Europe.

10. United States
Slavery may have been made illegal in 1865, but it still exists today—the CIA has estimated that over 100,000 people are enslaved. The State Department has estimated that close to 20,000 people are illegally trafficked into the United States for the purpose of forced labor. This includes (but is not limited to) working in agricultural fields, homes (as domestic help), as prostitutes and in the garment industry.

Most slaves are people from other countries who know little or no English and were promised employment in the United States (and transportation from their home countries to the U.S.). Once in the United States, they are forced to pay off a debt to cover inflated "costs" of their journey. Of course, with no resources or command of the English language and sometimes fear of the U.S. authorities, these people feel they have no way to escape their situation.

Too many other countries could make a case for being in this list.

Source of most data: U.S. Department of State, American Anti-Slavery Group, UNICEF and the International Labor Organization of the United Nations.

Countries without Constitutions
There are a few countries in the world currently without a constitution (or at least a formal one). In the cases of New Zealand and the United Kingdom, instead of a constitution, they have a combination of

statutes and "common law and practice" that acts as a constitution. At the other extreme, Afghanistan has no constitution or anything resembling one. Some of these countries had constitutions in the past that were suspended (and new ones were never implemented). In some nations, the constitution means far less than in others (for instance, Somalia technically has a constitution).

1. Afghanistan
2. Bhutan
3. Burma
4. Iraq *
5. Israel
6. New Zealand
7. Oman
8. Saudi Arabia **
9. Swaziland
10. United Kingdom

* Had one before the toppling of Saddam Hussein.
** Governed by Islamic law.

Source: CIA World Factbook 2003.

States That Forbid All Organized Gambling

Nearly all states have some sort of gambling, such as lotteries (38 states), sports betting, racetracks, traditional casinos, riverboat gaming and Indian gaming. With Tennessee's lottery beginning in 2004, only two states no longer have any legal gambling.

1. Hawaii
2. Utah

CHAPTER ELEVEN
Miscellaneous Geography

Finally, here is a chapter for those who like maximum topic variation. Topics from food to churches to classic rock to palms (all of which fit into geography somehow) can be found in Chapter 11. For those who want more structure in their lives, I recommend rereading Chapters 1 through 10!

Countries That Have the Highest Number of Available Calories per Person per Day

Europe and the United States have the most food available per person. However, the number of calories actually eaten is slightly less, as some food is wasted.

Country	Number of Daily Available Calories per Person
1. Portugal	3,768
2. United States	3,754
3. Greece	3,689
4. Ireland	3,649
5. Austria	3,639
6. Italy	3,629
7. Belgium *	3,625

8. France	3,575
9. Israel	3,542
10. Cyprus	3,487

* Statistics for Belgium include Luxembourg.

Source: Food and Agriculture Organization of the UN, 1999 data.

Countries That Have the Lowest Number of Available Calories per Person per Day

Poor countries of the world produce (and/or import) the fewest number of calories per capita.

Country	Number of Daily Available Calories per Person
1. Somalia	1,555
2. Burundi	1,628
3. Congo (Dem. Rep.)	1,637
4. Eritrea	1,646
5. Afghanistan	1,755
6. Comoros	1,800
7. Ethiopia	1,803
8. Angola	1,873
9. Kenya	1,886
10. Tajikistan	1,927

The country with the fewest available daily calories per person in the Western Hemisphere is Haiti, with 1,977 calories.

Source: Food and Agriculture Organization of the UN, 1999 data.

Countries Where the Highest Percentage of the Available Calories Comes from Meat (Not Including Fish)

This list contains a variety of nations. Some, like Finland or France, are affluent Western nations that can afford the higher cost of meat. Mongolia, lying mostly in a cold desert, produces few crops (and most vegetables must be imported, which is rare for a developing nation). Uruguay and Argentina are major beef-producing countries.

Country	Percentage of Available Calories from Meat
1. Mongolia	28.1
2. Uruguay	24.2
3. Bahamas	17.7
4. Argentina	17.5
5. Finland	15.7
5. New Zealand	15.7
7. France	15.4
7. Antigua & Barbuda	15.4
9. Iceland	15.2
10. Australia	14.6

The United States is ranked No. 25, at 12.0 percent.

Source: Food and Agriculture Organization of the UN, 1999 data.

Countries Where the Lowest Percentage of Available Calories Comes from Meat (Not Including Fish)

The people of the Indian subcontinent eat very little meat for economic, religious and cultural reasons. The remaining countries on this list are in Africa, where crops and other food are too precious to be fed to animals (which would later be killed for meat) instead of to people.

Country	Percentage of Available Calories from Meat
1. Bangladesh	0.6
2. Sri Lanka	0.7
3. India	0.8
4. Guinea	0.9
5. Sierra Leone	1.0
6. Rwanda	1.1
6. The Gambia	1.1
8. Burundi	1.2
8. Malawi	1.2
8. Nigeria	1.2

Source: Food and Agriculture Organization of the UN, 1999 data.

Countries Where the Highest Percentage of Calories Comes from Animal Products

These are the countries where the ratio of animal products to vegetable products eaten is highest. While mostly European countries rank high, a few desert nations where relatively few plants grow well also rank high. Uruguay ranks high due to its large production of beef.

Country	Percentage of Available Calories from Animal Products
1. Mongolia	44.7
2. Iceland	40.7
3. Somalia	39.9
4. Uruguay	38.7
5. Finland	38.0
6. France	37.8
7. Denmark	37.1
8. Netherlands	36.3
9. Serbia and Montenegro	33.7
10. Switzerland	33.3

The United States is ranked No. 32 at 28.0 percent. Animal products on this list include (among other items), meat, fish, dairy, eggs and animal fats.

Source: Food and Agriculture Organization of the UN, 1999 data.

Countries Where the Lowest Percentage of Calories Comes from Animal Products

Most of these countries are poor and thus must use their grains (and other crops) to feed people directly instead of animals. While these countries may appear to be the most "vegetarian" in the world, meat stocks and animal fats are still used in foods, albeit sparingly.

Country	Percentage of Available Calories from Animal Products
1. Malawi	2.4
2. Burundi	2.5

3. Rwanda	2.7
4. Congo (Dem. Rep.)	2.8
5. Mozambique	2.8
6. Nigeria	2.9
7. Bangladesh	3.0
8. Liberia	3.2
9. Guinea	3.3
10. Cote D'Ivoire	3.4

Animal products on this list include (among other items), meat, fish, dairy, eggs and animal fats.

Source: Food and Agriculture Organization of the UN, 1999 data.

Countries Where the Highest Percentage of Available Food Calories Comes from Sugar

The countries which rank highest produce (and consume) large amounts of sugar.

Country	Percentage of Available Calories from Sugar and Sweeteners
1. Cuba	25.0
2. Belize	23.3
3. Swaziland	22.1
4. Trinidad & Tobago	21.0
5. Costa Rica	20.9
6. Colombia	19.2
7. Brazil	18.5
8. Iceland	18.4
9. United States	18.3
10. Barbados	18.1

Includes calories from other sweeteners.

Source: Food and Agriculture Organization of the UN, 1999 data.

Countries Where the Lowest Percentage of Available Food Calories Comes from Sugar

Country	Percentage of Available Calories from Sugar and Sweeteners
1. Rwanda	0.6
2. Laos	0.8
3. North Korea	1.0
4. Congo (Dem. Rep.)	1.1
5. Sierra Leone	1.3
6. Guinea-Bissau	1.5
7. Burkina Faso	1.6
8. Togo	1.7
9. Nepal	1.8
10. Afghanistan	1.9

Includes calories from other sweeteners.

Source: Food and Agriculture Organization of the UN, 1999 data.

Countries Where the Highest Percentage of Available Food Calories Comes from Wheat

Wheat is clearly a staple in central Asia, where it originated.

Country	Percentage of Available Calories from Wheat
1. Tajikistan	61.9
2. Turkmenistan	60.2
3. Azerbaijan	60.0
4. Kyrgyzstan	58.0
5. Uzbekistan	55.9
6. Armenia	53.3
7. Afghanistan	52.0
8. Algeria	50.3
9. Tunisia	49.7
10. Yemen	47.7

Source: Food and Agriculture Organization of the UN, 1999 data.

Countries Where the Highest Percentage of Available Food Calories Comes from Rice

Rice is associated with Asia, where it was first domesticated. However, it is also commonly eaten in tropical sections of Africa.

Country	Percentage of Available Calories from Rice
1. Cambodia	76.4
2. Bangladesh	76.1
3. Burma	73.1
4. Laos	70.4
5. Vietnam	65.4
6. Indonesia	52.0
7. Sierra Leone	47.8
8. Madagascar	46.4
9. Thailand	41.6
10. Philippines	41.3

Source: Food and Agriculture Organization of the UN, 1999 data.

Countries Where the Highest Percentage of Available Food Calories Comes from Corn (Not Including Corn Oil)

Despite corn's domestication in North and Central America, it is actually the biggest component of the diet in some southern African nations.

Country	Percentage of Available Calories from Corn
1. Lesotho	56.7
1. Zambia	56.7
3. Malawi	54.2
4. Zimbabwe	47.4
5. Guatemala	42.3
6. El Salvador	38.0
7. Kenya	37.7
8. Bosnia & Herzegovina	36.4
9. Mexico	34.0
10. Honduras	31.0

Source: Food and Agriculture Organization of the UN, 1999 data.

Countries Where the Largest Amount of Bananas Is Available per Person

Bananas grow best in the tropics, so not surprisingly, the top countries here are all tropical. In Papua New Guinea, bananas comprise a large enough part of the diet that they supply nearly 10 percent of the total calories eaten.

Country	Available Pounds of Bananas per Person in 1999
1. Papua New Guinea	262.6
2. Sao Tome & Principe	235.3
3. Burundi	191.8
4. Comoros	180.4
5. Ecuador	153.0
6. St. Lucia	151.0
7. Kiribati	107.4
8. Cameroon	87.8
9. Bolivia	87.5
10. Dominican Republic	86.0

Source: Food and Agriculture Organization of the UN, 1999 data.

Countries Where the Largest Amount of Tomatoes Is Available per Person

While tomatoes are used in many cuisines around the world, it is the Mediterranean and Middle Eastern cuisines that feature them most prominently.

Country	Available Pounds of Tomatoes per Person in 1999
1. Greece	308.0
2. Libya	273.4
3. Egypt	186.5
4. Israel	170.2
5. United Arab Emirates	166.9
6. Lebanon	165.4
7. Italy	164.7
8. Turkey	160.3
9. Tunisia	157.9
10. Portugal	141.3

Source: Food and Agriculture Organization of the UN, 1999 data.

Countries Where the Largest Amount of Potatoes Is Available per Person

The Irish diet is famous for its potatoes, but some countries in Eastern Europe eat even more.

Country	Available Pounds of Potatoes per Person in 1999
1. Belarus	377.3
2. Estonia	331.4
3. Poland	302.5
4. Latvia	297.2
5. Portugal	284.7
6. Ireland	280.9
7. Croatia	278.7
8. Lithuania	277.4
9. Ukraine	268.1
10. Russia	260.2

The United States, despite its ravenous appetite for French fries, ranks only No. 34 with 136.9 pounds of potatoes per person per year (that's still about six ounces per day per person, though).

Source: Food and Agriculture Organization of the UN, 1999 data.

Countries Where the Smallest Amount of Potatoes Is Available per Person

Potatoes are very clearly unpopular (or at least not practical) in West Africa.

Country	Available Pounds of Potatoes per Person in 1999
1. Benin	less than 0.1
1. Guinea	less than 0.1
3. Burkina Faso	0.2
3. Ghana	0.2
3. Guinea-Bissau	0.2
3. Liberia	0.2
3. Mali	0.2
3. Sierra Leone	0.2

3. Somalia	0.2
3. Solomon Islands	0.2

Source: Food and Agriculture Organization of the UN, 1999 data.

Countries Where the Largest Amount of Cassava Is Available per Person

Cassava, a starchy tuber, is grown extensively in tropical areas with poor soil. In some areas, they provide a large percentage of the total calories (in the Democratic Republic of Congo, they provide 56 percent of the total available calories in food, more than in any other nation). While cassava is eaten most in Africa, it also is a staple food in parts of South America. In the United States, it is rarely eaten, though some Americans have had tapioca, which is a beady form of cassava used in puddings.

Country	Available Pounds of Cassava per Person in 1999
1. Congo (Dem. Rep.)	675.0
2. Congo (Rep.)	549.0
3. Ghana	543.8
4. Angola	491.1
5. Mozambique	481.6
6. Tanzania	440.1
7. Benin	391.4
8. Togo	348.8
9. Central African Rep.	323.5
10. Liberia	309.4

The highest ranking country outside of Africa is Paraguay, with 299.9 available pounds of cassava per person per year. In a blatant contrast to the countries above, the highest ranking country completely out of the tropics or subtropics (all land area north of 30 degrees North latitude or south of 30 degrees South) is New Zealand, with a paltry 2.0 available pounds.

Source: Food and Agriculture Organization of the UN, 1999 data.

Carbonated Cognomens: "Soda," "Pop," "Coke," or "Tonic"?

An Internet survey was created by Alan McConchie to determine where people call soft drinks "soda" versus "pop" (as well as "Coke," which is a brand name). Over 100,000 people filled out the Internet survey, which showed that, overall, people in the Northeast and parts of the Southwest were most likely to say "soda," people in the Midwest and Northwest were most likely to say "pop" and people in the South were most likely to say "Coke." A sizable minority in the Boston area responded with "tonic." Nationwide, "soda" drinkers just barely outnumbered "pop" drinkers (but in Canada, "pop" drinkers outnumbered "soda" drinkers by a greater than 20 to one ratio).

States with the Highest Percentage of People Calling Soft Drinks "Soda"

State	Percentage of People Calling Soft Drinks "Soda"
1. Rhode Island	95.0
2. New Jersey	94.6
3. Connecticut	94.4
4. Vermont	93.6
5. Maine	92.4
6. Hawaii	90.9
7. Delaware	90.3
8. New Hampshire	82.5
9. Maryland	78.2
10. California	74.0

Source: "The Pop vs. Soda Page" (www.popvssoda.com), 2003.

States with the Highest Percentage of People Calling Soft Drinks "Pop"

State	Percentage of People Calling Soft Drinks "Pop"
1. Michigan	89.1
2. Iowa	84.9

2. Ohio	84.9
4. Minnesota	84.8
5. Nebraska	81.6
6. South Dakota	81.2
7. Montana	78.9
8. North Dakota	78.5
9. Washington	75.3
10. Wyoming	72.5

Source: "The Pop vs. Soda Page" (www.popvssoda.com), 2003.

States with the Highest Percentage of People Calling Soft Drinks "Coke"

State	Percentage of People Calling Soft Drinks "Coke"
1. Alabama	85.3
2. Mississippi	84.1
3. Georgia	81.8
3. Tennessee	81.8
5. Arkansas	81.3
6. Texas	79.8
7. Louisiana	75.7
8. South Carolina	63.2
9. Kentucky	57.4
9. New Mexico	57.4

Source: "The Pop vs. Soda Page" (www.popvssoda.com), 2003.

States with the Highest Percentage of People Calling Soft Drinks "Tonic"

State	Percentage of People Calling Soft Drinks "Tonic"
1. Massachusetts	24.3
2. New Hampshire	12.7

Source: "The Pop vs. Soda Page" (www.popvssoda.com), 2003.

Toxic Terrain: States with the Highest Amount of Toxic Materials Released into the Environment

Now we move from "tonic" to "toxic." These are the states in which industry released the highest amount of chemicals, due mostly to mining, manufacturing and production of electricity, into the environment (including into the air, water and ground) in 2000. The four highest ranking states attained their status largely because of mining. Over 7 billion pounds of toxic chemicals were released in the United States in 2000.

Figures are given in millions of pounds and include toxins such as polycyclic aromatic compounds, mercury (and mercury compounds—just these alone make up about ⅓ of the U.S. total), PCBs (polychlorinated biphenyls), PBTs (persistent bioaccumulative toxins, such as tetrabomo-bisphenol A or hexachlorobenzene), various pesticides and dioxin.

State	Millions of Pounds of Toxic Chemicals Released into the Environment
1. Nevada	1,008 (yes, over 1 *billion* pounds)
2. Utah	956
3. Arizona	745
4. Alaska	535
5. Texas	302
6. Ohio	283
7. Pennsylvania	226
8. Indiana	204
9. Tennessee	163
10. North Carolina	157

Source: Environmental Protection Agency, data for 2000.

States with the Highest Amount of Toxic Materials Released into the Environment Due to Manufacturing

State	Millions of Pounds of Toxic Chemicals Released into the Environment by Manufacturing
1. Texas	246
2. Pennsylvania	139
3. Ohio	137

4. Louisiana	135
5. Indiana	134

Source: Environmental Protection Agency, data for 2000.

States with the Highest Number of Deaths by Accidents from Fire and Flames (per Million People)

On average, over 4,000 people are killed each year in the U.S. by accidents involving fire and flames (residential deaths account for 73 percent of all fire deaths). Many states with the highest date rates are in the South, but Alaska is the strong exception. The states below have the highest number of deaths per year per million people (1989–1998).

State	Average Number of Deaths per Million People per Year from Fire and Flames
1. Mississippi	40.6
2. Alaska	36.5
3. South Carolina	31.1
4. Alabama	30.1
(District of Columbia	28.6)
5. Tennessee	28.3
6. Arkansas	28.1
7. Oklahoma	27.2
8. Illinois	27.0
9. Kentucky	26.1
10. Louisiana	25.4

Source: National Center for Health Statistics, Center for Disease Control.

States with the Lowest Number of Deaths by Accidents from Fire and Flames (per Million People)

The West has the lowest death rate by accidents involving fire and flames. The reasons are not clear, but newer homes and fewer smokers are two possible contributing factors. Again, the death rate listed is per year per million people (1989–1998).

State	Average Number of Deaths per Million People per Year from Fire and Flames
1. Hawaii	5.5
2. California	8.5
2. Colorado	8.5
4. New Mexico	9.0
5. Utah	9.2
6. Washington	10.6
7. Arizona	10.9
8. Connecticut	11.4
9. Rhode Island	11.7
10. Florida	11.8

Source: National Center for Health Statistics, Center for Disease Control.

States with the Most Churches and Religious Groups per 10,000 People

The South has the most churches per capita, though some of the Plains states are not far behind. This list has the number of churches per 10,000 people (though, of course, some of these "10,000 people" do not attend church, even in these states).

State	Churches per 10,000 People
1. Mississippi	42.5
2. Alabama	41.0
3. South Carolina	40.7
4. West Virginia	37.0
5. North Carolina	36.8
6. North Dakota	36.7
7. Arkansas	36.5
8. South Dakota	33.9
(District of Columbia	33.4)
9. Tennessee	33.1
10. Iowa	30.6
10. Kansas	30.6

Source: Internet phone directories, 2002. A few churches may not be listed.

States with the Fewest Churches and Religious Groups per 10,000 People

The West and a few northeastern states rank lowest in churches per 10,000 people. This does not always mean the number of people who attend a church is smaller, as the average church size likely varies from state to state (rural states would probably have the smallest churches).

State	Churches per 10,000 People
1. Nevada	7.0
2. California	9.6
3. Arizona	10.7
4. Connecticut	12.0
5. Massachusetts	12.3
6. Hawaii	13.3
7. Colorado	13.8
8. Utah	13.9
9. New Mexico	14.0
9. Rhode Island	14.0

Source: Internet phone directories, 2002. A few churches may not be listed.

States with the Highest Percentage of Country-Music Radio Stations

Country stations are most numerous in the Plains states, though parts of the South (especially in areas adjacent to the Midwest) had a large number of country stations. Surprisingly, Tennessee came in at only No. 13 among the 50 states). This radio format was least common in the Northeast, California and Hawaii.

State	Percentage of Country-Music Radio Stations
1. North Dakota	39.5
2. South Dakota	30.9
2. Wyoming	30.9
4. Oklahoma	30.7
5. Kentucky	27.5
6. Nebraska	26.1
7. Missouri	25.7
8. Montana	25.2

9. Arkansas   24.2
10. Minnesota   23.8

Survey conducted in 2001.

States with the Highest Percentage of Religious or Gospel Radio Stations

Religious radio (including gospel stations) are much more common in the southeastern U.S. than in the North and West.

State	Percentage of Religious Radio Stations
1. North Carolina	25.0
2. Alabama	23.8
3. Tennessee	21.6
4. Georgia	21.2
5. Mississippi	20.5
6. South Carolina	20.3
7. Florida	19.4
8. Louisiana	19.1
9. Missouri	18.5
10. Virginia	17.9

Survey conducted in 2001.

States with the Highest Percentage of Oldies Radio Stations

Oldies stations are more common in rural states than urban states. However, there was little "directional" preference for this format.

State	Percentage of Oldies Radio Stations
1. Wyoming	12.3
2. New Hampshire	11.1
3. South Dakota	10.6
4. Louisiana	10.0
5. Oklahoma	9.0
6. North Dakota	8.6

7. Pennsylvania	8.3
8. Indiana	8.0
9. Iowa	7.9
10. South Carolina	7.5

Survey conducted in 2001.

States with the Highest Percentage of Classic Rock Radio Stations

The classic rock format is more common in northern states than southern states.

State	Percentage of Classic Rock Radio Stations
1. Wyoming	11.1
2. Montana	8.7
3. New Hampshire	7.4
3. North Dakota	7.4
5. Delaware	6.9
6. Minnesota	6.8
7. Hawaii	6.1
8. Wisconsin	5.9
9. Michigan	5.8
10. Missouri	5.6

Survey conducted in 2001.

States with the Highest Percentage of Radio Stations Broadcasting in Spanish

It is certainly no surprise that the states with large Latino populations (which, of course, are highest in the Southwest) are where one would find the highest percentage of stations broadcasting in Spanish. However (at least in 2001), in every state in the United States, except Maryland, the percentage of stations broadcasting in Spanish was lower than the percentage of people who were Latino (though the format is rapidly increasing among radio stations).

State	Percentage of Spanish-Language Radio Stations
1. Texas	20.3
2. California	15.2
3. Arizona	14.5
4. Nevada	9.0
5. New Mexico	8.6
6. Florida	7.1
7. Connecticut	5.9
8. New Jersey	5.8
9. Maryland	4.4
10. Washington	4.3

Survey conducted in 2001.

States with No Radio Stations Broadcasting in Spanish

1. Alaska
2. Hawaii
3. Iowa
4. Kentucky
5. Maine
6. Mississippi
7. Missouri
8. North Dakota
9. South Dakota
10. Vermont
11. West Virginia
12. Wyoming

Based on 2001 and 2003 data.

Countries with the Most FM Radio Stations

The United States is No. 1 on this list, but not by that wide of a margin. Much smaller Italy ranks No. 2, and in Rome, the FM dial is extremely crowded as local stations appear every 0.3 megahertz.

Country	Number of FM Radio Stations
1. United States	5,542
2. Italy	4,600
3. France	3,500
4. Argentina	over 1,000
5. Germany	787
6. Poland	777
7. Spain	715
8. Norway	over 650
9. Mexico	598
10. South Africa	590

Some values are approximate. The values given include "repeater" stations.

Source: CIA World Factbook, 2003 (most data from 1998–2001).

Countries with the Highest Density of FM Radio Stations

The FM dial is very crowded in these countries, most of which are highly urbanized European nations. Guatemala is the only Western Hemisphere representative. In addition to the high population density of Europe, the spacing between the frequencies of the stations is less (thus more stations can "fit" on the FM dial). In the Western Hemisphere (the Americas), frequencies for stations are typically set at a minimum of 0.2 MHz apart, while in the Eastern Hemisphere (Europe, Asia, Africa), they have half the spacing at 0.1 MHz, with 0.05 MHz spacing for some frequencies in Italy.

This listing is based on FM radio stations per 1,000 square miles. Small countries (less than 2,000 square miles) are not included as unusual cases occur, such as Vatican City's 4 FM stations in the space of well less than one square mile (though the primary audience is Italy).

Country	Number of FM Radio Stations per 1,000 Sq. Mi.
1. Italy	39.7
2. France	27.0
3. Taiwan	24.1
4. Denmark	21.3
5. Slovenia	20.5

6. Cyprus   20.0
7. Guatemala   11.7
8. Czech Republic   10.1
9. Switzerland   7.0
10. Belgium   6.7

Due to its large landmass, the United States has only 1.5 FM radio stations per 1,000 square miles.

Source: CIA World Factbook, 2003 (most data from 1998–2001).

Countries with No FM Radio Stations

Ethiopia is the largest and most populous country in the world to have no FM radio stations. Otherwise, these are countries with both a low land area and a low population. All of these countries have at least one AM station, however.

1. Ethiopia
2. Kiribati
3. Nauru
4. Solomon Islands
5. Tuvalu

Source: CIA World Factbook, 2003 (most data from 1998–2001).

Lush Lands: Countries in Which People Drink the Most Alcoholic Beverages

Europeans drink more alcoholic beverages (by weight) than in any other part of the world. In the Czech Republic, over a pound of alcoholic beverages (usually beer, where a serving is about a pound) is drunk each day by the average person. Given that beer usually has the lowest alcohol content by weight (thus it would be the heaviest for the amount of alcohol ingested), beer-drinking countries will rank higher on this list than countries primarily drinking other generally stronger alcoholic beverages, like wine or vodka.

The statistics below are for the amount of *available* alcohol per person per year. It should coincide closely with the amount drunk per person per year, since alcohol is not frequently wasted!

Country	Average Number of Pounds of Alcoholic Beverages Available per Person per Year
1. Czech Republic	386
2. Ireland	349
3. Denmark	338
4. Austria	334
5. Germany	333
6. Uganda	308
7. Portugal	282
8. Belgium *	276
9. Croatia	264
10. United Kingdom	262

The United States ranks No. 18 with 224 pounds of alcoholic beverages per person per year.

* Statistics for Belgium include Luxembourg.

Source: Food and Agriculture Organization of the UN, data for 1999.

Teetotaling Territories: Countries in Which People Drink the Fewest Alcoholic Beverages

All except two (Burma, Cambodia) of the below countries are at least 70 percent Muslim.

Country	Average Number of Pounds of Alcoholic Beverages Available per Person per Year
1. Bangladesh	less than 0.2
1. Iran	less than 0.2
1. United Arab Emirates	less than 0.2
4. Mauritania	0.2
5. Pakistan	0.4
6. Comoros	0.7
7. Burma	0.9
7. Niger	0.9
7. Sudan	0.9
10. Cambodia	1.5

10. Egypt   1.5
10. Indonesia   1.5

Saudi Arabia is tied at No. 13 at 1.8 pounds per person. Surprised that the amount of alcohol is not even lower? Even though alcohol is banned in that country, it is occasionally drunk by expatriates in compounds (such as Americans working for Saudi companies) and even bootlegged in small amounts. Of course, most Saudis are teetotalers.

One can compare these countries with the ones where alcohol is forbidden entirely (from page 315).

No data were available for Afghanistan, Bahrain, Kuwait, Libya or Qatar, countries that would likely rank high.

Source: Food and Agriculture Organization of the UN, data for 1999.

Two States That Have No Native Pines

1. Hawaii
2. Kansas

While neither Hawaii nor Kansas have any native pines, there are pines native to other areas planted in those states, including some tropical pines in Hawaii. Alaska, Iowa and North Dakota just barely have native pines. The lodgepole pine is only native to the far southeastern part of Alaska, the white pine is native to a small part of northeastern Iowa, and the ponderosa pine is native to a small part of extreme southwestern North Dakota.

Source: USDA, The PLANTS Database, 2001.

Timberlines in Different Mountainous Regions around the United States

Timberline is the highest elevation in a mountainous area at which trees will grow. Above timberline, summer temperatures are not sufficiently warm for tree growth. Average temperatures (both day and night combined) during the warmest month of summer will usually be at or slightly above 50°F at timberline.

Timberline varies by hundreds of feet in most areas due to variations in the local microclimates. The values given below are therefore approximate but show a general maximum elevation limit to any organized forest. Often, there will be areas below timberline which will be devoid of trees for a variety of reasons, including steep slopes, wind, dryness or glaciers. Occasionally, a few stunted trees will be found above timberline on sunny, wind-protected slopes, but these certainly do not constitute forests. The timberlines are usually lower to the north than to the south due to the shorter cooler summers. Winter temperatures have almost no effect on the elevation of the timberline, and timberlines are actually lower in coastal regions than inland areas (given equal latitudes) because summers are cooler (despite the coastal winters being milder). This is most notable in Alaska, where timberline along mountains above the southeastern coast is lower than in places much further north in the interior.

Location	Timberline (Ft. above Sea Level)
Deviation Peak (near Kiana, in Northwestern Alaska)	1,300
Mountains east of Anchorage, Alaska	2,400
Mountains near Ketchikan, Alaska	2,500
Mountains east of Mt. McKinley, Alaska	3,000
Southern foothills of Brooks Range, Alaska	3,200
Mount Katahdin, Maine	4,400
Mount Washington, New Hampshire	4,800
Mount Olympus, Washington	5,400
Mount Rainier, Washington	6,500
Mount Hood, Oregon	6,700
Glacier National Park, Montana	7,700
Mount Shasta, California	9,000
Teton Range, Wyoming	9,600
Mauna Kea, Hawaii	9,600
Mountains near Sun Valley, Idaho	10,000
Wind River Range, Wyoming	10,300
Medicine Bow Peak, Wyoming	11,000
Wheeler Peak, Nevada	11,300
Mount Whitney, California	11,300

Uinta Mountains, Utah	11,400
Mount San Gorgonio, California	11,450 (near crest)
Rocky Mountain National Park, Colorado	11,500
Humphreys Peak, Arizona	11,600
Mount Evans, Colorado	11,700
Pikes Peak, Colorado	12,000
Mount Elbert, Colorado	12,000
Wheeler Peak/Truchas Peak, New Mexico	12,200

A few stunted trees extend almost to the top of Truchas Peak, at around 13,000 feet above sea level.

States That Have Native Palms

These states have at least one palm tree (or shrub) native to at least part of the state. One might be surprised to see Arkansas and Oklahoma on the list, but a shrubby, yet rather hardy palm called the dwarf palmetto (*Sabal minor*) is native to small sections of those states. In a few states not listed below, palms can be grown with at least limited success (some examples are included in the next list).

1. Alabama
2. Arizona
3. Arkansas
4. California
5. Florida
6. Georgia
7. Hawaii
8. Louisiana
9. Mississippi
10. Nevada
11. North Carolina
12. Oklahoma
13. South Carolina
14. Texas

Source: USDA, The PLANTS Database, 2001.

Ten Surprising Places Where One Can Find Palms Outdoors

While places such as Miami, San Diego and Tahiti are well-known for having many palm trees outdoors, there are other places where people have planted palms (which have survived) that would surprise many. Most of these are near the cold limit for palms so that only a few types of palms are hardy out of doors, and some are mere shrubs. In addition, some people experiment with growing palms in areas that would otherwise not support palms (or experiment with growing a larger variety of palms than their climates would normally support) by providing protection or planting in the warmest spots in their yards. In the list below, all places have at least a few unprotected palms that can survive the winters.

1. Washington, D.C.

There is one type of palm that has been quite successful (with other types subject to experimentation and limited success) in Washington, D.C.—the needle palm (*Rhapidophyllum hystrix*). This is a shrubby palm native to the southeastern United States and can sometimes withstand temperatures below zero (Fahrenheit)! In the National Arboretum, a specimen planted in the 1970s is nearly 10 feet tall, and a needle palm near Dupont Circle is about seven feet tall. The needle palm looks different from most palms as most of the trunk is below the ground, and the large leaves spring up from just above the ground. It still looks quite tropical, especially when seen in a non-tropical city like Washington, D.C.

2. Seattle, Washington

Despite its northerly latitude and abundant conifers, the moderating influence of the Pacific Ocean allows some palms to grow here. The most common is the Chinese windmill palm (*Trachycarpus fortunei*), which can grow quite large in Seattle. In addition, the cabbage tree (*Cordyline australis*), which looks like a palm, grows and sometimes even flowers here.

3. Vancouver, British Columbia, Canada

One can see palms even north of the United States! As in Seattle, the Pacific Ocean has a strong moderating influence on Vancouver's climate so that Chinese windmill palms and European fan palms (*Chamaerops humilis*) can grow here.

4. Oklahoma

There are several instances in this state where the hardiest shrubby palms, such as the needle palm and some shrub palmettos (*Sabal minor,* also known as the dwarf palmetto, and *Sabal louisiana*) have survived many years outdoors, including in Tulsa and Oklahoma City. One can see several specimens of the dwarf palmetto at the Oklahoma City Zoo.

Most surprising is that the dwarf palmetto is actually native to a small part of extreme southeastern Oklahoma. These small shrubby palms, which here look more like yuccas from a distance, can be found in the countryside near Tom, Oklahoma, not far from where Oklahoma, Texas and Arkansas meet. The dwarf palmetto is native to parts of every former Confederate state, except Tennessee and Virginia.

5. St. George, Utah

Palms—in Utah? In the extreme southwest corner of Utah, palms can be found. After all, St. George is only a little bit more than 100 miles from palm-laden Las Vegas. St. George is at the northern limit, along I-15, and has unusually cold winter weather for a place with palms, including an all-time record low of -11 degrees F. While nearly all palms, hardy or not, will succumb to -11, most winters will have their coldest nights in the teens (above zero), and with many sunny mild winter days and low rainfall, several kinds of palms, including the Washington palm (*Washingtonia filifera*), native to parts of California, Arizona and possibly a very small part of Nevada, will grow large and survive for many years.

6. Bodensee (Lake Konstanz), on the German-Swiss border

The chilly winters in Europe's interior are just barely warm enough near some of the lakes to support a few palms. A botanical garden along the shores of the Bodensee has some Chinese windmill palms which persist winter after winter.

7. British Isles

Palms have been planted for centuries here, especially near the coast. Even London has some varieties of palms occasionally planted, not only the hardy Chinese windmill palm, but also the jelly palm (*Butia capitata*). The Chinese windmill palm is also occasionally seen in Dublin, Ireland. In coastal parts of Cornwall, in southwestern England, one has an even greater variety of palms, including the majestic Canary Island date palm (*Phoenix canariensis*). Even in parts of Scotland, a few palms can grow (likely the furthest north in the world).

8. Tokyo, Japan

Tokyo is more famous for its flowering cherry trees and bonsai evergreens, but a number of palms can survive here. Winters are cool with some occasional snowfall, but the snow usually melts fast and the coldest night during an average year is in the upper 20s, similar to that in Rome, Italy or Orlando, Florida. The main reason that palms are not particularly common here is that they are simply less popular in Japan than in other countries.

9. Plovdiv, Bulgaria

Some large Chinese windmill palms have survived here in central Bulgaria for many winters, some of which have encountered heavy snow and temperatures near zero. One person living here is attempting to develop a genetically hardy breed of Chinese windmill palm from seeds of the survivors of this climate.

10. Yalta, Ukraine

Most of the Ukraine has winters far too cold for palms, but at the tip of the Crimean peninsula, between some mountains and the Black Sea, is a place, sheltered by cold winds, that has a Mediterranean climate. The coldest winter nights are usually around 20 degrees F, which allows several types of palms to grow well here. In addition to the Ukraine, Russia also has a few palm-friendly spots along its part of the Black Sea coast where the Caucasus Mountains provide shelter from winds from the north and east.

States with the Highest Number of Native (Vascular) Plant Species *

Diverse environments result in diverse plants. Therefore, states with widely varying terrain and climate are high on the list here (with warmer climates usually being more favorable for plant diversity).

State	Number of Native Plant Species
1. California	5,498
2. Texas	4,598
3. Arizona	3,535
4. New Mexico	3,256
5. Oregon	3,168
6. Florida	3,153

7. Georgia	3,122
8. North Carolina	2,983
9. Alabama	2,968
10. Utah	2,941

* Includes vascular plants, such as trees, shrubs, subshrubs, vines, forbs/herbs and grasses. Only distinct species are included; subspecies and varieties are not.

Source: USDA, The PLANTS Database, 2001.

States with the Lowest Number of Native (Vascular) Plant Species *

These states have somewhat less plant diversity. However, that does not mean these states are "boring" (after all, how many botanists would consider Alaska and Hawaii "boring"?). In most cases, these states have less climate diversity, though not all—Alaska has large climate diversity (not all sections are bitterly cold; coastal southeastern sections rarely see temperatures below zero). In Hawaii, it is usually quite cold at the tops of places like Mauna Kea and Mauna Loa, though their isolation from other cold places results in fewer available plant species.

State	Number of Native Plant Species
1. North Dakota	1,197
2. Alaska	1,381
3. Nebraska	1,480
4. Rhode Island	1,495
5. South Dakota	1,501
6. Hawaii	1,537
7. Vermont	1,664
8. New Hampshire	1,674
9. Iowa	1,704
10. Delaware	1,716

* Includes vascular plants, such as trees, shrubs, subshrubs, vines, forbs/herbs and grasses. Only distinct species are included; subspecies and varieties are not included.

Source: USDA, The PLANTS Database, 2001.

States with the Highest Number of Native Tree Species *

Wetter and warmer states have a greater diversity of tree species than drier and colder states.

State	Number of Native Tree Species
1. Florida	371
2. Hawaii	351
3. Texas	342
4. Georgia	328
5. North Carolina	293
6. Alabama	287
7. South Carolina	263
7. Virginia	263
9. Pennsylvania	244
10. Illinois	242
10. New York	242

* Only distinct species are included; subspecies and varieties are not included.

Source: USDA, The PLANTS Database, 2001.

States with the Lowest Number of Native Tree Species *

Despite being the largest state, Alaska has the lowest number of tree species as the extreme cold over most of the state limits the variety.

State	Number of Native Tree Species
1. Alaska	53
2. North Dakota	70
3. South Dakota	77
4. Idaho	82
4. Montana	82
6. Nebraska	84
7. Wyoming	88
8. Washington	90
9. Colorado	92
10. Nevada	99

* Only distinct species are included; subspecies and varieties are not included.

Source: USDA, The PLANTS Database, 2001.

States with the Highest Number of Native Vine Species *

Most vines in the world love heat! That is quite obvious in this list, as all of these states are in the warmer southern half of the United States.

State	Number of Native Vine Species
1. Texas	254
2. Florida	249
3. Georgia	162
4. Hawaii	156
5. Alabama	151
6. Louisiana	139
7. South Carolina	135
8. Mississippi	134
8. North Carolina	134
10. Arizona	130

Puerto Rico, if it were a state, would be No. 1 with 323 vine species. The U.S. Virgin Islands have 167.

* Only distinct species are included; subspecies and varieties are not included.

Source: USDA, The PLANTS Database, 2001.

States with the Lowest Number of Native Vine Species *

Go to a tropical rainforest and you'll find vines everywhere. These states, of course, have little resemblance climatically to a tropical rainforest, even in summer (though the residents, who are adapted to colder weather, might think otherwise), so only a few hardy vine species can be found here.

State	Number of Native Vine Species
1. Alaska	15
2. Montana	28
3. Wyoming	31
4. Idaho	33
5. North Dakota	37

6. Maine	41
6. Vermont	41
8. Nevada	42
8. South Dakota	42
10. New Hampshire	45
10. Washington	45

* Only distinct species are included; subspecies and varieties are not.

Source: USDA, The PLANTS Database, 2001.

Countries with the Highest Percentage of Barren (or Nearly So) Land Area

These countries have large amounts of land with bare soil, sand, rocks or snow (though permanent snow and ice cover are treated in a separate list). In the areas considered barren, vegetation never covers more than 10 percent of the ground at any time of year. Not surprisingly, countries in the Sahara Desert rank highest.

Country	Percentage of Total Land Area That Is Barren
1. Egypt	94
2. Libya	90
3. Algeria	87
3. Mauritania	87
5. Oman	85
6. United Arab Emirates	77
7. Saudi Arabia	72
8. Kuwait	68
8. Qatar	68
10. Djibouti	63

If Western Sahara were an independent nation, it would rank No. 1 at nearly 100 percent.

Source: U.S. Geological Survey, Global Land Cover Characteristics Database, 2000 (data from 1992–1993).

Largest Countries to Have No Barren Lands

These highly vegetated countries are the largest (with land area) to have 10 or fewer square miles of barren lands. None of these countries have any deserts.

1. Indonesia
2. Papua New Guinea
3. Paraguay
4. Japan
5. Germany
6. Malaysia
7. Poland
8. Philippines
9. New Zealand
10. United Kingdom

Source: U.S. Geological Survey, Global Land Cover Characteristics Database, 2000 (data from 1992–1993).

Countries with the Highest Percentage of Their Land Area Covered by Ice and Snow throughout the Year

Mountain glaciers and ice caps will continue to decrease if global temperatures continue to increase. These figures are from the early 1990s, when glaciers were larger and more extensive than just 10 years later. Outside of Polar Regions, such as Antarctica, Greenland or northern Canada, persistent snow and ice cover are found as mountain glaciers.

Country	Percentage of Total Land Area Covered by Snow and Ice Year-Round
1. Iceland	24.4
2. Tajikistan	5.0
3. Switzerland	3.9
4. Canada	3.3
5. Chile	2.9
6. Pakistan	2.7
7. Nepal	2.3
8. Bhutan	1.9
9. Norway	1.2
10. United States	0.8

If Antarctica were an independent nation, it would rank No. 1 at about 98 percent (the few dry valleys in the interior or a very few ice-free coastal areas are probably the only acceptable places for an Antarctican capital city). Greenland would rank No. 2 at 91 percent.

Source: U.S. Geological Survey, Global Land Cover Characteristics Database, 2000 (data from 1992–1993).

Bibliography

iAbolish. American Anti-Slavery Group. 8 Aug. 2003 www.iabolish.com/default.htm.

Amnesty International. 1 Aug. 2003 www.amnesty.org/.

The World Factbook Central Intelligence Agency. 1 Nov. 2003 www.cia.gov/cia/publications/factbook/index.html.

Environmental Protection Agency. 1 Mar. 2003 www.epa.gov/.

Food and Agriculture Organization of the United Nations. 1 Feb. 2003 www.fao.org/.

Global Initiative to End All Corporate Punishment of Children. 2 Sep. 2003 www.endcorporalpunishment.org/.

International Labour Organization. 28 Sep. 2003 www.ilo.org.

International Station Meteorological Climate Summary. CD-ROM. National Climatic Data Center, 1996.

Inter-Parliamentary Union. 10 Oct. 2003 www.ipu.org/english/home.htm.

Kmart. 26 Jun 2003 www.kmart.com/.

Macmillan World Atlas. New York: Macmillan, 1996.

Mapquest.com. 1 Jan. 2002 www.mapquest.com/.

McConchie, Alan. *The Pop vs. Soda Page*. 1 Nov. 2002 www.popvssoda.com/.

McDonald's. 21 Feb. 2003 www.mcdonalds.com/.

Metschies, Gerhard P. *Fuel Prices and Vehicle Taxation (*PDF Files*).* German Agency for Technical Cooperation and the World Bank, 2001 www.zietlow.com/docs/Fuel%202000.pdf.

NASA Eclipse National Aeronautics and Space Administration. 3 Nov. 2002 sunearth.gsfc.nasa.gov/eclipse/eclipse.html.

National Center for Health Statistics, Center for Disease Control. 12 Oct. 2002 www.cdc.gov/nchs/.

National Climatic Data Center. 30 Sep. 2003 www.ncdc.noaa.gov/.

Office of Travel & Tourism Industries, International Trade Administration. 5 Oct. 2002 tinet.ita.doc.gov/.

Information Please Pearson Education. 30 Sep. 2003 www.infoplease.com.

Road Atlas, United States, Canada & Mexico. Skokie, Illinois: Rand McNally, 2001.

Ethnologue, Languages of the World SIL International. 22 Oct. 2003 www.ethnologue.com/.

Target. 26 Jun 2003 www.target.com/.

Topozone.com. 6 May 2002 www.topozone.com/.

UNICEF. 8 Jul. 2003 www.unicef.org/.

United States Census Bureau. 20 Aug. 2002 www.census.gov/.

U.S. Chess Online. United States Chess Federation. 25 Aug. 2003 www.uschess.org/.

United States Citizen and Immigration Services. 6 May 2003 uscis.gov/graphics/index.htm.

United States Consumer Product Safety Commission. 22 Dec. 2002 www.cpsc.gov/.

Copyright. United States Copyright Office. 30 Dec. 2002 www.copyright.gov/.

The Plants Database Page. United States Department of Agriculture. 1 Aug. 2001 plants.usda.gov/.

United States Department of State. 10 Jul. 2003 www.state.gov/.

United States Department of Transportation. 8 Dec. 2002 www.dot.gov/.

United States Fish and Wildlife Service. 29 Nov. 2002 www.fws.gov/.

"Topography maps: 7.5-Minute Series." *United States Geological Survey.*

United States Geological Survey. 1 Jul. 2001 www.usgs.gov/.

United States Naval Observatory Astronomical Applications Department. 22 Jan. 2002 aa.usno.navy.mil.

Wal-Mart. 26 Jun 2003 www.walmart.com/

Western Region Climate Center. 1 Oct. 2003 www.wrcc.dri.edu/.

World Almanac and Book of Facts. New York: World Almanac, various years (1953–2001).

World Tourism Organization. 30 Dec. 2002 www.world-tourism.org/.

YellowPages.com(SM). 1 Apr. 2003 www.yellowpages.com/.

Books Available from Santa Monica Press

Blues for Bird
by Martin Gray
288 pages $16.95

The Book of Good Habits
Simple and Creative Ways to Enrich Your Life
by Dirk Mathison
224 pages $9.95

The Butt Hello
and other ways my cats drive me crazy
by Ted Meyer
96 pages $9.95

Cats Around the World
by Ted Meyer
96 pages $9.95

Childish Things
by Davis & Davis
96 pages $19.95

Discovering the History of Your House
and Your Neighborhood
by Betsy J. Green
288 pages $14.95

The Dog Ate My Resumé
by Zack Arnstein and Larry Arnstein
192 pages $11.95

Dogme Uncut
Lars von Trier, Thomas Vinterberg and the Gang That Took on Hollywood
by Jack Stevenson
312 pages $16.95

Exotic Travel Destinations for Families
by Jennifer M. Nichols and Bill Nichols
360 pages $16.95

Footsteps in the Fog
Alfred Hitchcock's San Francisco
by Jeff Kraft and Aaron Leventhal
240 pages $24.95

Free Stuff & Good Deals for Folks over 50, 2nd Ed.
by Linda Bowman
240 pages $12.95

How to Find Your Family Roots and Write Your Family History
by William Latham and Cindy Higgins
288 pages $14.95

How to Speak Shakespeare
by Cal Pritner and Louis Colaianni
144 pages $16.95

How to Win Lotteries, Sweepstakes, and Contests in the 21st Century, 2nd Edition
by Steve "America's Sweepstakes King" Ledoux
224 pages $14.95

Jackson Pollock: Memories Arrested in Space
by Martin Gray
216 pages $14.95

James Dean Died Here
The Locations of America's Pop Culture Landmarks
by Chris Epting
312 pages $16.95

The Keystone Kid
Tales of Early Hollywood
by Coy Watson, Jr.
312 pages $24.95

The Largest U.S. Cities Named after a Food
by Brandt Maxwell
360 pages $16.95

Letter Writing Made Easy!
Featuring Sample Letters for Hundreds of Common Occasions
by Margaret McCarthy
224 pages $12.95

Letter Writing Made Easy! Volume 2
Featuring More Sample Letters for Hundreds of Common Occasions
by Margaret McCarthy
224 pages $12.95

Life is Short. Eat Biscuits!
by Amy Jordan Smith
96 pages $9.95

Marilyn Monroe Dyed Here
More Locations of America's Pop Culture Landmarks
by Chris Epting
312 pages $16.95

Movie Star Homes
by Judy Artunian and Mike Oldham
312 pages $16.95

Offbeat Food
Adventures in an Omnivorous World
by Alan Ridenour
240 pages $19.95

Offbeat Marijuana
The Life and Times of the World's Grooviest Plant
by Saul Rubin
240 pages $19.95

Offbeat Museums
The Collections and Curators of America's Most Unusual Museums
by Saul Rubin
240 pages $19.95

A Prayer for Burma
by Kenneth Wong
216 pages $14.95

Quack!
Tales of Medical Fraud from the Museum of Questionable Medical Devices
by Bob McCoy
240 pages $19.95

Redneck Haiku
by Mary K. Witte
112 pages $9.95

School Sense: How to Help Your Child Succeed in Elementary School
by Tiffani Chin, Ph.D.
408 pages $16.95

Silent Echoes
Discovering Early Hollywood Through the Films of Buster Keaton
by John Bengtson
240 pages $24.95

Tiki Road Trip
A Guide to Tiki Culture in North America
by James Teitelbaum
288 pages $16.95

Order Form 1-800-784-9553

	Quantity	Amount
Blues for Bird (epic poem about Charlie Parker) ($16.95)	———	———
The Book of Good Habits ($9.95)	———	———
The Butt Hello . . . and Other Ways My Cats Drive Me Crazy ($9.95)	———	———
Cats Around the World ($9.95)	———	———
Childish Things ($19.95)	———	———
Discovering the History of Your House. . . ($14.95)	———	———
The Dog Ate My Resumé ($11.95)	———	———
Dogme Uncut ($16.95)	———	———
Exotic Travel Destinations for Families ($16.95)	———	———
Footsteps in the Fog: Alfred Hitchcock's San Francisco ($24.95)	———	———
Free Stuff & Good Deals for Folks over 50, 2nd Ed. ($12.95)	———	———
How to Find Your Family Roots . . . ($14.95)	———	———
How to Speak Shakespeare ($16.95)	———	———
How to Win Lotteries, Sweepstakes, and Contests . . . ($14.95)	———	———
Jackson Pollock: Memories Arrested in Space ($14.95)	———	———
James Dean Died Here: America's Pop Culture Landmarks ($16.95)	———	———
The Keystone Kid: Tales of Early Hollywood ($24.95)	———	———
The Largest U.S. Cities Named after a Food ($16.95)	———	———
Letter Writing Made Easy! ($12.95)	———	———
Letter Writing Made Easy! Volume 2 ($12.95)	———	———
Life is Short. Eat Biscuits! ($9.95)	———	———
Marilyn Monroe Dyed Here ($16.95)	———	———
Movie Star Homes ($16.95)	———	———
Offbeat Food ($19.95)	———	———
Offbeat Marijuana ($19.95)	———	———
Offbeat Museums ($19.95)	———	———
A Prayer for Burma ($14.95)	———	———
Quack! Tales of Medical Fraud ($19.95)	———	———
Redneck Haiku ($9.95)	———	———
School Sense ($16.95)	———	———
Silent Echoes: Early Hollywood Through Buster Keaton ($24.95)	———	———
Tiki Road Trip ($16.95)	———	———

	Subtotal	———
	CA residents add 8.25% sales tax	———
	Shipping and Handling (see left)	———
	TOTAL	———

Shipping & Handling:
| 1 book | $3.00 |
| Each additional book is | $ .50 |

Name —————————————————————————

Address ———————————————————————

City ———————————— State ——————— Zip ————

☐ Visa ☐ MasterCard Card No.: _____

Exp. Date ——————————— Signature ———————————

☐ Enclosed is my check or money order payable to:

Santa Monica Press LLC
P.O. Box 1076
Santa Monica, CA 90406

www.santamonicapress.com 1-800-784-9553